Conceptualising 'Learning' in Applied Linguistics

Also by Paul Seedhouse

THE INTERACTIONAL ARCHITECTURE OF THE LANGUAGE CLASSROOM:
A Conversation Analysis Perspective

APPLYING CONVERSATION ANALYSIS (*co-editor with Keith Richards*)

LANGUAGE LEARNING AND TEACHING AS SOCIAL INTERACTION
(*co-editor with Zhu Hua, Li Wei. & Vivian Cook*)

CONVERSATION ANALYSIS AND LANGUAGES FOR SPECIFIC PURPOSES
(*co-editor with H. Bowles*)

Also by Steve Walsh

INVESTIGATING CLASSROOM DISCOURSE

IELTS RESEARCH REPORTS VOLUME 6 (*editor*)

IELTS RESEARCH REPORTS VOLUME 7 (*editor*)

THE VOCABULARY MATRIX (*with M. McCarthy and A. O'Keeffe*)

ELT ADVANTAGE (*with M. McCarthy and A. O'Keeffe*)

Conceptualising 'Learning' in Applied Linguistics

Edited By

Paul Seedhouse, Steve Walsh, Chris Jenks
Newcastle University, UK

palgrave
macmillan

First published 2010 by
PALGRAVE MACMILLAN

Palgrave Macmillan in the UK is an imprint of Macmillan Publishers Limited,
registered in England, company number 785998, of Houndmills, Basingstoke,
Hampshire RG21 6XS.

Palgrave Macmillan in the US is a division of St Martin's Press LLC,
175 Fifth Avenue, New York, NY 10010.

Palgrave Macmillan is the global academic imprint of the above companies
and has companies and representatives throughout the world.

Palgrave® and Macmillan® are registered trademarks in the United States,
the United Kingdom, Europe and other countries.

ISBN: 978-0-230-23254-9 hardback

This book is printed on paper suitable for recycling and made from fully
managed and sustained forest sources. Logging, pulping and manufacturing
processes are expected to conform to the environmental regulations of the
country of origin.

A catalogue record for this book is available from the British Library.

A catalog record for this book is available from the Library of Congress.

10 9 8 7 6 5 4 3 2 1
19 18 17 16 15 14 13 12 11 10

Printed and bound in Great Britain by
CPI Antony Rowe, Chippenham and Eastbourne

Contents

Illustrations

Tables

Notes on Editors and Contributors

Editors

Paul Seedhouse is Professor of Educational and Applied Linguistics in the School of Education, Communication and Language Sciences, Newcastle University, UK. His monograph *The Interactional Architecture of the Language Classroom* was published by Blackwell in 2004 and won the Modern Languages Association of America Mildenberger Prize. He also co-edited the collections *Applying Conversation Analysis* (Palgrave Macmillan 2005), *Language Learning and Teaching as Social Interaction,* (Palgrave Macmillan 2007) and *Conversation Analysis and Language for Specific Purposes* (Peter Lang 2007). He currently has a second grant from the IELTS consortium to study topic development in the IELTS speaking test.

Steve Walsh is Senior Lecturer in Applied Linguistics and TESOL and Postgraduate Research Director in the School of Education, Communication and Language Sciences at Newcastle University. He has been involved in English language teaching for more than 20 years and has worked in a range of overseas contexts including Hong Kong, Spain, Hungary, Poland and China. His research interests include classroom discourse, teacher development, second language teacher education, educational linguistics, and analysing spoken interaction. He has published extensively in these areas and is the editor of the journal *Classroom Discourse* published by Routledge.

Chris Jenks is Lecturer in Applied Linguistics at Newcastle University, where he teaches courses on conversation analysis and task-based learning. His current work is concerned with voice-based interaction in computer-mediated media, task-based interaction, English as a lingua franca interaction, and institutional discourse.

Contributors

Joachim Appel has graduated from the University of Constance. He holds an M.Sc. in Applied Linguistics (Edinburgh) and a PhD. (Munich). After teaching German at Edinburgh University he trained and worked as a secondary school teacher. He went on to teach English language teaching methodology and applied linguistics at Munich University and at the Pädagogische Hochschule Freiburg. He is currently Professor of Applied Linguistics and Language Teaching in the Department of English at the Pädagogische Hochschule Ludwigsburg. His current research interests include the teacher's experiential knowledge, and verbal interaction in language teaching.

Vivian Cook is Professor of Applied Linguistics at Newcastle University. His main interests are how people learn second languages, and how writing works in different languages. He is a co-editor of the new journal *Writing System Research*, and founder of the European Second Language Association. He has written books on the learning and teaching of English, on linguistics, and on writing systems, including popular books on English spelling and vocabulary; he has given talks in countries ranging from Chile to Japan, Canada to Iran, and Cuba to Norway.

Irina Elgort is Lecturer in Higher Education at Victoria University of Wellington, New Zealand. Her research interests include second and foreign language vocabulary acquisition, reading and computer assisted language learning, and flexible learning and educational technology. She teaches on the MA programme in TESOL and Applied Linguistics at Victoria University. Her PhD research in vocabulary acquisition won the Christopher Brumfit PhD/Ed.D. Thesis Award in 2007.

Rod Ellis is currently Professor in the Department of Applied Language Studies and Linguistics, University of Auckland, where he teaches postgraduate courses on second language acquisition, individual differences in language learning, and task-based teaching. He is also a visiting professor at Shanghai International Studies University (SISU) as part of China's Chang Jiang Scholars' Program. His published work includes articles and books on second language acquisition, language teaching, and teacher education. His most recent books are a second edition of *The Study of Second Language Acquisition* (Oxford University Press, 2008) and *Implicit and Explicit Knowledge in Second Language Learning, Testing and Teaching* (Multilingual Matters, 2009). He is also currently editor of the journal *Language Teaching Research*.

Diane Larsen-Freeman is Professor of Education, Professor of Linguistics, and Research Scientist at the English Language Institute at the University of Michigan, Ann Arbor. She is also a Distinguished Senior Faculty Fellow at the Graduate SIT Institute in Brattleboro, Vermont. Professor Larsen-Freeman's latest book, *Complex Systems and*

Applied Linguistics (co-authored with Lynne Cameron, Oxford University Press, 2008), was awarded the 2009 Kenneth W. Mildenberger prize from the Modern Language Association. In 2009, she was appointed Fulbright Distinguished Chair at the University of Innsbruck, Austria. Also in 2009, she received an honorary doctorate from the Hellenic American University in Athens, Greece.

Constant Leung is Professor of Educational Linguistics at King's College London, University of London. He is Chair of the MA English Language Teaching programme and Director of the MA Assessment in Education programme in the Department of Education and Professional Studies. He also serves as Deputy Head of Department. His research interests include language education in ethnically and linguistically diverse societies, second/additional language curriculum development, language assessment, language policy, and teacher professional development. He has written and published widely on issues related to ethnic minority education, additional/second language curricula, and language assessment nationally and internationally.

Florence Myles is Professor of French Linguistics and Director of the Centre for Research in Linguistics and Language Sciences at Newcastle University. Her research interests range from theory building in Second Language Acquisition (SLA), the development of morpho-syntax in French L2, the interaction between generative and processing constraints L2 development, the role of age in SLA, to the use of new technologies in SLA research. Together with her colleagues, she has developed large databases of oral learner French and Spanish, available on-line (www.flloc.soton.ac.uk; www.splloc.soton.ac.uk). She is co-author, with R. Mitchell, of the best-selling *Second Language Learning Theories*.

Paul Nation is Professor of Applied Linguistics in the School of Linguistics and Applied Language Studies at Victoria University of Wellington, New Zealand. He has taught in Indonesia, Thailand, the United States, Finland, and Japan. His specialist interests are language teaching methodology and vocabulary learning. A four-book series *Reading for Speed and Fluency* appeared from Compass Publishing in 2007. His latest books on vocabulary include *Learning Vocabulary in Another Language* (2001) published by Cambridge University Press, *Focus on Vocabulary* (2007) from NCELTR/Macquarie, and *Teaching Vocabulary: Strategies and Techniques* published by Cengage Learning (2008). Two books, *Teaching ESL/EFL Listening and Speaking* (with Jonathan Newton) and *Teaching ESL/EFL Reading and Writing*, have recently been published by Routledge and another book, *Language Curriculum Design* (with John Macalister), appeared in 2009.

Amy Snyder Ohta is Associate Professor at the University of Washington. She is co-editor of *Japanese Applied Linguistics* (with Junko Mori) and wrote *Second Language Acquisition Processes in the Classroom: Learning Japanese*. She is editor of the volume of Wiley-Blackwell's forthcoming *Encyclopedia of Applied Linguistics* entitled *Social, Dynamic, and Complexity Theory Approaches to Second Language Development*. Her research interests include classroom interaction, what learners think and do outside of the classroom and how that impacts their L2 development, interlanguage pragmatics and socio-cultural theory, bilingualism, and Japanese sociolinguistics. Professor Ohta is currently analysing data from a large interview study of Japanese-English bilingual development.

Simona Pekarek Doehler is Professor of Applied Linguistics at the University of Neuchâtel, Switzerland. Her research, drawing from conversation analysis and interactional linguistics, focuses on second language acquisition, specifically within the classroom, and the relation between grammar and interaction. She investigates how people use language as a resource to accomplish and coordinate social actions and how, through that use, they develop their linguistic and interactional competence. She is also interested in the conceptual and theoretical implications that emanate from such empirical observations for our understanding of SLA and, more generally, of language.

Manfred Pienemann is Professor of Linguistics at Paderborn University, Germany. He was previously Professor of Applied Linguistics at the University of Newcastle, and also at the Australian National University. He founded the Language Acquisition Research Centre at the University of Sydney and was one of the founding members of PacSLRF. Professor Pienemann has been involved in second language acquisition research since the 1970s, when he collaborated with Meisel and Clahsen. His main contribution to the field has been the development of processability theory, a cognitive approach to SLA that has been tested for a range of L2s, and applied to the profiling of L2 development.

Transcription Conventions

A full discussion of CA transcription notation is available in Atkinson and Heritage (1984). Punctuation marks are used to capture characteristics of speech delivery, **not** to mark grammatical units.

[	indicates the point of overlap onset
]	indicates the point of overlap termination
=	a) turn continues below, at the next identical symbol
	b) if inserted at the end of one speaker's turn and at the beginning of the next speaker's adjacent turn, it indicates that there is no gap at all between the two turns
(3.2)	an interval between utterances (3 seconds and 2 tenths in this case)
(.)	a very short untimed pause
<u>word</u>	underlining indicates speaker emphasis
e:r the:::	indicates lengthening of the preceding sound
-	a single dash indicates an abrupt cut-off
?	rising intonation, not necessarily a question
!	an animated or emphatic tone
,	a comma indicates low-rising intonation, suggesting continuation
.	a full stop (period) indicates falling (final) intonation
CAPITALS	especially loud sounds relative to surrounding talk
° °	utterances between degree signs are noticeably quieter than surrounding talk
↑ ↓	indicate marked shifts into higher or lower pitch in the utterance following the arrow
> <	indicate that the talk they surround is produced more quickly than neighbouring talk
( )	a stretch of unclear or unintelligible speech.
(guess)	indicates transcriber doubt about a word
.hh	speaker in-breath

hh	speaker out-breath
→	arrows in the left margin pick out features of special interest

Additional symbols

(T shows picture)	non-verbal actions or editor's comments
ja ((tr: yes))	non-English words are italicised, and are followed by an English translation in double brackets
[gibee]	in the case of inaccurate pronunciation of an English word, an approximation of the sound is given in square brackets
[æ]	phonetic transcriptions of sounds are given in square brackets
< >	indicate that the talk they surround is produced slowly and deliberately (typical of teachers' modelling forms)
X_____	the gaze of the speaker is marked above an utterance and that of the addressee below it. A line indicates that the party marked is gazing towards the other; absence indicates lack of gaze. Dots mark the transition from nongaze to gaze and the point where the gaze reaches the other is marked by X
T:	teacher
L:	unidentified learner
L4:	identified learner
LL:	several or all learners simultaneously

1
An Introduction to Conceptualising Learning in Applied Linguistics

Steve Walsh and Chris Jenks

The chapters which make up this volume have emerged principally from a two-day BAAL/CUP seminar, 'Conceptalising Learning in Applied Linguistics', held at Newcastle University in June 2008. The seminar brought together some of the leading names in SLA research and resulted in a stimulating and thought-provoking debate about the meaning and characteristics of learning in applied linguistics. We hope we have captured the essence of that debate in the chapters which follow.

The volume addresses a number of issues, all related in some way to the central theme of learning in applied linguistics. A central focus of the book is the ways in which conceptions of learning vary according to different research traditions, paradigms and epistemologies. Our view of what learning actually is varies according to the research tradition we subscribe to. A clearer understanding of this relationship will likely provide a closer understanding of what learning is. A second sub-theme relates to the assessment of learning, considering how different methods for evaluating learning relate to different conceptions of learning. Another focus is the relationship between features of a language and conceptions of learning: are certain approaches to learning better suited to some features of the language than others? Which conceptions of learning lend themselves to, for example, lexis, which to oral fluency? A fourth theme is that of new conceptions of learning. For example, under a conversation analytic perspective of learning, it might be possible to trace second language acquisition in the moment-by-moment unfolding of spoken discourse. Related to this theme is that of learning and data: what new insights to learning can be gained from close scrutiny of naturally-occurring data, both in and out of classrooms? Finally, the whole point of the seminar was to consider whether it is possible to produce conceptualisations of learning to which members of different schools of SLA will be able to subscribe.

In the field of applied linguistics, there are currently a number of differing conceptions of learning a second language. In the cognitive psychology tradition of SLA, learning tends to be regarded as a change in an individual's cognitive state. Changes over time may be tested and quantified by reference to discrete items or language chunks. On this view of learning, learners acquire new language through a largely individual, cognitive process and through exposure to input. While this process may entail interaction with others, learning is regarded very much as an individual endeavour. By contrast, in the social or sociocultural tradition of SLA, learning tends to be conceptualised rather differently. Here, the focus tends to be on the processes of language learning and on socially-distributed cognition, rather than on discrete items as products. Evaluation of learning can include a) comparing evidence of a learner's current ability with that demonstrated in scaffolded interaction; b) explicating the progress of the learning process; c) portraying the process of socially-distributed cognition; d) showing changes in patterns of participation.

While some chapters in this collection focus on the compatibility of social and cognitive notions of learning, others argue that the two paradigms cannot be brought together and that we should simply acknowledge this. A common theme which runs through the book, however, is that social and cognitive notions of learning are not mutually exclusive; it should be possible to develop a perspective which incorporates the best insights and procedures from both traditions. In formal contexts, conceptions of learning tend to vary according to which aspect of a language is being taught. If the focus is on introducing new syntactical structures to students, the conception of learning may logically focus on whether individual students are able to actively produce these structures correctly. By contrast, if the teaching focus is on developing the ability to communicate and to participate in social interaction, the conception and evaluation of learning will focus on changes in patterns of participation and interaction over time. Whatever the focus, the complexity of language learning cannot be ignored. Consider, for example, what it means to 'know' a word: mastering a word may require knowledge of its orthographical and phonological form, meanings, grammatical behaviour, associations, collocations, frequency, register, and so on (see Elgort and Nation's chapter, this volume, for example).

The book aims, then, to present different conceptions of learning in applied linguistics which are able to explicate and incorporate variation according to a) the aspect of a language or communication which is being used and/or taught; b) the view of learning which is being adhered to; and c) the paradigms, methodologies and epistemologies being subscribed to and employed.

The main objectives of the book are to:

- explore and unpack the different conceptions of learning involved in research into learning and teaching a language;
- develop awareness of how different conceptions of learning originate in different paradigms, methodologies and epistemologies;
- develop awareness of how different procedures for evaluating learning relate to different conceptions of learning;
- develop awareness of how conceptions of learning vary according to the particular aspect of language or communication which is being learnt or taught;
- explore notions of learning in non-institutional settings;
- present different conceptions of learning to which members of different schools of SLA will be able to subscribe.

The collection consists of this introduction and 13 chapters. The first three chapters provide overarching frameworks which are able to encompass varying conceptions of learning. Cook (Chapter 2) considers what is meant by 'second language learning' and how this relates to an independent discipline of SLA research. His chapter defines the three key elements of SLA: language, second language, and learning. Ellis's epistemic relativism and theoretical pluralism approach (Chapter 3) and Larsen-Freeman's complex systems approach (Chapter 4) provide encompassing perspectives which are able to incorporate cognitive and social approaches, and to portray learning as both a process and a product.

Pienemann (Chapter 5) offers a cognitive view of language learning, arguing that while the cognitive perspective is not the only view of learning, it is a necessary component in any theory of SLA. Moving to look in some detail at the 'what' of learning, Elgort and Nation (Chapter 6) focus on vocabulary, arguing that cognitive and social approaches to vocabulary learning can complement each other in creating a balanced approach to L2 vocabulary learning, both as a process and a product. Staying with the theme of learning as process and product, Pekarek Doehler (Chapter 7) presents a CA-for-SLA perspective of learning in which, using a conversation analytic methodology, she outlines some of the methodolgical challenges which need to be addressed when learning is viewed as both interactional and linguistic development.

The theme of classroom discourse is continued in Chapter 8 by Seedhouse and Walsh, who examine some of the conceptual and methodological problems involved in analysing how L2 learning is related to classroom interaction before proposing a conceptualisation of Classroom Interactional Competence (CIC).

In a departure to learning outside the classroom, while retaining a CA-based methodology, Jenks (Chapter 9) explores how interactants in online voice-based chat rooms learn to change their participation patterns according to established communicative norms and expectations. Using conversation analysis, Jenks shows that language learning is a process that is situated in the turn-by-turn moments of talk and interaction.

In Chapter 10, Ohta, using a sociocultural approach to L2 learning, considers the oral and literacy skills development of language learners by analysing their interview comments about the Zone of Proximal Development (ZPD). The chapter focuses on some of the limitations of social interaction for language learning as reported by learners.

Using an EAL (English as an Additional language) context, Leung (Chapter 11) offers a descriptive and analytical account of current policy positions in relation to additional language learning, using a piece of naturally occurring classroom data to illustrate some of these observations.

In Chapter 12, we return to the language classroom as Appel presents a microanalysis of participation in a young learners' language classroom. The discussion focuses on two issues: the collaborative setting-up of participation frameworks, and the relationship between participation structures and task structure.

Looking more towards the future, Myles (Chapter 13) proposes a conceptual map, suggesting how different approaches to learning in SLA can relate to each other. Finally, in Chapter 14, Seedhouse pulls together the different themes which have been developed in this volume and summarises the similarities and differences between conceptualisations which have emerged. A conceptualisation of learning is proposed which incorporates Ellis's epistemic relativism and theoretical pluralism (Chapter 2) and Larsen-Freeman's (Chapter 3) complex systems approach. The framework for conceptualising language learning developed is, of necessity, a loose one and consists of the three following components:

a) a definition of learning;
b) a protocol;
c) three complementary ways forward.

We believe that the main strength of the volume lies in the way it admits and explores diversity but is able to generate from this discussion a broad conceptualisation of learning to which the different schools of SLA are able to subscribe. We are confident that the collection of chapters presented here offers a broad framework for the conceptualisation of learning with which the proponents of different approaches to SLA will be able to feel comfortable.

2
Prolegomena to Second Language Learning

Vivian Cook

Introduction

The aim here is to discuss the 'second language' in second language acquisition (SLA) research. The phrase 'second language learning' involves three parameters of variation: the nature of language, the nature of a second language and the nature of learning. Prolegomena are the preliminary matters to be considered before the main work, as in Hjelmslev (1943, 1961) *Prolegomena to a Theory of Linguistics*. This chapter argues that discussions of learning depend on what is learnt – language – and what makes a language 'second'. Virtually no book on SLA today defines these two terms more extensively than the odd footnote on second versus foreign language learning. Yet they are the rationale for the existence of second language acquisition as a distinct area of enquiry. As VanPatten and Williams (2007: 7) say, 'Any theory about second language acquisition needs to be clear what it means by language'.

Is, say, the concept of language used in Universal Grammar-based L2 research the same as that in Vygotskyan studies? Is the language used in studying bilingual social networks the same as that in psycholinguistics processing? Is the language used in post-modern studies of discourse the same as in procedural/declarative models? Is the language in transfer studies the same as that used with emotion? If SLA research indeed has a framework within which it can reconcile all these views of language, it is a major intellectual feat. If not, then SLA research needs to state explicitly the meaning of 'language' that it is using in each area.

Meanings of 'language'

The English word 'language' has many different meanings. One danger is that its apparent translation equivalents in other languages convey

Table 2.1 Six meanings of 'language'

Lang$_1$	a human representation system
Lang$_2$	an abstract external entity
Lang$_3$	a set of actual or potential sentences
Lang$_4$	the possession of a community
Lang$_5$	the knowledge in the mind of an individual
Lang$_6$	a form of action

different implications, particularly troublesome in a field of multilingual researchers largely writing in English. For example, de Saussure's three-way French distinction between 'langue', 'langage' and 'parole' (de Saussure 1915, 1976) has been a stumbling-block for English translators and linguists for almost a century. Table 2.1 gives six thumbnail meanings of 'language', for convenience given the labels Lang$_1$ to Lang$_6$. The meanings of 'language' used here have been chosen to cast light on SLA rather than as watertight definitions; doubtless a more rigorous categorisation could be devised. A brief version of these has been presented in Cook (2007).[1] For once the Oxford English Dictionary (OED 2009) is not very helpful; the main entry for 'language' defines it as 'the system of spoken or written communication used by a particular country, people, community etc.', neatly bundling together the meanings to be deconstructed here (and disenfranchising sign languages).

Lang$_1$: Language as a human representation system

From Cicero in 55BC (*De Inventione*, I, IV) to Hauser et al. (2002), people have seen human beings as standing out from other creatures by having language – 'a species-unique format for cognitive representation' (Tomasello 2003: 13). This is not to say that there is agreement over what the human aspects of language actually are; any feature claimed to be unique to humans is soon found somewhere in the animal kingdom. Hauser et al. (2002), for instance, argued that the sole distinctive element of human language is recursive embedding, that is to say structures embedded within structures of the same type over and over again; soon after, Gentner et al. (2006) trained starlings to react to supposedly recursive embedding.

Interpreting second language learning as **second Lang$_1$ learning** leads to the question of 'the extent to which the underlying linguistic competence of learners or speakers of a second language (L2) is governed by the same universal properties that govern natural language in general' (White 2003: xi): does the 'language' in second language learning qualify as a human language? It has indeed been asserted that 'L2 learners are not only creating a rule system which is far more complicated than the native system, but which is not definable in linguistic theory' (Clahsen and Muysken 1986: 116). The consequence of second languages not being $Lang_1$ languages would be that SLA research could be investigated in the same way as the learning of any human cognitive abilities, like chess-playing, and would presumably be handled by psychologists within general human learning rather than by SLA researchers, as indeed happens in some psychological approaches. Second $Lang_1$ learning research is then concerned with the ultimate question of the species-specificity of language itself, not with the details of any individual second language.

$Lang_2$: Language as an abstract external entity

'Language' also refers to an abstract entity – objective knowledge in Popper's world 3 of abstract ideas (Popper 1972: 159), as in 'the English language' or 'the Chinese language'. A $Lang_2$ is something out there in the world of abstractions, like the rules of football – a creation of the human mind that stands outside any individual and that can be captured in codified rules in a dictionary and a grammar book – for example *Le Petit Robert* (2006) for French words or *A Grammar Of Contemporary English* (Quirk et al. 1972) for English grammar – and sometimes legislated for by institutions such as the French Academy. No single person knows a $Lang_2$ language as such – no speaker of English knows more than a fraction of the 263,917 entries and 741,149 meanings in the *Oxford English Dictionary* (OED 2009). $Lang_2$ entities are countable – English, Chinese and so on, up to the 6,912 in *Ethnologue* (Gordon 2005). A $Lang_2$ often becomes a symbol of a particular culture or country, and hence one language gets lauded over others: 'Most books on English imply in one way or another that our language is superior to all others' (Bryson 1991: 3). People are proud of their $Lang_2$ and loyal to it, even if they see their own knowledge of it as imperfect. $Lang_2$ has been used to justify wars of territoriality, as in Hitler's claims to German-speaking areas of Europe, fostered as part of the independence movement for minority groups such as Catalans, imposed upon conquered territories as in the imposition of Japanese names on Koreans in 1939, and used as a unifying lingua franca to fight against its native speakers, as in the Black People's Convention in South Africa (Biko 1978).

The L2 user does not know a complete $Lang_2$ language any more or less than the monolingual. The relationship between the abstract $Lang_2$ entity and the speaker is as indirect and as debatable in a second language as in the first. The object learnt cannot be defined as a $Lang_2$ as this is not actually knowable by any human being. Methodologically, for instance, it is unsafe to take the description of the past tense in English in Quirk et al. (1972) as being what any individual speaker of English knows, even if there is an indirect relationship involved. When people have compared L2 users with native speakers, there has always been the danger of ascribing $Lang_2$ knowledge to the native user (Cook 1979): for instance, when I tested the UG-related syntax area of subjacency I found that 15% of native speakers did not know it – which led to me to abandon that line of research.

The $Lang_2$ to which L2 learning relates is usually taken to be the status spoken or written dialect within a particular country, say standard English with an RP accent rather than Geordie, or Mandarin dialect for Chinese rather than Taiwanese. Or it could be a choice between local standards, say Patagonian Welsh versus Welsh Welsh or Indian English versus British English. SLA research has usually only related to the standard national language; variation and acceptability of non-status dialects or local varieties are ignored. Status differences between $Lang_2$s also have to be taken into account, for example whether the $Lang_2$ in question counts as peripheral (local), central, supercentral or hypercentral (De Swaan 2001), since second language learning typically ascends rather than descends this hierarchy (Cook 2009). Research then relates to a particular abstract $Lang_2$ entity with particular political and social attributes. SLA research has to ensure that the L2 users it is studying have indeed been exposed to the standard form it is testing; for example English L2 users who make a distinction between singular *you* and plural *yous*, or who omit present tense third person – *s*, may be following Geordie or Norfolk practice rather than the standard.

$Lang_3$: Language as a set of sentences

In the $Lang_3$ sense, a language is a set of sentences: all the sentences that have been said or could be said make up the language – 'the totality of utterances that can be made in a speech-community' (Bloomfield 1926, 1957: 26) or 'a set (finite or infinite) of sentences, each finite in length and constructed out of a finite set of elements' (Chomsky 1957: 13). English is the name for one such set of sentences, Chinese for another. $Lang_3$ seems to be the sense in which language is internalised in usage-based learning (Tomasello 2003): language knowledge emerges from the array of data that the learner encounters, distilled from a corpus. Lang$_3$ is not an abstraction but a concrete object, made up of physical sounds, gestures or written symbols. Patterns can be extracted from these primary data, whether by the linguist or the learner. But they remain patterns of data rather than systems of knowledge or behaviour.

Second Lang$_3$ learning concerns the second language as a set of recorded phenomena, for example 'the utterances which are produced when the learner attempts to say sentences of a TL [target language]' (Selinker 1972). The relevant evidence for Lang$_3$ research is L2 users' sentences, as in the Vienna Oxford International Corpus of English (VOICE) (Seidlhofer 2002), and the L2 spelling corpora of van Berkel (2005). The overall research questions concern the regularities and frequencies in L2 language data.

The unique problem for second Lang$_3$ learning research is how to categorise the set of sentences produced or encountered by a L2 user as belonging to one Lang$_3$ language or another. Weinreich (1953. 7) said that 'A structuralist theory of communication which distinguishes between speech and language ... necessarily assumes that every speech event belongs to a definite language'; a recent variant is 'I define *bilingual input* as dual-language input consisting mainly of substantial numbers of utterances that both lexically and structurally belong to one language only' (De Houwer 2005: 31). But how do you tell which bits belong to which language? How can the total set of sentences produced by an L2 user be divided neatly into two 'languages' without invoking a meaning of language other than Lang$_3$? The L1 sentences a L2 user produces, for example, often differ from those of a monolingual native speaker. Second Lang$_3$ learning needs to include the whole set of sentences produced by the learner; only later can they be assigned to languages according to other criteria. Bilingual speech therapists have indeed long argued that therapy should be based on the child's first language, as well as on their second: you can't tell what's wrong with either if you don't look at both (Stow and Dodd 2003). Second Lang$_3$ learning research consists of the description and analysis of occurring language data.

Lang$_4$: Language as the shared possession of a community

Lang$_4$, the possession of a language community, is often seen as complementary to Lang$_5$, the knowledge in the individual's mind: 'although languages are thus the work of *nations*...they still remain the self-creations of *individuals*' (Humboldt 1836, 1999: 44) or 'le langage a un côté individuel et un côté social, et l'on ne peut concevoir l'un sans l'autre' ('language has an individual side and a social side, and one cannot imagine one without the other') (de Saussure 1915, 1976: 24). Lang$_4$ is a social phenomenon, a cultural product shared among a group – 'the English-speaking world', 'native speakers of Chinese', and so on. Possession of a language confers membership of a particular group. The language community is often equated with the nation – people born in Korea tend to speak Korean. But in many cases it is an imaginary community, unconstrained by political borders (Anderson 1983): Kurdish is spoken by nine million people in Iraq, Turkey and Iran, though there is no modern country of Kurdistan (Gordon 2005). Indeed Anderson (1983) argues that the equation of language with nation only arose in the nineteenth century; the inhabitants of the Austro-Hungarian Empire did not primarily see themselves as speakers of German; many Kings and Queens of England have been speakers of French, German and Dutch, a tradition continuing with Prince Philip, who was born in Corfu and christened Philippos.

Second Lang$_4$ learning, then, depends upon the concept of the language community. 'Language acquisition and use are viewed here as indicators of individual and group integration into the host society and/or alienation from it' (Dittmar et al. 1998: 124). As this quotation illustrates, the normal community is typically assumed to be monolingual: 'An individual's use of two languages supposes the existence of two different language communities; it does not suppose the existence of a bilingual community' (Mackey 1972: 554). SLA researchers, language teachers, and indeed many L2 users themselves have seen the L2 user as petitioning to join the monolingual community of native speakers. The alternative view is now starting to be heard that there are bilingual communities in which speaking more than one language is the norm. As Canagarajah (2005: 17) says of Sri Lanka:

> One can imagine the difficulty for people in my region to identify themselves as native speakers of 'a' language. People may identify themselves as speakers of different languages very fluidly, based on the different contexts of interaction and competing claims on their affiliation.

Second Lang$_4$ learning research has to decide whether the community that its research is dealing with is monolingual or multilingual – the multi-competence of the community (Brutt-Griffler 2002; Cook 2007, 2009).

Lang$_5$: Language as knowledge in the mind of the individual

Language is also the mental possession of an individual, Lang$_5$: 'a language is a state of the faculty of language, an I-language, in technical usage' (Chomsky 2005: 2), the other side of the coin to Lang$_4$. An individual has a mental state, consisting of rules, weightings, principles or whatever, which constitutes their language – competence in other words 'the speaker-hearer's knowledge of his language' (Chomsky 1965: 4). Speakers of Lang$_5$ English possess something that allows them to connect the world outside to the concepts inside their minds in a particular way. Competence then contrasts with performance – 'the actual use of language in concrete situations' (Chomsky 1965: 4). Partly the competence/performance distinction recognises the difference between Lang$_3$ sets of sentences and Lang$_5$ mental knowledge, partly between competence as a declarative state and actual speech production.

Second Lang$_5$ learning involves what the L2 user knows: 'the goal is to provide a clear and accurate account of the learner's competence' (R. Ellis 1994: 38). Lang$_5$ is perhaps the most typical meaning of 'language' underlying SLA research, as stressed in Firth and Wagner (1997). If mental knowledge is equated with Chomskyan linguistic competence, the problem has always been how this relates to performance. Data from any form of performance is dubious evidence for competence, a gap as hard to bridge in SLA research as in any other area of language. To go over familiar ground, Lang$_3$ performance data are full of mistakes and disfluencies (the degeneracy of the data); many mental rules of grammar are not derivable from the properties of Lang$_3$ sets of sentences (the poverty-of-the-stimulus). Hence competence is not derivable neatly from sheer Lang$_2$ data through discovery procedures (Chomsky 1957), as usage-based linguistics would have it (Tomasello 2003). Second Lang$_5$ learning research is concerned with testing and specifying internal invisible contents of the mind.

Lang$_6$: Language as action

The Lang$_6$ tradition of language as a form of action goes from Malinowski's assertion that language 'is a mode of action and not an instrument of reflection' (Malinowski 1923: 312) through to Schegloff et al. (2002: 5): 'People use language and concomitant forms of conduct to *do* things, not only to transmit information'. Language as action is an integral part of Vygotskyan theory: language starts as external social action by the child, and development consists of internalising this external action (Vygotsky 1934, 1962). In a sense this might seem to combine other meanings already discussed, say elements of external Lang$_3$ with social Lang$_4$ and mental Lang$_5$. There is nevertheless a tenable view that language is a set of observable actions, an external cultural construction.

Second Lang$_6$ learning is about how people act in second languages: 'a competence-in-action ... socially situated, collaboratively established and contingent with regard to other competencies' (Pekarek Doehler 2006b), distinct both from the neutral descriptions of Lang$_3$ and from the community-based Lang$_4$ in its assertion of an individual sociality. In its Vygotskyan guise, 'sociocultural research seeks to study mediated mind' (Lantolf 2000: 18).

Finally an orthogonal point has to be mentioned, that whichever meaning of 'language' is used, SLA research needs a rigorous analysis of its subject matter, language. Dealing with language as the possession of human beings, Lang$_1$, entails a precise specification of what this consists of, whether principle and parameter syntax, phonemes, weightings of connections or whatever. For Lang$_3$, analysing the properties of a set of language means having well-defined categories and procedures, as in say Pattern Grammar. And so on for all the other meanings: each implies a particular form of description and analysis. As Cook (2008) observed, much psycholinguistics research 'utilises descriptive terms such as phonemes ("the building blocks" ...), syllables, words, meanings, as if these were primitive concepts that were unproblematic and unrelated to any linguistic theory'. The definition of 'word' for instance, much relied on in SLA research, has proved a sticky problem: increasingly words have been seen as an artifact of writing systems that use word spaces, rather than a universal category (Aronoff 1992); the word is hard to use as a category in Chinese, which separates morpheme-related characters by spaces, not words. Like 'phoneme', 'word' may be an indispensable label; but, compared to say 'lexical item' or 'lexical entry' or even 'lemma', it needs a definition to give it scientific status. Choosing a meaning for 'language' does not absolve us from using scientifically acceptable tools for analysing it, varying according to the meaning involved. If we believe that language consists of words and phonemes, we look at how words and phonemes are acquired; if we believe language is abstract rules and parameters, associations of stimulus and response, weighting of connections, competition between elements, schemas for social interaction, or any of the milliard of alternatives, we need to rigorously describe these constructs before looking for ways in which they may be learnt.

To come back to the general argument, the six meanings of 'language' can now be applied to language learning. Tomasello (2003: 7), for example, states that 'the principles and structures whose existence is difficult to explain without universal grammar ... are theory-internal affairs and simply do not exist in usage-based theories of language – full stop'. Exactly: statements about $Lang_3$ are not statements about $Lang_5$, any more than swallows are fish; why should they be? The usual linguists' criticisms of connectionism are not that it is wrong, but that it is not about language as conceived of by linguists; $Lang_3$ and $Lang_5$ are incompatible once again, but is that a reason for denying a universe in which $Lang_3$ exists?

In other words, views of language learning based on a particular meaning of 'language' are often incompatible with views of language learning based on another meaning. Only those who are proselytising for the dominance of a particular view of language need to spend time arguing it against all rivals; most of us can continue to cultivate our own gardens without throwing weedkiller over the fence into the one next door. Paradis (2009: 3) talks of:

> ... the arrogant attitude of those who are convinced that they hold the Truth and who treat anyone with diverging views as muddle-headed, using intimidation to impose their views – only to discover a decade or less later that they were wrong, at which point they go on to defend and try to impose the new Truth with the same determination and contempt for diverging views.

Unless people agree on the underlying meaning of 'language', these arguments are unwinnable – or both sides claim victory because the opposition cannot account for some aspect of language learning whose very existence the other denies, say the $Lang_1$ principles denied by usage-based learning or the $Lang_5$ abstract structures denied by connectionists. Take the continuing debate initiated by Firth and Wagner (1997: 2007) that SLA research has stressed individual psychology at the expense of social interaction. Interpreted as a plea for more work on $Lang_4$ and $Lang_6$ rather than an exclusive concentration on $Lang_5$, this seems timely. It may be historically true that syntactic development did preoccupy many 1970s researchers (with the exception of discourse work by Hatch and her associates (Hatch 1978)) and still dominates generative SLA approaches, as reported in White (2003). It is desirable for SLA research to investigate a greater range of areas and explore different interpretations of 'language', though one should extend this brief beyond social interaction to gestures, writing systems, neurolinguistics, and doubtless many other newly-thriving areas.

There is little point in refuting a theory based on one idea about language with arguments based on another. Firth and Wagner (2007) document the reactions to their original chapter, which amount largely to 'my view of language is right':

> Long, Kasper, Poulisse and Gass ... lay down the law by defining SLA's 'proper' intellectual territory (e.g., 'learners', 'language', 'cognition'), delineating its 'key concerns' (e.g., 'acquisition', not 'use', 'language', not 'communication'), and by pointing to its borders (e.g., by stipulating what is 'inside' and 'outside' SLA).

In the Feyerabend approach to science, all avenues should be explored simultaneously rather than abandoned prematurely (Feyerabend 1975).

To show how multiple meanings of 'language' occur in the same discourse, let us take a seminal SLA chapter by Diane Larsen-Freeman (1997); this brought to SLA research for the first time the ideas of chaos theory, and started an influential line of thinking which has continued to this day. It consisted half of a presentation of chaos theory, half of speculations how these ideas might be used in SLA research. It admits its wide coverage of 'language, the brain, and second language acquisition' and insists that it is not a matter of either X or Y, but of both X and Y: 'chaos/complexity theory encourages a blurring of boundaries in SLA – to see complementarity and to practise inclusiveness where linguists have seen oppositions and exclusiveness' (ibid: 158); the multiple meanings of 'language' are then a conscious choice.

Table 2.2 presents a selection of citations from the chapter arrayed according to the meaning of 'language' they seem to use. While this is hard to do, some clearly belong more to one meaning of language than another. Statements like 'language is a fractal' (ibid: 150) presumably belong to $Lang_1$ human language; statements about change like 'anything borrowed into the language' (ibid: 150) seem to refer to $Lang_2$ abstract entities; many of the uses of 'language' envisage it as a constantly changing pool of elements: 'every time language is used, it

Table 2.2 'Language' in Larsen-Freeman (1997)

Lang$_1$	'language is also complex' p.149; 'if language is as complex as it is' p.154 'language is a fractal' p.150; 'the fractality of language' p.150 'language and language acquisition are like other complex systems in the physical sciences' p.152 'ILs, like all natural languages, are unstable' p.156
Lang$_2$	'the changes which languages undergo diachronically' p.147 'the source language, the target language' p.151 'anything borrowed into the language' p.150
Lang$_3$	'language can be conceptualised as aggregations of paradigmatic and syntagmatic units' p.147 'every time language is used, it changes' p.148 'language use and language change are inseparable' p.158 'Zipf's law is not only applicable to a language in general' p.150
Lang$_4$	'proficient speakers of a given language' p.151
Lang$_5$	'we might call UG the initial state of human language' p.150 'why do we not each wind up each creating our own language ...?' p.153
Lang$_6$	'language as a dynamic system' p.147 'language grows and organises itself from the bottom up in an organic way' p.148

changes' (ibid: 148), clearly a Lang$_3$ view of language as a set of actually occurring pieces of spoken or written text. Lang$_4$ community is implied by the attribution of 'proficient speakers of a given language' (ibid: 151), Lang$_5$ mental state by 'UG the initial state of human language' (ibid: 150). The recognition that 'language is a dynamic system' (ibid: 147) and similar claims seems to belong to Lang$_6$ language as action.

So Chaos theory affects our ideas of the nature of language, of individual language change, of language as a set of sentences, of language in the community and in the mind, and of language in action. 'Language' is being used here with complex interrelated meanings. SLA researchers have to decide whether to take on the full spectrum of meanings in their research, as in this chapter, or to limit themselves to a particular meaning. The scope is much greater than an either/or choice between 'cognitive' Lang$_4$ and 'action' Lang$_6$, with knock-on consequences for the evidence they accept and the methods they use to obtain it. But whatever they decide, they need to be consciously aware of the meanings of 'language' they have taken on.

Counting languages

We now turn to the word 'second' in 'second language learning'. The rare discussions of this in SLA research only concern the 'second/foreign language' distinction, with the exceptions of Stern (1983) and Block (2003). Talking about 'first' and 'second' languages is not just counting how many there are with cardinal numbers like 'one' and 'two', but also putting languages in an order with ordinal numbers like 'first' and 'second'; *Language Two* (Dulay et al. 1982) is in principle a different concept from *Understanding Second Language Acquisition* (Ortega 2009). There is a curious paradox that SLA researchers say 'L2 learners' aloud as 'L two learners' rather than 'Second L learners', switching from cardinal to ordinal. Of course the 'first' in 'first language acquisition' is equally problematic since monolingual children never go on to a second language; my wife was not very pleased to be referred to as my first wife.

What kinds of order could 'first' and 'second' represent?

Official first language by fiat

Politics has often used 'first' and 'second' language alongside 'official' language. Countries adopt their national languages by constitution – the European Union currently has 23 official languages, having the most multilingual institutions in the world (De Swaan 2001: 144). In Canada, 'English and French...have equality of status and equal rights and privileges as to their use' (Official Languages Act 2006: preamble); all Canadian citizens belong to one or other or both of the two official language communities, regardless of their mother tongue (Churchill 2004). The official language of a country has little to do with whether many people speak it as their $Lang_4$ or $Lang_5$; French is the official language of Senegal, though 75% of the population speak Wolof. Singapore by constitution has four official languages, Malay, Mandarin, Tamil and English, and one national language, 'the Malay language...in the Roman script', yet Bahasa Malaysia is spoken by only 14% of the population. Officialdom may also lay down which language should be the first, and indeed second, foreign language.

Official languages are examples of countable $Lang_2$ nation-bound entities: it is taken for granted that the language of England is English. Though the definitions of official and foreign languages vary from one country to another, these concepts nevertheless have to be allowed for in SLA research, if only to facilitate communication with the organisations that administer language policy. But it is particularly important, when asking L2 users what their first language is, to know what they mean by 'first language'; a student from Taiwan may say 'Chinese' (which is ambiguous among many 'dialects'), 'Mandarin' (the official language) or 'Taiwanese' (a local 'dialect' of Min Nan Chinese spoken by 70% of the population).

First and second as sequence of acquisition

The numbering of languages may also correspond to the chronological order of an individual's development or acquisition: 'the learning of the "second" language takes place sometime later than the acquisition of the first language' (Mitchell and Myles 1998: 1). The first language is thus acquired before the second in the lifetime of the individual; Joseph Conrad learnt Polish before he learnt French, making Polish his L1, French his L2. This applies both to the individual gaining membership of a second Lang$_4$ community and to them gaining a second Lang$_5$ mental system: one language comes before another in their life-history. Simultaneous early bilingualism in which the baby handles two languages from birth is something else, covered in Swain's memorable phrase 'bilingualism as a first language' (Swain 1972).

The use of 'second' should not be taken too literally. Many sources maintain that it subsumes later languages; Doughty and Long (2003: 3) enumerate how SLA includes 'second (third, etc.) languages and dialects'; Lightbown and Spada (2006: 204) say a 'second language…may actually refer to the third or fourth language'. In this sense English was Conrad's L2, although he learnt it as his third. The implication is that learning of languages beyond the second is no different from learning a second language. However, this has been strongly denied by those working with trilingualism or multilingualism, whose goal is 'to work out the differences and similarities between SLA and TLA [Third Language Acquisition]' (Jessner 2008: 19) rather than to take their identity for granted. It may be necessary to order languages beyond second, rather than having second subsume all later-acquired languages.

Sequence of acquisition thus involves several meanings of 'language'. One is the official standard language that the person encounters first, a Lang$_2$ – English before French, say. A second is the Lang$_4$ community the person belongs to first compared to a community they join later, say belonging to the Chinese community in Singapore before joining the English-speaking bilingual community. A third is the Lang$_5$ mental system that the person acquires after their first Lang$_5$. The multi-competence approach argues, however, that the mind is a single linguistic system at some level; it is arbitrary to divide up this complex mental system into bits labelled 'first' and 'second', rather than treating it as a whole.

First and second by priority

'First' and 'second' can also be a matter of value judgement: something which comes first is better than something which comes second – 'first choice', 'First Lady', 'first class degree'. Your first language is the language you command best; your second is therefore worse: 'second language' indicates a lower level of actual or perceived proficiency' (Stern 1983: 13).

A much-explored topic over the years has been language dominance: 'We use the terms "first language" and "second language" to refer to relative language dominance' (Chee et al. 2004: 15270). This could be the dominance of one Lang$_4$ community over another: 'A language used by a socio-economically dominant group in society or which has received a political or cultural status superior to that of other languages in the community' (Hamers and Blanc 2000: 373). French was the dominant language in England from 1066 to 1385, yet undoubtedly most people spoke English, just as most people in India spoke Indian languages during the British Raj. Nor is the mother tongue necessarily closest to one's identity; Myhill (2003: 84) points to 'Hebrew in Israel and Yiddish in Ultra-Orthodox communities, in both of which cases native language is a distant second in terms of centrality to identity'.

More often, dominance has meant psychological dominance of one Lang$_5$ language in the individual mind – 'the second, and less dominant, language' (van Hell and Dijkstra 2002: 780). Considerable effort was expended to establish a speaker's dominant language, reviewed in Flege et al. (2002), for example the test batteries by Lambert (1955), leading to the concept of balanced bilinguals as 'those equally fluent in two languages' (Grosjean 1982: 233). However, the L2 repertoire of an L2 user may be wider than their L1; they cannot be judged just on how well they can carry out L1 functions in the L2: Greek students in England, for example, say that they can only write essays in English since essay-writing did not feature in their L1 education.

These senses of dominance give priority to the first language. The dominance of one community over another is not relevant to multilingual communities where several languages are in balance. As Canagarajah (2005: 16) points out:

> Although the now discredited notions such as native speaker or mother tongue speaker require us to identify ourselves according to our parental language or language of infancy, even the alternatives such as L1 and L2 force us to identify a single language as receiving primacy in terms of our time of acquisition or level of competence.

Nor does the dominance of one Lang₅ language in the individual's mind square with the idea that the two languages form an interrelated system. It is only in these senses that your first language may change into your second when it becomes dominant in your external or internal life; otherwise a second language will remain second for evermore.

Second and foreign by situation

We can now come back to the second versus foreign language distinction, introduced into EFL teaching in the 1950s (Howatt 1984). A typical definition can be found in Klein (1986: 19):

> ... 'foreign language' is used to denote a language acquired in a milieu where it is normally not in use ... A 'second language' on the other hand, is one that becomes another tool of communication alongside the first language; it is typically acquired in a social environment in which it is actually spoken.

This incorporates two contrasts. One is function: a second language meets a real-life need of the L2 user, say to communicate with the majority community – for example a Chinese speaker using English in Newcastle upon Tyne; a foreign language fulfils no current need for the speaker – for example a Newcastle schoolchild learning French. The other contrast is location: a second language is learnt in a milieu where it is used by native speakers – for example German in Berlin; a foreign language is learnt in a place where it is not widely used – for example German in Japan. Block (2003) draws out the further contrast that a second language is acquired naturalistically; a foreign language is learnt in a classroom.

Much SLA discussion does not take the second/foreign distinction on board, either rejecting it explicitly (Mitchell and Myles 1998: 2), or playing safe by referring to 'the learner of a second or foreign language' (Council of Europe 1997: 12), or using alternative formulations such as 'first' versus 'foreign' (Johnson 2001). The second/foreign distinction is far from transparent. I used to teach English as a foreign language in London to students intending to return shortly to their own countries despite currently using it as a second language; students at English-medium universities may effectively be using it as a second language, whether in Saudi Arabia or the Netherlands.

De Groot and Hell (2005: 25) perceive a difference between North American usage, where a language not native to a country can be either 'foreign' or 'second', and British usage, where 'foreign' means not spoken in a country and 'second' means not 'native' but used widely as medium of communication, say English in Nigeria. There is the additional confusion that what is referred to as 'foreign language teaching' in North America is often called 'modern language teaching' in Europe. Stern (1983: 10) sums up: ' "foreign language" can be subjectively "a language which is not my L1" or objectively "a language which has no legal status within the national boundaries" '.

The distinction was useful for EFL teachers in capturing two broad perspectives on their work. It applies most easily to languages that are confined to one locale: Finnish is either a foreign language outside Finland, or a second language for people acquiring it within Finland. It is more problematic when it concerns languages that are widely spoken by non-native speakers to other non-native speakers across the globe (Berns 1990). A second language is presumably a $Lang_4$; acquiring a second language allows you to join another community. A foreign language, however, in one sense is the $Lang_2$ abstract entity laid down as a goal by education, in another the individual's $Lang_4$ or $Lang_5$ potential stored up for future use.

A wide variety of people are learning second languages in diverse situations for multiple functions. 'First language' or 'second language' are historical terms which are inadequate to cover the complexity of language in our societies and in our minds. The second/foreign language distinction oversimplifies the myriad dimensions of second language learning, as the chapters in VanPatten and Lee (1990) bear out. In particular, it applies uneasily to heritage language learning where people are acquiring a language that is culturally important to them, say Mandarin for those of Chinese origin (who may speak other Chinese dialects such as Cantonese), or Polish for those of Polish descent in London: 140,000 people are attending heritage Chinese classes in the United States (Brecht and Rivers 2005). The reason for learning a heritage language is not primarily to use it as a second or foreign language, but to identify with a particular cultural tradition. Similarly, while school teaching of a modern language has often been seen as involving a 'foreign' language, many students will never use it for second or foreign purposes; it is just a subject on the academic curriculum, and neither a second nor foreign language.

Many researchers manage perfectly well without the second/foreign distinction. R. Ellis (1994: 12) nevertheless claims 'it is possible there will be radical differences in both what is learnt and how it is learnt' in second and foreign language situations. True as this may be, without more evidence we cannot tell if this two-way distinction is more crucial than any of the others. Cook (2009) argues for a spectrum of at least six groups of language users. Rather than a simple opposition of second and foreign, we need multiple distinctions to capture the range of people acquiring second languages. While SLA research is doubtless stuck with the word 'second' in its name, this does not mean it cannot be more rigorous in the ways it actually approaches the diverse situations of second language learning.

Conclusion

This chapter has tried to demonstrate that discussion of second language learning depends on getting straight what is learnt and the circumstances in which it is learnt, that is, 'language' and 'second'. Communication depends on a shared set of meanings, whether between people or between rival theories of language learning. There may be occasions when different meanings of 'second language' can be fruitfully combined. But in each case it has to be shown that there is sufficient compatibility between them. Without agreement over 'second language', SLA researchers perforce have to follow separate paths on different maps. The danger is that SLA researchers often do not realise that they are working from different maps, and exhaust their energy quarrelling over differences in basic assumptions or patiently defending them against their critics. These prolegomena have suggested that SLA research needs to base itself on the foundations of specific notions of 'language' and 'second' before it ventures to tackle the idea of 'learning'. The word 'learning' indeed covers an array of processes, conditions and states in different theories; a simple division such as Krashen's 'acquisition' (natural, unconscious, and so on) versus 'learning' (formal, conscious, and so on) (for example, Dulay et al. 1982), now enjoying a second life as Paradis' distinction between conscious learning and unconscious acquisition (Paradis 2009), is as vast an oversimplification of 'learning' as 'language' and 'second' have turned out to be, as the other chapters in this volume readily demonstrate.

Note

1. This analysis has benefited from comments from many colleagues and from anonymous referees in earlier incarnations.

3
Theoretical Pluralism in SLA: Is There a Way Forward?

Rod Ellis

Introduction

In 1990 Long published a well-received article entitled 'The least a second language acquisition theory needs to explain'. His idea was to establish a set of 'facts' that any theory of second language (L2) acquisition would need to explain and, thereby, provide an empirical basis for evaluating the plethora of theories that were current at that time. Such an approach is admirable, as perhaps the one evaluation criterion that all SLA researchers would sign up to is the need for a theory to be compatible with established empirical findings. The problem, of course, is that the 'facts' themselves are often in dispute. While it is often possible to agree on broad generalisations (for example, 'age differences systematically affect how successful learners are in learning an L2'), it is less easy to reach agreement on more specific statements (such as 'there is a critical period for learning an L2, beyond which it is not possible to achieve native speaker competence'). While some researchers (DeKeyser 2000) claim the existence of a critical period has been clearly established, others (for example Bialystok and Hakuta 1999) dispute its existence while yet others (for example Birdsong 1999) have changed their opinion over time. Even apparently well-established facts have been challenged. For example, Lantolf (2005) queried the existence of acquisition orders and sequences. While it might be an overstatement to claim that just about all the major 'findings' of SLA have been subjected to doubt and revision, it is clear that this is a field where disagreement is rife.

It is, therefore, not surprising that SLA is characterised by theoretical pluralism. The multiplicity of theories is evident in the surveys of SLA that have appeared over the years. In Ellis (1985) I reviewed seven theories, McLaughlin (1987) considered five, Larsen-Freeman and Long

(1991) also examined five (although not the same five as McLaughlin), Mitchell and Myles (1998) discussed six general theoretical 'perspectives' and VanPatten and Williams (2006) examined ten. Furthermore, this theoretical pluralism shows no signs of abating, for, as Spolsky has observed, 'new theories do not generally succeed in replacing their predecessors, but continue to coexist with them uncomfortably' (1990: 609). It is clear that there is no consensus regarding what theory (or even what type of theory) should guide the field forward.

In recent years, a debate has arisen centred around not specific theories but rather the general approach to theory-building in SLA. SLA has become a site of controversy, with some researchers viewing SLA as essentially a cognitive enterprise and others seeing it as a social phenomenon. As Firth and Wagner (2007) put it:

> It appears that SLA has, over the last decade in particular, undergone a bifurcation between a cognitive SLA (which is being termed mainstream in a number of publications) – represented perhaps most clearly in the work undertaken by, for example, Doughty and Long (2003: 4), who see SLA as a 'branch of cognitive science' – and a sociocultural/ sociointeractional SLA.

These two perspectives lead to very different ways of describing, understanding and explaining L2 acquisition. Whereas the former is foremost in the surveys of SLA referred to above, the latter has attracted increasing attention in recent years, dating in particular from Firth and Wagner's (1997) seminal article attacking many of the assumptions that underpin cognitive SLA.

I will begin by identifying what I see as the major differences between 'cognitive' and 'social' SLA. I will then ask whether this controversy represents incommensurate and irreconcilable positions, or whether there is a way forward. A way forward might be achieved by (1) considering which position is 'right' (or at least 'preferred') by invoking and applying a set of evaluation criteria, or (2) asking whether it is possible to integrate the two positions.

Cognitive and social SLA compared

Illustrating the differences

In a special issue of *Modern Language Journal* that revisited the debate centring around the original Firth and Wagner article, Firth and Wagner (2007) spent some time discussing the extract in (1) below from a telephone conversation between a Danish cheese exporter and an Egyptian importer. I will begin by using this extract to illustrate the difference between a cognitive and social perspective on theorising in SLA.

(1)

1. A: we don't want the order after the cheese is uh::h blowing
2. H: see, yes
3. A: so I don't know what I can we can do uh with the order now. (.) What do you think we should do with this is all blowing Mister Hansen (0.7)
4. H: I am not uh (0.7) blowing uh what uh, what is this uh too big or what?
5. A: No the cheese is bad Mister Hansen (0.4) it is like (.) fermenting in the customs cool rooms
6. H: ah it's gone off
7. A: yes, it's gone off

(transcript modified from Firth and Wagner 2007)

From a cognitive perspective this extract illustrates how a negotiation of meaning sequence involving two non-native speakers creates an opportunity for acquisition. A's utterance in (3) contains the word 'blowing', which triggers an indicator of non-understanding on the part of H in (4). This leads to A providing a paraphrase of the troublesome word in (5) – first 'bad' and then 'fermenting'. As a result, A is able to understand the meaning of 'blowing' and demonstrates uptake in (6) by providing his own synonym ('gone off'). Finally, A confirms this paraphrase.

From a social perspective, this exchange reflects the way language is used and acquired in the kinds of multilingual settings that characterise the use of English today. Firth and Wagner (2007) discuss it in this way. In (2) H makes public his lack of familiarity with 'blowing', leading to A explaining its meaning by means of reformulation in (3). H then displays his understanding with his own reformulation in (4) and finally A confirms that shared meaning has been achieved in (5).

On the face of it, the similarities in how such an extract is described in cognitive and social SLA outweigh the differences. Both acknowledge there is a communication problem that is resolved through interaction. There are, however, some fundamental differences between how a cognitive and a social account view such sequences in terms of acquisition. From a cognitive perspective, such sequences assist acquisition because they connect input to internal mechanisms by means of such processes as noticing, noticing-the-gap, and rehearsal (see, for example, Long 1996) and in so doing enable learners to acquire target-language forms. However, such sequences do not in themselves demonstrate that acquisition has taken place. To show this, it is necessary to provide evidence that A stored the word 'blowing' in his/her long-term memory and could recognise its meaning and/or produce it unaided on a later occasion. Producing a new form such as 'blowing' is not acquisition; it merely makes acquisition possible. From a social perspective, such sequences need to be understood in terms of the social context in which they occur and the social relationships of the interlocutors. When two non-native speakers such as A and H are speaking they create their own linguistic resources (which may or may not correspond to target-language norms[1]) in the course of achieving intersubjectivity, and in so doing demonstrate acquisition taking place in flight. Use is acquisition and acquisition is use; it is not possible to draw a clear distinction between 'acquisition' and 'participation' (Sfard 1998).

The dangers of a broad-brush approach

Firth and Wagner (2007) specified what they saw as the main differences between the two perspectives. For them cognitive SLA focuses on 'errors', emphasises the importance of input modification for learning, views the learners' first language (L1) as a source of 'interference', views 'fossilisation' as common if not inevitable for most learners, and adopts an etic stance (that is, focuses on the universal conditions and properties of learning). In contrast, social SLA emphasises the importance of collaboration between learners, sees learning as characterised by invention (as illustrated by the 'blowing' sequence) and as taking place <u>in</u> rather than <u>through</u> social participation, and adopts an emic perspective (that is, focuses on individual learners using and learning the L2 in specific, localised contexts).

This broad characterisation of the two perspectives is helpful but not altogether accurate. In particular it stereotypes both social and cognitive SLA. Cognitive SLA, for example, is more likely to view the L1 as a resource for learning rather than as a source of interference, and certainly does not see fossilisation as inevitable. Social SLA is also a more complex phenomenon than Firth and Wagner acknowledge. It does not constitute a single, homogeneous line of enquiry but rather, like sociolinguistics itself, is evident in a number of different approaches. Coupland (2001) distinguished two main types of sociolinguistic enquiry both of which are reflected in social SLA. What he calls 'socio-structural realism' is evident in social approaches to SLA that seek to explain how macro social factors such as social class and ethnicity impact on the success of individual L2 learners. Examples of this approach are Schumann's (1978) acculturation theory and Gardner's (1985) socio-educational theory. This type of social SLA is entirely compatible with cognitive SLA and, indeed, has figured conspicuously within it. The other main type of sociolinguistic enquiry involves a 'social action perspective'. This assumes that 'social life and our entire experience of society are best seen as structured through local actions and practices' (Coupland 2001: 2). This approach views acquisition as arising in the interactions that learners participate in, and emphasises the importance of identity and communities of practice. It was perhaps first evident in Giles and Byrne's (1982) adaptation of accommodation theory to account for L2 acquisition, and is clearly what Firth and Wagner have in mind when they refer to 'social SLA'. It is worth bearing in mind, however, that there has always been a strong social vein in mainstream SLA, albeit of the socio-structural realism kind. A close look at 'cognitive' and 'social' SLA, then, suggests that broad-brush characterisations of differences, as offered by Firth and Wagner (2007), are misleading, as noted in Seedhouse's concluding chapter in this book.

Elaborating the differences

Nevertheless, there are clear differences that can be discerned in terms of how cognitive and social SLA conceptualise (1) language, (2) representation, (3) the social context, (4) learner identity, (5) the learner's linguistic background, (6) interaction, (7) language learning and also, crucially, (8) the methodology they employ to research L2 acquisition. These differences are summarised in Table 3.1.

These various differences can be summed up in the following two quotations.

> A cognitive theory of second language acquisition seeks to explicate the psychological mechanisms that underlie comprehension and production and the means by which competence develops in the mind of the learner. (Harrington 2002: 124)

> In situated social practices, use and learning are inseparable parts of the interaction. They appear to be afforded by topics and tasks and they seem to be related to specific people, with particularised identities, with whom new ways of behaving occur as the unfolding talk demands. (Firth and Wagner 2007: 812)

In the first, defining cognitive SLA, the key words are 'mechanisms', 'competence', and 'mind'. In the second, defining social SLA, the key terms are 'use', 'specific people', 'identities', and 'new ways of behaving'.

Table 3.1   A comparison of cognitive and social SLA

Dimensions	Cognitive SLA	Social SLA
Language	Language viewed as either a set of formalist rules (as in Chomskyan linguistics) or as a network of form–function mappings (as in functional models of grammar of the Hallidayan type).	Language viewed not just as a linguistic system but as 'a diverse set of cultural practices, often best understood in the context of wider relations of power' (Norton and Toohey 2002: 115).
Mental representation	Two views: (1) as a set of rules that comprise the learner's linguistic competence; (2) as an elaborate network of connections between neural nodes.	In some social theories representation is not considered at all. Vygotskyan approaches emphasise the semantic ('conceptual') rather than the formal properties of the language that learners internalise.
Social context	A broad distinction is made between 'second' and 'foreign' language contexts. Social context is seen as influencing the rate of acquisition and ultimate level of proficiency achieved but not affecting the internal processes responsible for acquisition.	The social context is seen as both determining L2 use and developmental outcomes (as in variationist studies) and as something that is jointly constructed by the participants. The social context is where learning takes place.
Learner identity	The learner is viewed as a 'non-native speaker'. Learner identity is static.	The learner is viewed as having multiple identities that afford different opportunities for language learning. Learner identity is dynamic (see Norton (2000)).
Learner's linguistic background	The learner has full linguistic competence in his/her L1.	Learners may be multilingual and may display varying degrees of proficiency in their various languages.

Continued

Table 3.1 Continued

Dimensions	Cognitive SLA	Social SLA
Input	Input is viewed as linguistic 'data' that serves as a trigger for acquisition. Input is viewed as related to but distinguishable from 'interaction'.	Input is viewed as contextually constructed; it is both linguistic and non-linguistic.
Interaction	Interaction is viewed as a source of input.	Interaction is viewed as a socially negotiated event and a means by which learners are socialised into the L2 culture. Input and interaction are viewed as a 'sociocognitive whole' (Atkinson 2002).
Language learning	L2 acquisition occurs inside the mind of the learner as a result of input that activates universal cognitive processes.	L2 acquisition is 'learning-in-action'; it is not a mental phenomenon but a social and collaborative one. It is an 'interactional phenomenon that transcends contexts while being context dependent' (Firth and Wagner 2007: 807).
Research methodology	Typically, atomistic, quantitative and confirmatory – aims to form generalisations about groups of learners.	Holistic, qualitative and interpretative – focuses on individual learners and specific interactional sequences.

It would seem then that cognitive and social SLA constitute incommensurate paradigms and this is indeed how they have presented themselves. Advocates of social SLA, often seeing themselves as combating an established and 'mainstream' paradigm, have sought to establish their credentials through critiques of cognitive SLA. Even in cases where there are apparent points of contact protagonists of social SLA have insisted on the differences (as for example in Dunn and Lantolf's (1998) exegesis of the difference between Krashen's i+ 1 and Vygotsky's ZPD). Advocates of cognitive SLA have not been slow to respond to the critiques. Long (1998), in particular, writing dismissively of Firth and Wagner's (1997: 92) initial attack, comments:

> Instead of dismissing all work as 'narrow' and 'flawed', and simply asserting that SLA researchers should therefore change their data base and analyses to take new elements into account, [critics] should offer at least some evidence that, for example, a richer understanding of alternative social identities or people currently treated as 'learners', or a broader view of social context, makes a difference, and a difference not just to the way this or that tiny stretch of discourse is interpretable, but to our understanding of acquisition.

Given the strident tone of this debate, it is worth asking how it might be resolved. My purpose in the next section is to consider ways of achieving a resolution. How do we decide which paradigm SLA should adopt in the years ahead?

Resolving the debate

There are a number of ways in which we might seek a resolution to the debate:

1. Adopting a rationalist approach (that is, identifying a set of criteria by which to evaluate the claims of theories based on the alternative paradigms).
2. Adopting a non-judgmental relativist position (that is, accepting that the two paradigms afford different but equally valid and insightful perspectives on the complex phenomenon of L2 acquisition).
3. Assuming an epistemic relativist position (that is, by acknowledging that theories are designed for specific purposes and therefore need to be evaluated in relation to how successful they are in fulfilling their purpose).
4. Developing a composite theory (that is, constructing a theory that incorporates both a cognitive and social perspective).

I will now examine each of these approaches.

The rationalist approach

Rationalists assume that there are objective truths to be discovered and that the goal of a theory is to explain these. Gregg (2000: 389) staked out the standard rationalist position:

> Scientists test claims. They test them by making predictions about the world, which they try to confirm or disconfirm by experiment and observation.

It follows from such a position that a good theory is one that can account adequately for the known empirical truths (what Long (1990) called 'established findings') while a bad (or less satisfactory) theory is one that does not. It also follows that once a theory has been identified as unsatisfactory it should be 'culled'. Long (1993) argued that theory 'culling' was necessary to enable SLA to advance from what Kuhn (1962) called the 'pre-paradigm stage' to the 'normal science stage'. He argued that the history of science shows that successful sciences are those that are guided by a 'dominant theory'. Thus, in Long's opinion, only when researchers can agree on a particular theoretical approach are they be able to get on with the business of solving more and more problems and expanding knowledge without wasteful expenditure of energy in fruitless controversies. Beretta (1993) adopted a similar position, noting the advantages of advocating a 'tribal model' – that is, a theory that is aggressively promoted so that it stimulates others to explore and elaborate. Gregg's advocacy of a theory based on Universal Grammar and Long's promotion of the Interaction Hypothesis can both be seen as attempts to establish a tribal model.

If culling is to take place and tribal models established then it is necessary to establish a basis for deciding which theories should survive and which should perish. One way of achieving this entails identifying a set of criteria that can be applied to all theories as a way of eliminating those that are unsatisfactory. This, according to Beretta (1991) and Long (1993), should be the goal of SLA research. Various criteria have been proposed (see Jordan 2003; Long 1993; McLaughlin 1987; Mitchell and Myles 1998; Towell and Hawkins 1994). In R. Ellis (2008) I attempted a synthesis of the main criteria, which are listed and commented on in Table 3.2 below. It must be acknowledged, however, that there is no universally agreed set of criteria. Social SLA theorists, for example, might well make out a case for including the social value of a theory as a key criterion.[2]

Table 3.2   Criteria for evaluating theories

Criterion	Commentary
Scope of the theory	There is general agreement that a theory with a broad scope is preferable to a theory with a narrow scope. McLaughlin proposed that a theory should fit the body of established knowledge about L2 acquisition. Both Mitchell and Myles, and Jordan, explicitly mention the need for a theory to be broad in scope. Towell and Hawkins are more specific, identifying five 'core areas' that a theory should account for.
Empirical support	McLaughlin, Long, Mitchell and Myles, and Jordan all recognise the importance of this criterion. A good theory must be compatible with what is known about L2 acquisition.
Internal consistency	Long and Jordan both consider that the extent to which the theory is internally consistent (that is, coherent and cohesive) is important. Long sees internal consistency as a criterion that should be applied prior to empirical testing.
External consistency	A theory that is consistent with other recognised theories is better than one that is not. However, this does raise the question as to what theories the theory being evaluated should be compared with. McLaughlin refers to 'related theories' and Long to 'accepted theories in other fields'. However, the question then arises how to establish 'relatedness' and 'acceptability' in other fields.
Fruitfulness	McLaughlin, Long, and Jordan all consider that an indicator of a strong theory is whether it motivates substantial research and is likely to continue to do so in the future. The theory should help to establish new knowledge and to challenge established knowledge.
Simplicity	Jordan claimed that a theory 'with the simplest formula, and the fewest number of basic types of entity postulated, is to be preferred for reasons of economy' (p. 97). However, Gregg (2003) considered 'simplicity' a 'red herring' and noted that it not easy to determine what constitutes relative simplicity, given the difficulty of comparing theories that are formulated in different ways.
Falsifiability	This is widely invoked in accordance with a Popperian view of theory development, but is generally seen as problematic. Beretta (1991), for example, argued that it is impossible to obtain neutral, objective data with which to test theoretical claims and that theories tend to be formulated in such a way that they allow for *ad hoc* or auxiliary hypotheses as a way of immunising initial hypotheses against disconfirming evidence.

Applying such criteria with a view to identifying, on rationalist grounds, the strengths and weaknesses of theories and determining which should be culled is highly problematic for a number of reasons. First, all the criteria are framed in very general terms and cannot be easily operationalised. For example, how broad in scope does a theory have to be? How does one determine 'breadth'? How does one determine whether a theory is internally consistent? How can the criterion of external consistency be applied in evaluating theories drawn from entirely different paradigms which by definition must be incommensurate? How does one determine whether a theory is compatible with the empirical facts when the facts themselves (and even what constitutes a 'fact') are often disputed? And even if one could agree on the facts, as Sfard (1998: 12) noted, 'empirical evidence is unlikely to serve as an effective weapon in paradigm wars'. Perhaps the only criterion for which objective assessment is possible is 'fruitfulness', where it might be possible to use a citation index as a measure. Second, as Table 3.2 makes clear, some criteria (in particular 'simplicity' and 'falsifiabilty') are inherently problematic, with very different views about their validity as evaluative criteria. Third, even if it is possible to apply the criteria, how does one decide the weighting of the different criteria? What is the relative importance of internal and external consistency, for example?

These problems, however, have not prevented rationalists such as Jordan from proceeding to conduct evaluations of different theories. Thus, with some doubts, I too will attempt an evaluation of a cognitive theory (the Interaction Hypothesis) and sociocultural theory (as evidenced in the work of Lantolf). My evaluation is presented in Table 3.3. What seems clear to me from such an exercise is the impossibility of determining which theory to keep and which to cull. In their own terms, each theory holds up well against the criteria.

In conclusion, it does not seem to me that a rationalist solution to the debate between advocates of a cognitive and a social SLA is possible. First, there is no universally accepted set of criteria. Acknowledgement of this is a recurring refrain in the commentaries on SLA theory evaluation. Beretta (1991) concluded his discussion of the various evaluative criteria with the assertion that there are no foolproof, indispensable criteria available. Jordan (2003: 97), some 12 years later, commented that 'there are no golden rules for theory assessment, no hard and fast rules, except the obvious requirement that a theory has empirical content'. Nor is it likely that any consensus will be reached in the years ahead, given the philosophical disagreements about such fundamental issues as 'objective evidence'.[3] Second, even if a set of criteria (such as those listed in Tables 3.2 and 3.3) could be agreed upon, there is no widely

Table 3.3 Applying the criteria to a cognitive and social theory of L2 acquisition

Criterion	Interaction Hypothesis (IH)	Sociocultural SLA theory (SCT)
Scope	Narrow (that is, it views 'interaction' narrowly in terms of the negotiation of meaning and does not seek to be a complete theory of L2 acquisition).	Broad (that is, it views interaction much more broadly and seeks to account for how all aspects of language are acquired).
Empirical support	There is now a substantial body of empirical research documenting how negotiation assists acquisition (see, for example, Mackey 2007).	There is a growing body of research examining L2 interactions from the perspective of SCT but, in general, theory has outrun empirical evidence.
Internal consistency	The IH is internally consistent with the underlying view that language/acquisition is a mental phenomenon.	SCT is internally consistent with the view that language/ acquisition is essentially a socio-psychological construct.
External consistency[4]	The IH is consistent with other cognitive accounts of L2 acquisition (for example, Schmidt's (1994) Noticing Hypothesis).	SCT is based on and compatible with Vygotskyan theory of the mind and with activity theory.
Fruitfulness	The IH has proved highly fruitful, leading to a large number of empirical studies.	SCT is increasingly fruitful as reflected in the growing number of empirical studies based on it.
Simplicity	The variables are pre-determined, specific, and limited in number.	Variables are broad (for example, 'private speech'), not easily operationalised, and emerging rather than fixed.
Falsifiability	Potentially falsifiable but the theory has shifted over time to accommodate new variables leading to controversy (for example, regarding the role of modified output).	Potentially falsifiable in some aspects (for example, the role of corrective feedback in assisting self-regulation – see Aljaafreh and Lantolf 1994); other aspects (for example, the role of private speech) are less easily falsifiable.

accepted procedure for applying them to the evaluation of specific theories. Thus, while it might be useful to subject theories to rational evaluation as a means of examining their strengths and weaknesses, it is very doubtful if such an evaluation can provide a basis for culling some theories and keeping others, let alone deciding which paradigm should prevail.

Non-judgmental relativism

Non-judgmental relativism (often referred to as cultural relativism) is the standard approach in modern anthropology, where the aim (as far as is possible) is to examine cultures in their own terms without making any value judgments. Applied to theory-building in SLA this amounts to acknowledging that each theory (or paradigm) has validity in its own right and therefore that it is not possible to claim that one theory (or paradigm) is superior to another. It would follow from such a position that we should 'let all the flowers grow': the title of Lantolf's (1996) article, where he argued in favour of broadening the scope of SLA beyond what he termed a 'computational model'.

SLA has not been short of non-judgmental relativists. Many researchers are quite happy to beaver away within the confines of their own preferred theoretical orientation and leave others to do the same in theirs. In effect these are *de facto* non-judgmental relativists. Other researchers have more explicitly embraced non-judgmental relativism, spawning an often acrimonious debate with the rationalists in the field.

Schumann (1993: 301), for example, argued that theory development should be seen as a process of 'exploration' involving 'efforts to expand, revise, alter, and ultimately to understand and assess the validity of the construct'. Schumann considered a 'reductionist' approach that accommodates explanation at different levels as preferable to a 'closurist' approach of the kind favoured by the rationalists. Block (1996) took objection to what he saw as a ruling clique in SLA. He challenged the assumptions which he viewed as strangling SLA enquiry – namely that there is such a thing as 'normal science' and that there is an 'ample body' of 'accepted findings' – and he argued that the multiplicity of theories in SLA is not problematic. In his book, Block (2003: 7) again confronted the 'self-proclaimed authorities/gatekeepers of SLA' (that is, Long, Gass et al.) and sought to 'circumvent exclusionary stances'. He argued for a broadening of SLA with regard to what is understood by the terms 'second', 'language', and 'acquisition' – an approach adopted by Cook in his chapter in this book. In effect, Block sought to broaden SLA's frame of reference to include a social perspective on L2 acquisition. The relativist position was most clearly articulated by Lantolf (1996: 721) in the article referred to above. Lantolf argued that theories are inherently metaphorical – 'theories are metaphors that have achieved the status of acceptance by a group of people we refer to as scientists' – and argued that SLA researchers needed to create new metaphors to represent multiple realities. Lantolf explicitly favoured a plurality of theories, seeing relativism as a defence against what he saw as the hegemony of a dominant theory (that is Chomsky's). Firth and Wagner (2007), despite their obvious allegiance to the social paradigm, argued for a theoretical, methodological and epistemological broadening of SLA rather than the replacement of the cognitive paradigm with a social one. Seedhouse (see Chapter 14) similarly argues for theoretical eclecticism.

Unsurprisingly this advocacy of non-judgmental relativism has not been to the taste of rationalists.[5] Gregg, Long, Jordan, and Beretta (1997) responded to Block (1996). Gregg (2000) responded to Lantolf (1996). He dismissed the postmodernist and constructivist arguments that underlie relativism, concluding that relativists need to 'get real'. According to Gregg, SLA researchers should act as scientists by recognising that the 'goals of scientific enquiry include the discovery of objective empirical truths' (Fodor 1998: 189). Lantolf (2002) followed up with 'a commentary from the flower garden', reaffirming the relativist case, while Gregg (2002) was given the last word – 'a garden ripe for weeding'. Long (2006: 156) reviewed this exchange of views, concluding that 'it is not true that a multiplicity of theories in a field is unproblematic' and arguing that to adopt such a position is 'tantamount to a declaration of irresponsibility or else a belief that progress is unattainable'.

There is no obvious resolution to this debate, which clearly underscores the cognitive/social SLA divide. Cognitive theorists align themselves with what they see as a rationalist 'scientism'. Social theorists belong to the relativist camp, although they also clearly believe in the superiority of their own broader, societal view of SLA perhaps because they view their relativist arguments as a strategy for obtaining entry to the 'closed shop' of SLA. It is clear, however, that the rationalists have not succeeded in putting up the barriers as, increasingly, research articles based on a social epistemology of one kind of another are appearing in the academic journals. Does this mean, therefore, that 'anything goes'? There is an obvious danger of absolute relativism for, as Firth and Wagner (2007: 813) observed, the field may not be able to 'withstand the current bifurcations, competing methods, critiques, and internal tensions, and remain generally cohesive'. One possible way out of this quagmire is to adopt an epistemic relativist stance.

Epistemic relativism

Reading through the critiques and counter-critiques of the cognitive and social SLA apologists, I am struck by just how locked into their own way of characterising and investigating L2 acquisition the two camps are. This antithetical positioning is reflected very accurately in Parrini's (1998: 35) definition of epistemic relativism:

> The core of epistemic relativism is the idea that scientific knowledge is set within a conceptual scheme more or less uniformly shared by a community of individuals engaged in certain scientific-cognitive practices. This epistemic framework is a research perspective which is closely tied to the structure of the language which is used, incorporates a 'thought style' concerning a variety of more or less clearly characterised phenomena, delimits the class of legitimate problems and sets standards of acceptable solutions.

It is not difficult to spot the 'conceptual schema' of the two camps, to identify the 'community of individuals' in each camp, and to distinguish their 'scientific-cognitive practices', their choice of language, their 'thought-styles', the 'problems' they choose to address, and the 'standards' they set for 'acceptable solutions'. Indeed, this is exactly what I set out to do in an earlier section of this chapter.

Parrini goes on to contrast epistemic relativism with what I have called absolute relativism by emphasising that epistemic relativism acknowledges that scientific thinking is necessarily contextual (that is, takes place within a 'provisionally accepted conceptual scheme') and allows for the possibility of evaluating 'alternative presuppositional frameworks' that lie within that scheme. I take this to mean that while it may prove impossible to evaluate different paradigms, it is possible to evaluate the strengths and weaknesses of different theories within the same paradigm.

This corresponds to the position I have taken in R. Ellis (1995, 2008). I argue that theories should be evaluated in relation to the context in which they were developed and the purpose(s) they are intended to serve. By way of example, I suggested that a UG-based theory is to be understood in terms of the field of Chomskyan linguistics from which it was developed, and thus needs to be evaluated with regard to the contributions that it makes to that field. It would seem to me entirely inappropriate to try to understand and evaluate such a theory from the point of view of a foreign language teacher. In contrast, sociocultural SLA has been developed by researchers interested in language pedagogy;

constructs such as mediation and the zone of proximal development have obvious relevance to teachers.

An approach to evaluation that acknowledges that theories are contextually determined allows for an acceptance of complementarity without a commitment to absolute relativism. It can still be argued that among theories constructed for the same purpose and context, one does a better job than another because it is more complete, fits the facts (if these can be agreed upon) better, affords more interesting predictions, is more consistent with other theories, and so on. For example, among early cognitive theories, Bialystok's Theory of L2 Learning (see Bialystok 1978) might be considered a better theory than Krashen's Monitor Theory (see Krashen 1981) because it allows for an interface between explicit and implicit knowledge, for which there is growing empirical support. Similarly, it could be argued that, among social theories, sociocultural SLA (as in Lantolf and Thorne 2006) provides a fuller and more convincing account than the sociointeractional theory promoted by Firth and Wagner (1997, 2007) because it seeks to explain not just how learning arises in social activity but how it becomes subsequently internalised. The importance of accounting for 'internalisation' is something I will return to later.

Recognising that theories are necessarily contextual and purposeful raises the key issue of who should be the arbitrator of whether a particular theory is valid (that is, of practical use). I would argue that ultimately it is not the SLA theorist who should decide whether a particular theory is relevant to a particular purpose, but the consumers of the theory. SLA is in essence an applied discipline, and any attempt to evaluate its products without reference to their applications is doomed to failure. This is why SLA theories are not usually abandoned as a result of empirical study or powerful argumentation, but rather slip slowly and gently into oblivion if and when they are no longer seen as useful. Over the years, it is possible to detect a gradual waning of influence of some theories (such as the Monitor Theory (see Krashen 1981), or my own Variable Competence Theory[6]) and the continued support given to others (for example, the Interaction Hypothesis – see Long (1996) – and sociocultural theory). Ultimately, it is not that the unsuccessful theories fail to match up to rationalist criteria while successful theories do (although evaluating theories within a paradigm against such criteria may be of value); it is rather that some theories are found to be useful by researchers and/or practitioners and others are not.

An epistemic relativist stance, therefore, affords a possible way of escaping the confrontation between cognitive and social SLA, while avoiding the philosophical (and practical) problems associated with absolute relativism. It allows for the co-existence of the two paradigms, while allowing for theories within each one to be examined critically. There remains, however, a final possibility; one that perhaps holds out more hope for SLA, as it may prevent the field bifurcating and splitting apart – that is, the development of a paradigm that reconciles the cognitive and social dimensions of L2 acquisition. It is this possibility that is explored in a number of the chapters in this book (see Larsen-Freeman's and Myles' chapters in particular).

Developing a composite theory: Sociocognitive SLA

A composite theory of L2 acquisition will need to ensure:

> ...a focus on real persons, rather than on learners as theoretical abstractions; a focus on the agency of the individual person as a thinking, feeling human being, with an identity, a personality, a unique history and background, a person with goals, motives and intentions; a focus on the interaction between this self-reflective agent, and the fluid and complex system of social relations, activities, experiences and multiple micro- and macro-contexts in which the person is embedded, moves and is inherently part of. (Ushioda 2007)

In other words, a composite theory will need to account for how peoples' cognitive and social worlds coalesce and how this helps to construct contexts-of-acquisition. The theory that holds the greatest promise for achieving this is sociocognitive theory.

In making the case for a sociocognitive approach to both L2 use and acquisition, Batstone (2010) wrote:

> When we adopt a sociocognitive perspective on language use, we subscribe to the view that the social and the cognitive are not merely co-present (a point which few scholars would take issue with) but interdependent. Sociocognition is based on the view that all forms of language use always have both a social and a cognitive dimension, that understanding language acquisition involves understanding how these two dimensions interrelate, and that acquisition cannot be adequately explained any other way (for example, through the view that acquisition is essentially cognitive, or entirely social).

For Batstone, the essence of a sociocognitive theory lies in acknowledging the distinction between performance (a social phenomenon) and competence (a cognitive phenomenon), but viewing them as not separable but as 'continually related through co-constructed interaction'. That is, when communicating, we draw on our 'prior conceptions' (our schematic knowledge, the scripts we have developed from previous interactions, and our personal identities) while simultaneously attending to what Gumperz (1982) has called 'contextualisation cues' (that is, the linguistic signs that signal how speakers are orienting to the discourse in terms of the identity they have chosen to enact in a particular context). In this way, speakers achieve what sociocultural researchers have termed 'intersubjectivity' – a convergence of the speakers' internal and external worlds. This convergence may entail an equal meeting of minds or be asymmetrical, where one speaker's schema takes precedence over that of another, as often occurs in service encounters between immigrants and native speakers.[7]

Batstone makes a useful contrast between a 'sociocognitive' and a 'sociolinguistic' theory. The former acknowledges the distinction between performance and competence, and seeks to account for how they are interrelated. The latter rejects the notion of cognition (or at least treats it as insignificant), arguing that 'competence' is a social rather than cognitive issue (that is, language should be seen as 'speech' rather than as an abstract linguistic system – see Johnson 2004). In these terms, it is clear that Firth and Wagner's sociointeractional approach to SLA is essentially sociolinguistic.

It is of course one thing to make a case for a sociocognitive theory of language use and entirely another to show how sociocognition can explain L2 acquisition. Much of what Batstone has to say about sociocognition concerns language use but he also addresses how it can inform acquisition. He makes the important point that a sociocognitive theory of L2 acquisition needs to explain both lower-order aspects of language (that is, sounds, vocabulary and grammar) and higher-order aspects (that is, genres and interactional competence as manifested through identity). In other words, as Cook in Chapter 2 of this book and Seedhouse in Chapter 14 argue, it is essential to define exactly what is meant by 'language' and to recognise that the goal of SLA is not just to explain how learners acquire lower-order aspects. Sociocognitive theory can be distinguished from a purely cognitive theory of the kind advanced by Pienemann (see Chapter 5), which traditionally has addressed only lower-order features of language, and a sociolinguistic theory of the kind that underlies Doehler's study (see Chapter 7) that has focused on higher-order features. But how can a sociocognitive theory account for acquisition other than through the rather simplistic (and uninformative) claim that acquisition arises out of the use of the L2? To address this question Batstone discusses what he sees as 'a fundamental characteristic of learning – transfer'. This addresses how performance of a specific interactional competence in one context comes to be generalised to performance in other contexts. Batstone comments that 'it is very difficult to see how we can explain generalisation without recourse to cognition' and goes on to quote Sfard (1998: 9):

> Our ability to prepare ourselves today to deal with new situations we are going to encounter tomorrow is the very essence of learning. Competence means being able to repeat what can be repeated while changing what needs to be changed. How is all of this accounted for if we are not allowed to talk about carrying anything from one situation to another?

Sfard concluded that we need both metaphors – 'participation' and 'acquisition'. Batstone, however, sees the distinction as a divisive one, and argues that sociocognition provides for a connection between the two. He suggests that a key construct for making this connection is 'identity', which he sees as both a cognitive and a social phenomenon. It is cognitive because it constitutes a stored representation of the self, and it is social because it is enacted (and modified) through interaction. But the question remains as to how learners actually acquire the linguistic resources of an L2 (in the sense that transfer and generalisation become evident, and new forms and functions of language emerge in new contexts) and how a sociocognitive theory can account for this. Batstone recognises that 'grammar ought to loom large in sociocognition', but is not able to explain how, beyond proposing that rules are acquired as a result of recurrent social practices where linguistic rules serve as 'a useful if not essential resource'. So what is missing from Batstone's account is any detailed explanation of how a sociocognitive theory can explain how (and when) 'change' in some aspect of linguistic representation takes place.

A number of theories can lay claim to being sociocognitive in nature – socialisation theories that draw on Lave and Wenger's (1991) notion of 'communities of practice', theories of interactional competence (for example, Young 1999), sociocultural theories (for example, Lantolf and Thorne 2006), chaos/complexity theory (Larsen-Freeman and Cameron 2008a; see also Chapter 4) and a theory that specifically calls itself 'sociocognitive' (Atkinson 2002; Atkinson et al. 2007). For reasons of space, I will focus on Atkinson's theory here.

Atkinson's starting point is much the same as Batstone's:

> Neither language acquisition nor language use – nor even cognised linguistic knowledge – can be properly understood without taking into account their fundamental integration into a socially-mediated world. (Atkinson 2002: 534)

Like Batstone, he argues for the inseparability of the social and the cognitive. A sociocognitive event is 'profoundly integrative' (Atkinson 2002). Thus, the simple activity of exchanging greetings involves 'facial expression, physical orientations, affective stance, a conventionalised social scene in a social setting with a social purpose performed by social actors and the effective deployment of the social tool of language' (ibid: 531–2). For Atkinson, language is simultaneously in the world and in the learner's head and thus is neither 'social' nor 'cognitive', but both simultaneously. Nor does he accept the sociocultural view of the relationship between the social and the cognitive – namely that language originates in social interaction but is subsequently internalised as the learner achieves self-regulation. For Atkinson, language never takes on a purely internal, mental function but always co-exists in cognitive and social space.

How then do learners come to acquire a second language? Atkinson's (2002) article has little to say about this, focusing instead on what is wrong with cognitive SLA in much the same way as social theorists do. However, in Atkinson, Nishino, Churchill and Okada (2007: 171), this question is addressed head-on. They key construct is 'alignment', defined as:

> ...the means by which human actors dynamically adapt to – that is, flexibly depend upon, integrate with, and construct – the ever-changing mind-body-world environments posited by sociocognitive theory.

Language learning, like any other kind of learning, arises as a result of human attempts to survive in an unpredictable environment through alignment of their resources in interaction. This later article, however, seems to also accept the need for a more clearly articulated cognitive dimension of learning, for learning involves more than alignment – it also entails incorporating the experience obtained through the effort to align into 'flexible models, strategies, networks and perspectives' (ibid: 171). But these are terms taken from cognitive SLA and do not do justice to the integrative model of learning that Atkinson and his co-authors seek to develop, so learning is finally redefined as:

> ... trajectories of ecological experience and repertoires of participation, gained in the process of adaptive dynamics. (Ibid: 172)

This is a very abstract conceptualisation of learning but, fortunately, Atkinson et al. go on to suggest how it might be investigated and examine how alignment can create the 'trajectories of ecological experience and repertoires of participation' that constitute learning. They describe a series of interactions between a Japanese high-school student (Ako) and her aunt as they work collaboratively on an English exercise, practising the 'have you ever' construction. In accordance with their view that learning entails the synchronisation of world-body-mind they adopt a methodology that includes the detailed examination of the artefacts they jointly produce, their postures as they interact, and transcriptions of their interactions, to demonstrate Ako's 'growing ability to participate meaningfully in conversations using the *Have you (ever) experience* construction' (ibid: 182).

A sociocognitive theory of the kind described by Batstone and Atkinson holds considerable promise for bridging the divide between a purely social and an essentially cognitive theory by taking as axiomatic that 'what goes on between is of equal importance to what goes in' (Atkinson et al. 2007). However, as yet, there is scarcely any empirical evidence to demonstrate this, nor is it yet clear what methodology is needed to investigate it. As things stand, Long's demand that researchers show how identity or 'a broader view of social context' can contribute to our understanding of acquisition (see quotation on p. 30) has not yet been convincingly addressed. In the next section, I would like to consider how researchers working within a sociocognitive frame of reference might set about satisfying Long and other cognitivists.

Towards a methodology for sociocognitive SLA

A key issue in developing a methodology for investigating sociocognitive SLA, is whether sociocognitive activity is viewed as 'situated cognition' (that is, holistically), as in Atkinson's approach, or as a composite of social and cognitive processes (that is, synthetically), as in Batstone's approach. In the case of the former, no clear distinction between performance and competence can be drawn (as in other socially-oriented approaches), while in the latter, social and cognitive processes are distinguished while also seen as inevitably co-occurring in language use and learning. This distinction between a holistic and a synthetic approach needs to be reflected in how sociocognitive activity is investigated. If language learning is viewed as 'situated cognition', the methodology will be that of discourse/conversation analysis (that is, interactional sequences will be submitted to careful analysis with a view to demonstrating how language learning arises in the act of communicating). However, if language learning is viewed as the integration of distinct social and cognitive processes, a different methodology will be needed. It will still be necessary to demonstrate how learning evolves out of interaction through discourse/conversation analysis, but in addition, it will require a demonstration of the cognitive processes that are involved in communicative exchanges and that, potentially, are changed in the course of conducting them. Below I will outline the methodological procedures that the holistic and the synthetic views of sociocognition entail. First, though, I will address a methodological issue that is common to both.

Any theory of L2 acquisition – and a sociocognitive theory is no exception – must necessarily account for change in the learner's use of the L2 over time. It is simply not possible to talk about 'acquisition' (however defined) without acknowledging that it involves change. As Larsen-Freeman (2007: 783) noted, 'any definition of learning must involve the transcendence of a particular time and space'. What is needed then is a clear operational definition of what 'change' involves. I would like to suggest that to demonstrate change it is ideally necessary to show that:

1. the learner could not do x at time a (the 'gap');
2. the learner co-adapted x at time b ('social construction');
3. the learner initiated x at time c in a similar context as in time b ('internalisation/ self-regulation');
4. the learner employed x at time d in a new context ('transfer of learning');

where x refers to some micro or macro feature of language (for example, a specific lexical item or a particular genre). This definition assumes that change (and therefore acquisition) can occur at three different levels. Level 1 is where change originates in social activity – it is a scaffolded construct. To demonstrate this, it is necessary to provide evidence that the learner could not perform x prior to the occasion when its jointly constructed use becomes evident. Level 2 is where the learner demonstrates the ability to use the newly acquired feature in a similar context to that in which it first appeared, but independently of any interlocutor's scaffolding. Level 3 occurs when the learner can extend the use of the feature to an entirely different context. These levels reflect 'depth' of acquisition. In other words, acquisition should not be viewed as an all-or-nothing phenomenon (that is, the learner 'knows' or 'does not know' something), as demonstrated so clearly for vocabulary acquisition in Elgort and Nation's chapter in this book, but as incremental and continuous. Arguably, acquisition is never complete, as the potential for transfer of learning (what I have called Level 3) is ever-present – a view that is compatible with a dynamic systems view of language acquisition (Larsen-Freeman and Cameron 2008a; Chapter 4).

Let us now see how this operational definition of change/acquisition plays out in an analysis of learners' use of language in communication. Extract (1), considered earlier, involved an interaction between a Danish cheese exporter communicating with his Egyptian customer by telephone about a problem with a consignment of cheese. In this extract we can see clear evidence of Level 1 change. That is, H manifests a 'gap' in his understanding of 'blowing', a gap that is subsequently addressed by his interlocutor (A) to the point where he indicates his comprehension of this word. There is, however, no evidence of Level 2 or Level 3 change. Firth and Wagner (2007), however, provide a further extract involving these two speakers, when two days later they again address the problem about the cheese. This extract is shown in (2):

(2)

A: yes (.) mister Hansen
H: Hello Mister Akkad (.) hh we haf some informations for you about the cheese (.) with the blowing
A: yes mister Hansen

On this occasion H is able to produce 'blowing' without any assistance from A, demonstrating Level 2 change. Firth and Wagner (2007: 808) comment that this second encounter shows how learning 'is carried over in time and space' and that 'H has now learned this lexical item in a way that extends beyond the concrete local context where he first became acquainted with it' (ibid: 809). However, the context in (2) is essentially the same as in (1) – that is, the medium of communication is the same (telephone), the interlocutors are the same, and the topic is the same. For this reason, I do not think it is possible to claim that

Level 3 change has been shown. To achieve this it would be necessary to provide evidence of H's ability to use 'blowing' in a new and different context (for example, when addressing a different topic with a different interlocutor).

Many of the differences between social and cognitive SLA have arisen because researchers working in these paradigms differ in how they conceptualise and operationalise 'acquisition'. If there is acceptance of the operational definition I have outlined above – a definition that I would argue is inherently sociocognitive – then it may indeed be possible to bridge the paradigm divide. Armed with this definition, I will now return to the question of the methodologies needed to investigate acquisition within the holistic and synthetic versions of socio-cognitive SLA.

Situated cognition can only be investigated by examining the authentic social interactions that learners participate in – as Atkinson et al. (2007: 173) put it, 'in a real-world, real-time case of doing-thinking-learning'. Atkinson et al.'s methodology for achieving this involves the analysis of video-taped recordings of interactions supported by detailed background information about the participants and of the physical and social learning contexts in which they were located.[8] Also included in the analysis are the artefacts that the participants make use of while interacting (in this case the worksheet that Ako, the high-school student, completed). The analysis itself takes the form of a running commentary on excerpts from the totality of the interaction, selected because they are revealing of the process of learning-through-speaking. The running commentary incorporates reference to posture, gesture, actions, what is said, how it is said (for example, aloud or *sub voce*), and the artefacts present. The aim is to provide as complete a picture as possible of what transpires between the interlocutors – 'the whole complex repertoire of meaningful action within and across multiple semiotic fields' (ibid: 177). The aim is to demonstrate 'learning in flight' where learning is conceptualised as 'repertoires of participation' rather than as internalised thought (a sociocultural construct) or decontextualised grammar rules (a cognitive construct). In other words, learning is evident in Ako's growing ability to participate in exchanges using the grammatical construction that is the focus of her interaction with her aunt. In order to document this development Atkinson et al. examine interactions at both a single point in time and also across time. Such an analysis aims to capture the 'shared cognition' of the participants but, interestingly, it seeks to achieve this almost entirely in terms of the language we associate with the description of social interaction (for example, 'scaffolding', 'repetition', 'elaboration', 'co-constructed nego-tiation' and 'other-completions') with almost no reference to cognitive constructs such as 'knowledge' or 'attention'. In 'situated cognition' it is the social rather than the cognitive that dominates.

A synthetic approach to investigating L2 acquisition as sociocogni-tion offers more opportunity for examining cognitive aspects. As with the holistic approach, the actual interactions that learners participate in will constitute the primary data for analysis. But if we want to find how the learners draw on their existing knowledge and on such cogni-tive processes as attention and rehearsal, we need to do more than sim-ply infer what goes on mentally from the social actions that we observe. The obvious tool to use here is stimulated recall. This allows us – albeit retrospectively – access to how learners cognised specific interactional events. As Gass and Mackey (2000) point out, the use of stimulated recall is controversial given the difficulty of determining whether it is actually capable of capturing the thought-processes of participants, but it is surely preferable to obtain participants' own reports on their mental processing rather than simply inferring them from the text of an interaction.

To conclude, a methodology for investigating acquisition as sociocog-nition should ideally include the following:

1. Longitudinal data collected from naturally-occurring social events that will enable the researcher to demonstrate to what extent 'change' takes place over time.
2. Rich analyses of specific interactions involving learners, based not just on the texts they produce but also on detailed information about the participants, their physical location and their artefacts. These analyses will need to examine a wide range of behaviours – paralin-guistic as well as linguistic.
3. Data that directly address the cognitive aspects of sociocognitive events (for example, stimulated recall protocols).

Finally, to reiterate a point made earlier, the focus of sociocognitive research will include both micro and macro aspects of language.

It should be clear that sociocognitive research will be difficult to accomplish. It will be time- consuming and require painstaking analy-sis. It will almost certainly need to allow the data collected to deter-mine which aspect of language to investigate, given the difficulty of obtaining authentic data containing pre-determined target features. For this reason sociocognitive research is likely to follow Atkinson et al.'s example, and be ethnographic and interpretative in style rather than experimental and confirmatory.

Conclusion

Theoretical pluralism – always endemic in SLA – has coalesced around two paradigms in the last ten years or so. Cognitive SLA seeks to explain the universal properties of L2 acquisition in terms of a computational metaphor according to which input is processed internally, resulting in some form of mental representation of the L2 which is then drawn on in output. In the cognitive paradigm, a clear distinction is drawn between 'use' and 'acquisition'. Social SLA views L2 acquisition as highly variable, reflecting the socio-histories of individual learners. In this paradigm, the emphasis is placed on the contextual and interactional dimensions of language use. The goal is to track acquisition as it arises through learners' participation in naturalistic encounters involving the L2. Thus, no clear distinction is made between 'use' and 'acquisition'. Each paradigm gives rise to a number of different theories. In the cognitive paradigm, for instance, different theories posit a symbolic or connectionist modelling of L2 knowledge. Social theories differ in the extent to which they view learners as constructed by their social worlds, or as agents who actively shape their participation in it. These within-paradigm differences are real and substantial, but the between-paradigm differences are arguably greater as they lead to fundamental discrepancies in how language, context, the learner's identity and background, interaction, and learning itself are conceptualised and, consequently, in the methodology used to investigate language use/learning. The question arises, therefore, as to whether SLA can withstand the existence of such apparently incommensurate approaches to the discipline – marked by calls from social SLA theorists for a fundamental reconceptualisation of the field and by the reaffirmation of SLA as an essentially cognitive field of enquiry by cognitive SLA theorists – or whether it should endeavour, in one way or another, to resolve the epistemological and methodological controversies that have arisen.

SLA is no different from any other social science (and perhaps no different from the physical sciences) in spawning multiple theories. Given the difficulty of agreeing exactly what the 'facts' of L2 acquisition are, and the complexity of the phenomena under study, theoretical pluralism is arguably inevitable. This should not be considered grounds for claiming that SLA is an 'immature' field of study. Rather it should be acknowledged as a reflection of the intense interest that L2 acquisition has generated in a world where the importance of communication between speakers of different languages, and therefore the need for language learning, has never been greater. I have always preferred to view the plethora of theories in SLA as evidence of the field's vibrant health.

Nevertheless, it does seem to me that there is a need to consider how the often antagonistic debates that theoretical pluralism generates can be resolved. Thus, in this chapter I have examined a number of ways of addressing theoretical differences, focusing on the recent debates between cognitive and social SLA. I have argued that the rationalist evaluation of theories based on an explicit set of criteria is very unlikely to succeed, given the problems in both determining what the criteria should be and in applying them. I have also argued against absolute relativism (an 'anything goes' approach) on the grounds that it runs the risk of allowing SLA to divide into separate camps that refuse to speak to each other. Instead, I have examined two proposals that might provide a way forward. The first – epistemic relativism – acknowledges that theories are contextual and purposeful, and thus need to be evaluated in terms of what they seek to explain. Such an approach would admit that cognitive and social theories both have a place in a broadly-defined SLA, as they have been framed to account for different populations of learners and to emphasise different (but equally important) dimensions of learning. As Larsen-Freeman (2007: 781) put it 'in some way both positions are correct'. I would argue that the co-existence of cognitive and social theories points to the fact that consumers of SLA find both useful, and that it is entirely appropriate that 'each side pursue its own research agenda, each accounting for a different dimension' (Larsen-Freeman 2007). The second and perhaps the more attractive solution, is the development of a composite theory of L2 acquisition that includes both social and cognitive elements. By way of illustration of how this might be achieved, I examined the arguments that have been advanced for a sociocognitive theory of L2 acquisition, drawing on recent work by Batstone (2010) and Atkinson (2002; Atkinson et al. 2007). Such a theory, while promising, remains embryonic given that different views exist as to whether sociocognition is best viewed holistically or synthetically.

Irrespective of whether a resolution of the debate is sought and how it is achieved, there is an obvious need to seek agreement on what constitutes the object of SLA – 'acquisition'. To this end, I have proposed an operational definition of 'acquisition' based on different levels of 'change' in language use. The challenge facing both cognitive and social SLA researchers is to demonstrate that change has taken place. In a sense, then, the fundamental problem is the same for both paradigms. Cognitive SLA researchers are currently debating the validity of their instruments for measuring acquisition (see, for example, Norris and Ortega 2003), querying the over-reliance on discrete-item tests that do not tap learners' ability to use L2 features spontaneously in natural-like contexts. Social SLA researchers, such as Firth and Wagner (2007), now acknowledge that it is not possible to simply equate use and acquisition and that longitudinal studies are needed to show how use leads to change over time. If there can be agreement on what is needed to demonstrate acquisition there is much less danger of SLA disintegrating into warring epistemological camps.

Finally, it is worth noting that throughout this chapter I have assumed that 'interaction' constitutes the site where acquisition either arises or is initiated, and that by 'interaction' I have meant 'social interaction'. Indeed, this appears to be the position adopted in most of the chapters in this book: acquisition entails social interaction. However, acquisition is not dependent on social interaction. It can also be sited in the intrapersonal interactions that occur when learners respond to oral or written input (for example, when listening to or reading a play). Any theory, then, must account for the role of intrapersonal as well as interpersonal interaction in L2 acquisition, a fact that has perhaps been lost sight of in the fervour of the debate that surrounds the role of social interaction.

Notes

This chapter is based on a talk given at a seminar organised by BAAL/CUP on 'Conceptualising Learning Styles in SLA' at Newcastle University England, June 2008.

1. 'Blowing' is not found in a dictionary of English, suggesting that it constitutes a neologism created by these learners. However, 'blown', applied to cheese, is found, with exactly the meaning ascribed to it by A and H in this extract.
2. Vygotsky, for one, argued that a theory must have social value. In accordance with Marx's philosophy, he saw the role of theory as contributing to beneficial changes in the material circumstances of people's lives.
3. Not all SLA researchers would accept that the debate cannot be resolved empirically. Tarone (2000), for example, argued that one way of deciding between the two positions would be to ask whether different social settings result in different interlanguage grammars. In Tarone and Liu (1995) she set out to provide evidence that social setting does influence the inter-language grammar. However, this study apart, there is scant evidence to support or refute this claim.

4. Larsen-Freeman (2007: 779), following her own comparison of the two paradigms, concluded that 'it is clear that each view is internally consistent'.
5. Not all rationalists have opposed the multiplication of theories; however, Jordan (2003), while pleading for SLA researchers to unite into 'a broad rationalist community', was in favour of 'unlikely' theories being developed, arguing that SLA researchers should be encouraged to 'fly any kite' they like.
6. However, although some theories fade with the passing of their summer, some of their underlying constructs and hypotheses can live on and become incorporated into later theories. For example, my views on variability have been incorporated into emergentist accounts of L2 acquisition (see N. Ellis 2002b).
7. Batstone illustrates asymmetrical encounters with an example taken from Bremer et al. (1996). In this example, an immigrant (Abdelmalek) misinterprets a travel agent's question regarding 'how' he wants to travel to Morocco as querying 'why' he wants to do so because he is used to having his motives queried by native speakers in service encounters.
8. For a further example of a methodology that seeks to provide a rich, descriptive and longitudinal account of acquisition-in-flight, see Markee and Kasper's (2004) arguments in support of the use of conversation analysis.

4

Having and Doing: Learning from a Complexity Theory Perspective

Diane Larsen-Freeman

Introduction

An initial consideration in thinking about learning is defining what it is that is being learned. This is no small order in applied linguistics, for definitions of language are abundant and diverse (see, for example, Cook and Seidlhofer's 12 definitions (1995: 4) or Cook's six (this volume). In order to limit the discussion, I will represent two dominant conceptualisations of language in applied linguistics by adapting Sfard's (1998) distinction between acquisition and participation metaphors. Each of these metaphors can be used to represent a particular view of language and of learning. Following this discussion, I will present a 'middle ground' position, one inspired by Complexity Theory, which sees language as a complex adaptive system (CAS) (Ellis and Larsen-Freeman 2009b). The remainder of this chapter fleshes out what language learning looks like, given such a CAS view of language.

Having-doing continuum

In Figure 4.1, I have placed Sfard's binary distinction on a continuum, assigning each member of the pair a position at opposite poles. At one end of the continuum there are theories that see language as 'having something'. Such accounts are commonplace in applied linguistics. They represent linguistic knowledge as a collection of context-independent symbols, such as words, accompanied by morphosyntactic rules that specify the relationship between them. In second language acquisition (SLA) terms, we could say – very broadly speaking – that once we have learned an L2 word or rule, we *have* it.

Having	Doing
Acquisition Metaphor	Participation Metaphor
(Language is something that one has)	(Language is something that one does)
For example, verb tenses; head parameter; the principle of 'merge'	For example, becoming participants in discourse communities

Figure 4.1 The having-doing continuum (Based on Sfard 1998)

Indeed, teachers speak of whether or not their students 'have' the past tense, for instance, and SLA researchers report acquisition orders and staged sequences of development, which suggest that one form is 'had' before another. The (at least) implicit goal of teaching and research from this perspective is to explain language acquisition as a process of taking in of linguistic forms as a mental act, albeit one that takes place through interaction with others. As learners acquire forms, they can then do something with them.

Of course, it is well-known in SLA research that establishing when something is acquired, that is, available for use at another time, is complicated, due to the commonly observed phenomenon of 'backsliding'. What is used on one occasion is not used on a subsequent occasion despite its appropriateness. Another explanation for why it is difficult to establish acquisition with surety is the well-known phenomenon of restructuring. One form may seem secure, but when a new, competing form is introduced, the semantic space they both occupy needs to be reallocated. In the meantime, the gains that appear to have been made with regard to the first form seem to disappear. This is commonly observed behaviour in learners who appear to understand and be able to use simple past tense in English; however, when the present perfect is introduced, it disrupts, at least temporarily, the learners' correct use of the past tense.

In recognition of the nonlinearity of the learning process, SLA researchers have gone to considerable lengths to define the point at which it could safely be said that a form has been acquired. For example, early after the founding of SLA as a separate area of inquiry, researcher Hakuta (1974) adapted Cazden's definition to his own longitudinal study of L2 morphological acquisition. In doing so, he defined his research subject's point of acquisition as the 'first of three consecutive two-week samples in which the morpheme is supplied in over 90% of obligatory contexts'. Notice that this definition centres on consistency of native-like use over time.

Another 'having' theory of language is generative grammar, both in its original transformational-generative form – positing rules that could be manipulated to derive surface structure from deep structure – and, in a later version, principles with binary parameters, the values of which would be set when children come into contact with their native language. It would also include Chomsky's more recent minimalist position, where is posited a very limited number of principles, perhaps only one (merge), which is said to underlie all languages and to be possessed by all humans. Of course, whether or not a UG (universal grammar) is 'had' only for L1 acquisition or is accessible for L2 is a matter of some dispute (for example, Epstein et al. 1996; Schwartz and Sprouse 1996).

As we saw with Hakuta's definition, the 'having' view of language proficiency is usually measured by the degree to which an L2 learner matches a corresponding baseline performance of a native speaker of the target language. This may be problematic because conforming to native-speaker use may not be the learners' goal at all, as with learners who study international lingua franca languages, which are most often put to service in communication among non-native speakers. It is also true that defining language acquisition in terms of native-speaker norms may cause us to overlook the mechanisms that account for changes as learners move through successive stages on their way to full acquisition, the goal of SLA research according to Long (1990). This is particularly hard to do within a symbolic view of language. As Dörnyei (2009) writes:

> ... one obvious problem with linguistic-symbolic accounts of language is that although they give a clear and intuitively convincing description of the main components of language and their properties, they have little to say about the gradual process by which these symbols are developed and how symbolic knowledge changes. The process of L2 acquisition, for example, is seen in most linguistic theories as a movement through successive grammars (inter-languages), without specifying the transition (Hulstijn 2007).

The quest to identify change mechanisms is particularly problematic for SLA researchers who adopt a generative grammar view of language. White (2007: 46) acknowledges this:

> It is important to understand that UG is a theory of constraints on representation ... UG determines the nature of linguistic competence;

principles of UG (constraints) guarantee that certain potential analyses are never in fact adopted. This says nothing about the time course of acquisition (L1 or L2) or about what drives changes to the grammar during language development. Similarly, the theory of parameter setting does not, in fact, provide a theory of language development even though it is often seen as such. The concept of parameter resetting in L2 presupposes that some kind of change takes place in the interlanguage grammar, from the L1 parameter to some other parameter value ... However, the precise mechanisms that lead to such grammar change are not part of the theory of UG.

Let me now briefly discuss the conceptualisation of language represented at the opposite end of the continuum. I have called this the 'doing' perspective because, according to theories that cluster at this end of the continuum, language is not a commodity one has acquired as a result of a mental act, but rather language is something one does, such as by participating in a social interaction. From this perspective, language learning involves holistically increasing participation in discourse or speech communities. Rather than conceiving of the learning process as a mental one involving acquiring entities, it is instead looked at as an activity in which one participates – in other words, 'the permanence of *having* gives way to the flux of *doing*' (Sfard 1998: 6). Unlike the acquisition metaphor, the participation metaphor rejects the idea that there is a clear endpoint to the process of learning.

... While the AM [acquisition metaphor] stresses the individual mind and what goes 'into it', the PM [participation metaphor] shifts the focus to the evolving bond between the individual and others. Learning is taking part and at the same time becoming a part of a greater whole.

Sfard points out that the acquisition metaphor and the participation metaphor do not inevitably correspond to a psychological-social dichotomy. The reason for this is that the acquisition metaphor makes no distinction between the internalisation of rules of language and the internalisation of social concepts. Psycholinguistic rules and sociolinguistic concepts can both be objects of learning, something to be possessed. Furthermore, whereas the social dimension is salient in the participation metaphor, it is not necessarily absent from research informed by the acquisition metaphor. This is, after all, how some of the mainstream SLA researchers have responded to Firth and Wagner's criticism of the scope of their research (see also the interactionist perspective in SLA, for example, Gass 1997).

In any case, adherents of the participation metaphor also face the challenge of demonstrating change, sometimes seeking to do so at a more global level, such as showing changes in patterns of participation and comparing a learner's ability to accomplish some task with and without the scaffolding provided by a more competent partner. At other times, those who subscribe to the participation metaphor focus narrowly on a particular communicative episode in an attempt to give a detailed emic description of a single conversational excerpt. Showing change over time is also challenging for those whose research has mainly focused on conversational interaction at one time because any definition of learning must involve the transcendence of particular time and space, something that the new move of CA (conversation analysis) for SLA proposes to take up (Markee and Kasper 2004). Thus, 'doing' researchers, too, must show how the changed resources are henceforth available (see Pekarek Doehler, this volume). As Long (1997: 319), wrote, they do 'not evaporate'.

Having/doing: Complexity Theory

Leaving SLA for the moment, I suggest that one way out of the having/acquisition versus doing/participation oppositional stance is to find a midpoint on the continuum. This I find in Complexity Theory.[1] A Complexity Theory (CT) view of language dissolves dichotomies that have been axiomatic in linguistics and applied linguistics, such as the one between having and doing, and yields insights into the nature of language and its learning that these dichotomies have obscured.[2] Dichotomising has contributed to static conceptualisations of language, on the one hand, or to process-oriented views which do not address the transcendence issue on the other. A CT view instead conceives of language as an open dynamic system of language-using patterns (Larsen-Freeman and Cameron 2008a). It is not that the patterns are acquired so that they can be used; neither is it that they are used so that they can be acquired. The processes are not sequential, but simultaneous.

The language-using patterns, form-meaning-use composites, are everywhere, at all levels of scale. They are variegated in shape, ranging from words and morphemes to fixed and semi-fixed lexical patterns with their attendant phraseology, to grammar constructions (such as verb-argument constructions; see below), to turn-taking patterns in conversations and written discourse patterns in different genres. Their boundaries are graded, not categorical. These patterns do not necessarily conform to the categories of linguists, and they are continually being transformed through use. Of course, some patterns, such as 'freezes' and 'frozen' collocations, change slowly; others change more rapidly. The point is that a language at any point in time is the way it is because of the way it has been used, and any use of language changes it, even if the change only takes place at the neurological level, one not yet manifest overtly in performance.

There are other consequences of this view. Concepts such as 'end-state' grammars become anomalous since language is an open system, and open systems are constantly undergoing change, sometimes rather rapidly. The openness does not mean that there is no structure to language, for without it, both communication and acquisition would be difficult, if not impossible (Givón 1999). However, what is different is that structure in language is seen as an epiphenomenon of interaction (Hopper 1988). Language-using patterns are emergent stabilities or attractor states in the dynamic system, where the state of a complex system refers to current patterns of behaviour, not to stasis. As speakers employ language patterns, the patterns become more available as resources for the next communicative or language-using act.

The system of language-using patterns is an adaptive system, that is, speakers' behaviour is based on their past interactions, and current and past interactions together feed forward into future behaviour. Furthermore, a speaker's behaviour arises from sorting out competing factors ranging from perceptual constraints to social motivations. The structures of language emerge from interrelated patterns of experience, social interaction, and cognitive mechanisms (Ellis and Larsen-Freeman 2006, 2009a). It can also be said that the learner's language resources develop through use (see below).

Connectionist accounts are useful for envisioning some aspects of language development because they aim to account for having and doing in one and the same system. Certain nodes in connectionist networks are strengthened as language data are taken in; others are weakened. Language can thus be seen as a statistical ensemble of interacting elements (Cooper 1999: ix), constantly changing. However, because forgetting in most connectionists learning is 'catastrophic', whereby the learning of something later replaces the learning of something earlier, connectionist models of a certain sort (those that operate with a back-propagation algorithm) do not lend themselves to models of second language acquisition (Nelson 2007). Further, in the end, connectionism is still associated within a decontextualised, disembodied computational metaphor of brain/mind. It is useful, but there are limits to its usefulness. At this point, it would be hard for it to account for social participation, for instance.

Nevertheless, a key idea from this brief treatment of connectionism, which I would not want to lose sight of, is the simultaneity of having and doing. This process leads to strengthening of certain connection weights in a neural network, which in turn make the pattern more readily retrievable the next time. It also means that other patterns become less available. In this way, language use is probabilistic. Of course, what we know and choose to employ in our use of language is not merely a reflection of the frequency of the patterns in the language we have encountered. Cue contingency is also important (Ellis 2006). Clearly, our choices as intentional human beings can override any 'imprinting' from the environment. Furthermore, we have the ability to abstract from stored exemplars so that we can analogise to create and to understand novelty. Nevertheless, there is abundant psycholinguistic research that demonstrates that language processing in all domains is exquisitely sensitive to frequency of occurrence (Ellis and Larsen-Freeman 2006). Another helpful feature of connectionist networks is that the representation of knowledge is distributed, and in this way, connectionist models portray more accurately the architecture and processing of the human brain than simple input-output models.

A non-connectionist way to render the same account of language learning is as follows: when faced with a need to communicate, individual language users 'soft assemble' (Thelen and Smith 1994) their language resources. In other words, taking advantage of the affordances present in the situation, speakers employ an extemporaneous 'make-do' solution to the communicative challenge, using patterns that are most readily at hand. The assembly is said to be 'soft' because the elements being assembled, as well as the specific ways in which they are assembled, can change at any point during the interaction. This is why it is important to give attention to the micro level of interaction in the way that conversation analysis does (see chapters by Seedhouse and Walsh; Jenks in this volume). A language user responds in the moment to the communicative pressures at hand. We simply need to know more about how this occurs. Also, we also need to be able to see how this transient transaction affects the language resources of *all* participants over time. The effect of one speaker's deploying his or her language resources is not unilateral. As two language users interact, they adapt to each other. This co-adaptation process results in a transformation of the language resources of each participant, and ultimately, on a longer time-scale and at another level, across a speech community. It is these local interactions that transform the state space of the language system, for how could it be otherwise? From a CT perspective, systems are self-organising, which means that 'order emerges from the interactions of the components of a system without direction from external factors and without a plan of the order embedded in any individual component' (Mitchell 2003a: 6). The self-organising property of complex systems, when applied to language, suggests that we do not need to view the emergence of complex rules as the unfolding of some prearranged or innate plan (Tucker and Hirsh-Pasek 1993: 364) because all that is required to account for their complexification is a sensitive dependence on initial conditions, and a context in which the system can adapt and change. Any structure arises in a bottom-up fashion from frequently occurring patterns of language use rather than as *a priori* components of fixed, autonomous, closed and synchronic systems. In this way CT provides an explanation for the emergence of macroscopic order and complexity from microscopic behaviour of language speakers (Port and van Gelder 1995: 29).

Indeed, implicit in this claim is that such an explanation extends to the phylogenetic evolution of language. Linguistic structure emerges as a complex adaptive system from the verbal interaction of hominids attempting to communicate with each other. Individuals organise lexical items into patterns and if the patterns are useful, therefore frequent and learnable, then their use will spread throughout the community and become grammaticised over time. Bybee (2006) uses the *be going to* construction to illustrate this point. As a particular lexical item, here *go*, enters with increasing frequency into an existing construction, here the present progressive, it begins to gain strength. With increasing frequency of use in social interaction, it moves away from its source construction (the present progressive) and begins to take on the inferred meaning of intention/futurity. Because of the frequency of use, phonological reduction also takes place, resulting in the form *gonna*. Notice that the same two words 'go' and 'to' cannot be pronounced this way in the present progressive (cf. *'I am gonna the park.'). It is only in the now autonomous new construction, *be going to*, that this is possible. Social interaction modifies the patterns to fit the brain rather than requiring the brain to evolve a genetically based mechanism designed to specify the form of the language (Lee and Schumann 2005).

Christiansen and Chater (2008: 498) amplify this essential point:

Instead of puzzling that humans can only learn a small subset of the infinity of mathematically possible languages, we take a different starting point: the observation that natural languages exist only because humans can produce, learn and process them. In order for languages to be passed on from generation to generation, they must adapt to the properties of the human learning and processing mechanisms; the structures in each language form a highly interdependent *system*, rather than a collection of independent traits. The key to understanding the fit between language and the brain is to understand how language has been shaped by the brain, not the reverse.

L1 development

Turning now to the matter of L1 development, given the discussion so far, it makes sense to ask what is it about language that facilitates its learning? An important quality of the language that learners have to work with is that it is well-suited for humans' psychoperceptual processes. One important property of language in this regard is its Zipfian profile. Zipf (1935) observed that the more common words in a given language accounted for geometrically more word tokens in that language than do less common ones. In other words, word distributions in a language obey a power law; language is a fractal (Larsen-Freeman 1997). This is no less true for other types of language resources (see below for the Zipfian profile of syntactic patterns in conversation). L1 acquisition researchers, such as Tomasello (2003) and Goldberg (2006), have demonstrated the significance of this observation.

For instance, Goldberg (2006) has conducted research investigating 28-month-old children learning English as their native language. Using transcribed data of mother-child interactions from the CHILDES corpus, Goldberg reports that prototypical verbs were used more frequently than all others in a particular verb-argument construction. In the case of the intransitive motion construction (for example, 'We are going home.'), it was the verb *go*. For another construction, the caused-motion construction, the verb *put* was used far and away more commonly than any other verb ('Let's put the toys away.'), and for the ditransitive construction, it was the verb *give* ('I'll give you a cookie.'). Goldberg suggests that these frequency-skewed data facilitate the learning of these constructions. The children had the opportunity to encounter a few verbs very often, verbs that were semantically consistent with the semantics of the construction with which they are associated. These verbs are also short (another effect of their frequency as noted by Zipf's law), and their meaning is concrete. The combination of frequency, short length, and concreteness makes constructions with these verbs easier to learn.

In addition, the psychology of category learning suggests that acquisition is optimised by the introduction of an initial, low-variance sample centred on prototypical exemplars (Elio and Anderson 1981, 1984). This low-variance sample allows learners to get a 'fix' on what will account for most of the category members (Ellis and Larsen-Freeman 2006); then later, children can generalise the semantics of the construction through 'inheritance' (Goldberg's term) to include the full breadth of exemplars.

I offer these psychoperceptual, categorisation, and generalisation processes as evidence to support my earlier claim that language development proceeds through cognitive processes. However, I have also included the social dimension. There is ample evidence now that children need to be interacting with others in order to learn. For example, they do not learn much language from watching television. For this reason, the social dimension of language interaction is indispensable. However, it is not merely a source of 'input' to the system. For one thing social contexts (and their inherent routines, artefacts, and grammatical constructions) 'serve to constrain the interpretative possibilities' available to the child (Tomasello 2003: 90). For another, our language resources are multivoiced, populated with others' intentions until we make them our own (Bakhtin 1981). Social interaction allows us to do so.

Another significant contribution of the social context to L1 development, from a CT perspective, is the possibility it affords for co-adaptation between an infant and an 'other', early on its caretaker. As a child and its caretaker interact, the language resources of each are dynamically altered, as each adapts to the other. Dynamic system theorists refer to this as the *coupling* of one complex system to another. This is not about the acquisition of rules, nor is it about conformity to uniformity (Larsen-Freeman 2003). It is also not about the acquisition of *a priori* concepts, which cannot be known separately from our perception of their emergence in the ongoing flow of experience (Kramsch 2002). It is about a mutually constituted shared system between interlocutors.

Cameron's (2003) study of talk between a teacher and her class of 9–11-year-old students captures the emergence of a shared metaphor in the dynamics of classroom discourse. Just as we saw how the *be going to* construction arises from use over time, Cameron shows how the metaphor 'lollipop trees', to refer to the way in which the children in the classroom draw trees, arises at one point in time. The teacher gave feedback to a student on her drawing of trees which were sketched in an overly simple way as circles on top of vertical lines. The feedback consisted of a comparison with 'a lollipop'. Cameron goes on to show how this metaphor of *lollipop trees* is taken up by other members of the class. It has become a shared concept. This co-adaptation is an iterative process, with each adjusting to the other over and over again.

Gleitman et al.'s (1984) early work showed how the quality of child-directed speech changes as the child grows, coming to approximate more closely adult-directed speech, importantly, though, never becoming isomorphic with it. Here is evidence that caretaker speech and the child's developing patterns of language use are mutually-constitutive, with each changing to accommodate the other through co-adaptation. This characterisation of environmental language is different from static depictions that tend to regard the environment as a triggering mechanism, fostering the maturation of innate structure. It also differs from theories that regard the input as primary and which suggest that the communicative context and highly structured input propel the system forward (Tucker and Hirsh-Pasek 1993).

To illustrate this point, let me cite some recent research by Dale and Spivey (2006) using three English corpora from the CHILDES database. The researchers showed how the child and his or her caregiver produce sequences of words or syntactic phrases, during a conversation, that match those being heard (a process they call 'syntactic coordination'). Especially interesting from my perspective is that the researchers found a Zipf-like distribution in the patterns that were shared with each child and caregiver pair. In other words, there are highly frequent sequences of word classes guiding the recurrent patterns in conversation. The other important finding is that advanced children are often leaders, whereas children earlier in development might be guided by caregivers. Therefore, who initiates the behaviour that is adapted to is not always the caretaker; the child is actively involved in shaping the context, particularly when the child reaches a higher level of grammatical development.

Thus, 'The act of playing the game has a way of changing the rules' (Gleick 1987: 24) in a complex adaptive system. There is upward emergence of the patterns of individuals interacting, which is nevertheless 'downwardly' entrained due to both the historic trajectory of the system and by its present-day sociocultural norms. The opportunities afforded by language use support children's language development through repeated experiences in regularly occurring communicative activities with their caregivers.

As Tucker and Hirsh-Pasek (1993: 362) put it:

[T]here is no attempt to appeal to the existence of information either in the environment or in the individual, as innate structure, to account for development. Structure or form (information) is *constructed* in development, and arises through the successive organisational adaptation of systems components to a specific context.

What is striking from a CT viewpoint is that the child produces language that is richer or more complex than the language addressed to the child (van Geert 2003: 659). This is a commonly observed property of all complex systems – systems in which the complexity emerges not from the input to the system nor from an innate blueprint, but rather from the creation of order, as happens when a creole develops from a pidgin. Viewing language development as self-organisation or structure formation in a dynamic system means that different learners may develop different language resources even when the ambient language is similar (Mohanan 1992). As Mohanan (1992: 653–4) puts it, 'Suppose we free ourselves from the idea that [first] language development is the deduction of the adult grammar from the input data, and think of it as the formation of patterns triggered by the data ...'

L2 development

Extending this perspective to SLA, consistent with CT is the position that previous experience shapes the present in significant ways. Such shaping in SLA has traditionally been referred to as transfer, whereby learners' initial experience in using their first language leads to a neural attunement to the first language (MacWhinney 2006), which affects their second language learning experience (Ellis and Larsen-Freeman 2006). Of course, the effects of this experience can occur in third and subsequent language acquisition as well, making the mix of these dynamic systems all the more complex.

There are many factors responsible for the visible effects of the experience with the first language: the typological proximity of the languages, the learners' perception of the proximity, the competition in frequencies among lexical items from the languages, the amounts of exposure to the languages, the learners' proficiency, the learners' orientation and goals, the cognitive and social demands of a given task, and so on. There are not only many factors, each on its own contributing a part, but also the factors interact, sometimes overriding each other, sometimes converging as powerful multiple effects (Andersen 1983; Selinker and Lakshmanan 1992).

These multiple effects converge to make for quite well-entrenched patterns, ones that are difficult to overcome by engaging in target language use alone. Such is the case with U, a Chinese speaker who was studying English at a large Midwestern university in the United States. On four separate occasions, at six-week intervals over a six-month period, U was asked to tell her teacher a story of her choice. She was also asked to write the story shortly after telling it. Her story was then arrayed by idea units on a grid. The results afford an opportunity to view the distribution of U's language resources over time. Perhaps because Chinese speakers do not distinguish between the meanings of 'in' and 'at', in the same way that English speakers do, U could benefit from some targeted instruction on the patterns that the English prepositions 'in' and 'at' enter into. In other words, the volatility of her performance, as compared with her use of other language patterns, suggests that implicit learning is insufficient (at least in the short run) to overcome the language-using patterns of her L1 (Table 4.1).

Table 4.1   The first idea unit in U's story at four times

June	August	October	November
Two years ago, I lived in Detroit.	Two years ago, I lived at Detroit.	I lived in Detroit two years ago.	When I came to the USA three years ago, I lived at Detroit.

Thus, it is important to note that especially in these two ways, L1 transfer and the limitation of implicit learning, SLA differs from first-language development. There are no doubt other differences in second-language acquisition, given the great variety of contexts in which SLA takes place around the world. Indeed, I should also acknowledge that the assumption of monolinguals speaking the same language acquiring an equally homogeneous target language is another one of those convenient reductionisms that are often adopted by researchers. As we know though, with increasing globalisation, initial language development, and certainly subsequent language development, is increasingly taking place in environments where multilingualism and heterogeneous language use are the norm.

Nevertheless, there are also ways in which L1 and L2 development are parallel. One of them appears to be that both types of learners are potentially aided by the Zipfian profile of language. Although the evidence is slim at the current time, recent research by Ellis and Ferreira-Junior (2009) confirms the Zipfian distribution of verb–argument structures in both learner speech and their native-speaking interlocutors' speech. The researchers used the ESF corpus and pulled from it 234 sessions' worth of speech samples for 7 ESL learners over time. Then, following Goldberg, they analysed the data for the presence of verb–argument constructions. Just as Goldberg had reported, Ellis and Ferreira-Junior found that Zipf's law applies to L2 data as well. The highest frequency exemplar within each verb–argument construction was the one that was most prototypical in meaning, perhaps optimising the opportunity for L2 learners to learn the pattern.

There is a second way that L2 development is similar to first – it is shaped by the soft assembly of resources that learners employ at a particular point in time and over time. Language use is both iterative, occurring over and over again, and recursive, in that it uses what results from one instance of use to begin again. The result is that a structure is built up of patterns at different levels of scale (Agar 2005), which is precisely the way that structure emerges in a CAS.

This by no means implies a linear process approaching some static native-speaker norm. Below is the second idea unit from learner U to illustrate my point. From the vantage point of native speaker performance, here we see U 'improving' in the use of initial time adverbials and in the use of articles. However, she seems to 'backslide' from October to November in using the infinitive form of the verb following 'to' (cf. 'to celebrate' in October and 'to celebrated' in November). I think few would deny, however, that U's language resources have changed (Table 4.2).

I recognise that asking learner U to tell the same story again biases the data, even while it facilitates a comparison over time. And yet, I cannot help but think that a great deal of second language use takes place in exactly this same way, that is, the same process works over

Table 4.2 The second idea unit in U's story at four times

June	August	October	November
Someday, my friends invited me to go to a celebration for a for a Chinese Holiday.	One day I went to a party for celebrating Chinese holiday.	One day, one friend invited me to a party to celebrate a Chinese holiday.	Two years ago, one of my friends invited me to a party to celebrated Chinese New Year.

and over again. Of course, we do not tell a particular story or enact the linguistic routines of our lives identically each time. For one thing, our language resources change. For another, we use our resources differently with different individuals. While our language resources are not bounded, they are nevertheless shaped by the interactions in which we engage. As Thelen and Bates (2003) note, the patterns are created and dissolved as tasks and environments change. Preferred patterns become stabilised through frequency of use and the strengthening of connection weights in neural networks (Hebb 1949). In this way, it can be said that the learning of language is never complete (Larsen-Freeman 2005). Furthermore, there is no homogeneity. We create new patterns from old by analogy when we want to make new meanings – we go beyond what is present in the input (Larsen-Freeman 1997). We also use our language resources differently with different others. There is no single homogenised language competence. Thus, teaching a language does not involve the transmission of a closed system of knowledge. Learners are not engaged in simply learning fixed forms or sentences, but rather in learning to adapt their behaviour to an increasingly complex environment. In some cases, morphogenesis, or the creation of new patterns, results. One motivation for their creation is some discrepancy between what the learner wants to say and what she or he is able to say in the way he or she wishes to say it. In addition, it is the role of the teacher, in negotiation with students, to establish the constraints and opportunities that will help learners to further develop their repertoire of language-using patterns. Doing so will likely be facilitated through syntactic coordination, Zipfian profiles, and interactional recursion.

Learners learn to use language through repeated activity in slightly different situations. Learning is not a linear, additive process, but an iterative one. When we say that someone 'has' some linguistic structure, we mean that the contextual and individual conditions are such that the learner has zoomed in on some stable, but not static, pattern. Linguistic structures do not only symbolise reality; they are used to actively construct reality in interaction with others (Kramsch 2009). Because the patterns emerge from language use, they are characterised not only by linguistic features, but also sometimes accompanied by gestures, prosodics, and by affective, cognitive, episodic associations. It follows, then, that learning is not only embodied, it is also situated and inextricably linked to history.

Often SLA research has proceeded from a 'having' perspective that is, as if a static and complete set of grammar rules were available and that its acquisition was the goal of language acquisition. Such projections as the learner's acquisition of verb tenses, and so on, continue as if the learner were filling out details of an already existent paradigm. But this is not likely to be the case from the learners' perspective. From a CT perspective not only do we get a more variegated portrayal of language-using patterns, we also get a different, more emic, or learner-centred, account of their development. Learning is not the taking in of linguistic forms by learners, but the constant adaptation of their linguistic resources in the service of meaning-making in response to the affordances that emerge in the communicative situation, which is, in turn, affected by learners' adaptivity. Individuals' perceptual, conceptual, and linguistic systems are continually being updated by what they perceive and contribute to the ongoing flow of experience. Thus, learning does not add knowledge to an unchanging system – it changes the system (Feldman 2006).

Conclusion

In conclusion, there are many ways to conceptualise learning in applied linguistics. One way that has occupied centre stage for some time is to conceive of language learning as a process of taking language forms in. I have called this the 'having' view. A second conceptualisation adopts a more functional approach to language. Language learning is developing discursive routines through participation in speech or discourse communities. I have called this the 'doing' view.

In this chapter, I have tried to make the case for a doing/having view. Such a view sees language as a complex adaptive system in which every use of language changes the language resources of the learner/user, and the changed resources are then potentially available for the next speech event. These resources are patterned at every level of scale – from individual words and their morphemes to discursive routines. Rather than preceding language use, one's language resources emerge from locally-situated, culturally-embedded, and discursively-patterned uses.

Some learner adaptations, because of their frequency and utility, become stabilised and endure. It is these that have been described by linguists. However, because they are always provisional, partial, and subject to change, I prefer to consider them not as evidence for a rule-based competence, but rather as evidence for a structured network of dynamic language-using patterns, stored in the memory (Larsen-Freeman and Cameron 2008a). Experience shapes our neural networks (Watson-Gegeo 2004). This view suggests a unity not only between doing and having, between real-time processing and development, but also between language use and evolution.

Notes

This chapter is based on an invited presentation given at a seminar at Newcastle University, organised by BAAL/CUP on 'Conceptualising "Learning" in Applied Linguistics', June 2008.

1. In terms of Ellis's (this volume) categorisations, it inspires an integrative sociocognitive view, where the social is a social action perspective.

2. Following Cook's taxonomy (this volume), it might be said that the 'having' views of language I have presented here correspond to definitions two and five, and the 'doing' view corresponds to definition six, and perhaps four. However, I fear that Cook will not be happy with the following treatment of language in complexity theory any more than he was with the way I dealt with it in my 1997 article. Defining what is being acquired is important (and I have also said so at the outset of this chapter and elsewhere), certainly for research studies. But in a theoretical discussion such as the one here, where I am trying to make the case for a new understanding of language and learning, I find that the taxonomy forces me to corral language and to make a choice, where I do not wish to make one. A CT perspective encourages a holistic perspective. It sees language inhabiting different levels of scale in nested fashion – from neural processing to the language of a speech community. It also sees language occurring at different times – from present-in-time use to evolution over time. It makes the claim that the different levels of scale and different time spans are interconnected. CT is abstract enough to provide a container for accommodating different ways of thinking about language.

5
A Cognitive View of Language Acquisition: Processability Theory and Beyond

Manfred Pienemann

Introduction

The purpose of this chapter is to give an overview of one cognitive view of language acquisition, Processability Theory (PT), which focuses on the development of grammar in L2 learners. The key assumption is that the development of L2 grammar is constrained by the language processor and that L2 grammatical development can be explained by the architecture of the language processor.

In this perspective, grammar is seen as a core component of language that facilitates discourse and interaction. Therefore, the ultimate objective of PT is to make explicit the interface between the learner's developmental grammar and its effect on discourse and interaction.

In our cognitive perspective, language learning is seen as consisting of two aspects:

a) the development of language-processing procedures that permit new linguistic forms to be processed, and
b) the discovery of new linguistic forms.

This view is related to, but rather different from, the traditional rationalist perspective on language learnability which assumes that a learnability theory must specify how a learner develops from an initial state to the target grammar with the available input and the given learning device (cf. Wexler and Culicover 1980; Pinker 1979). The rationale for assuming these components is rooted in the way in which learnability theory has been formulated in response to the 'logical problem' in language acquisition (cf. Wexler 1982). The logical problem basically describes the following paradox: children acquire in a relatively short period of time and on the basis of limited linguistic input the basic principles of their native language, and many of these principles are said to be impossible to be inferred from the input observed by the learner. In other words, the rationalist approach proposed by Wexler (1982) characterises a theory of language learnability as a solely linguistic problem of the relationship between the representation of linguistic knowledge and the acquisition of that knowledge.

In my opinion, such a perspective ignores the fact that this problem has to be solved, not by an unconstrained computational device, but by a mind that operates within human psychological constraints. PT (Pienemann 1998, 2005) adds to learnability theory the perspective of language processing. In my view, the logico-mathematical hypothesis space in which the learner operates is further constrained by the architecture of human language processing.

This assumption has repercussions not only for explaining developmental sequences but also for explaining how learners discover new linguistic forms. In the traditional learnability perspective the 'initial state' is assumed to be very rich, and it is explained with reference to aspects of universal grammar, whereas functionalists assume a far less prestructured initial state. They also assume that linguistic forms are discovered on the basis of the input observed by the learner. In other words, rationalists place more weight on the initial state, and functionalists place more weight on the input. In the PT perspective, the discovery of linguistic forms is aided by constraints on processability which radically limit the choices of linguistic forms available to the learner. For instance, I will show below in this chapter that the initial hypothesis of syntax in L2 acquisition follows from massive constraints on processability and the shape of the input. PT also implies that the sequence in which the target language (TL) unfolds in the learner is determined by the sequence in which processing routines develop that are needed to handle the TL's components.

The PT view on language learning has been utilised in a large number of empirical studies of SLA (cf. Pienemann 2005 for an overview), most of which are based on large corpora of natural or elicited interlanguage discourse. The operationalisation of this conception of learning follows logically from its objective to account for the way in which the target-language grammar unfolds as the learner's language develops. The focus is on emerging interlanguage forms. More specifically, PT utilises the so-called 'emergence criterion' which has been found to be more reliable in corpus studies than accuracy-based acquisition criteria. The emergence criterion avoids a one-to-one comparison with the target language not only in terms of accuracy but also in terms of TL forms, since it is based on an analysis of form and function in the interlanguage.

Table 5.1 may serve to illustrate this approach. Table 5.1 shows the percentage of occurrence of the morphemes '-s', '0' (that is, no morpheme) and '-x' (unspecified morpheme) on nouns in two different functional contexts, plural and singular. Table 5.1 shows that in the imaginary L2 sample in 40% of the plural contexts the morpheme '-s' (on nouns) is used, in 50% the zero morpheme is used, and in 10% an unspecified morpheme (for example, '-ren'). For the singular context the corresponding figures are 10%, 80% and 10%. The 40% use of plural '-s' would not satisfy most accuracy criteria. However, Table 5.1 shows that the morpheme '-s' is used far more often in plural contexts than in singular contexts, and this distribution suggests a regularity to be present in the form-function relationship between plural and '-s' in the sample. A full distributional analysis would also include a list of all nouns and all morphemes contained in the sample. The emergence criterion requires the same noun to be used with the plural morpheme in plural contexts and with the singular morpheme ('zero') in singular contexts, and the percentage of usage to be significantly different. In other words, the emergence criterion can pick up regularities in developing interlanguages far earlier than accuracy-based criteria, and it serves to describe the interlanguage on its own terms.

Obviously, the emergence criterion requires a complex distributional analysis which is designed for empirical studies and not for the classroom. However, this approach has been implemented into a computer-based screening procedure called Rapid Profile (Pienemann and Keßler 2007) which permits the teacher/analyst to generate a profile of a learner's developing grammar based on a 10-minute L2 sample. Currently, a fully automatic version is being developed for written data.

In a nutshell, the PT view on SLA focuses on cognitive processes in language acquisition, in particular on a hierarchy of processability which

Table 5.1 Form-function analysis

	N-s	N-0	N-x
Plural context	40	50	10
Singular context	10	80	10

accounts for L2 development in any L2. Evidence of L2 grammatical learning can be gathered from learners' oral language production using a detailed distributional analysis that identifies the point at which a structure emerges in the L2. In practice, this analytical approach can be simplified and sped up using Rapid Profile, as mentioned in the previous paragraph.

A brief outline of PT

The logic underlying PT (Pienemann 1998, 2005) is the following: at any stage of development the learner can produce and comprehend only those L2 linguistic forms which the current state of the language processor can handle. It is therefore crucial to understand the architecture of the language processor and the way in which it handles a second language. This enables one to predict the course of development of L2 linguistic forms in language production and comprehension across languages.

The architecture of the language processor accounts for language processing in real time and within human psychological constraints such as word access and human memory. The incorporation of the language processor in the study of SLA therefore brings to bear a set of human psychological constraints that are crucial for the processing of languages. The view of language production followed in PT is largely that described by Levelt (1989).

The core of PT is formed by a universal processability hierarchy that is based on Levelt's (1989) approach to language production. PT is formally modelled using Lexical Functional Grammar (LFG; Bresnan 2001). In other words, PT is a universal framework that has the capacity to predict developmental trajectories for any second language. The notion 'developmental trajectory' implies a developmental dimension known as 'staged development' as well as a variational dimension accounting for individual differences between developmental trajectories, as illustrated in Figure 5.1.

Figure 5.1 shows two different developmental trajectories, T1 and T2, which are based on the same set of developmental stages (indicated by the dotted horizontal lines). The two developmental trajectories differ with respect to the interlanguage varieties that are developed at each stage (indicated by vertical lines).

In this paradigm, each stage represents a set of grammatical rules that share certain processing routines, and each interlanguage variety represents a specific variant of the grammatical rules. For instance, in ESL

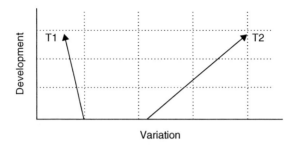

Figure 5.1   Different developmental trajectories

question formation the following developmental sequence has been
found (for example, Pienemann 1998):

Structure	Example
4. Aux-second	Where has he been?
3. Copula	Where is he?
2. WH+SVO	Where he is?
1. SVO question	He live here?

Learners attempting to produce 'Aux-second' at level 3 (that is, before
they are ready for this structure) have been found to produce the following interlanguage variants:

A   Where he been?

B   Where has been?

C   Where he has been?

D   He has been where?

Variants A to D have in common that they get around placing the
auxiliary in second position after an initial Wh-word. In other words,
they constitute different solutions to the same learning problem. In
Figure 5.1, each of the different solutions is represented by a vertical
line. It is important to bear in mind that for each structural learning
process there is a limited set of variable solutions. In the course of L2
development, the learner accumulates grammatical rules and their
variants, allowing her or him to develop an individual developmental
trajectory while adhering to the overall developmental schedule.

In this way, PT defines a two-dimensional space for the formation of processable hypotheses. Both dimensions of this space (that is, 'Hypothesis Space') are constrained by the processability hierarchy, which can be applied to any L2 using LFG.

Key claims and constructs

Processability Theory entails the following key claims:

a) Second language development follows universal stages that are constrained by the processability hierarchy.
b) Interlanguage variation is limited and regular, and this limitation and regularity is caused by the constraints inherent in the processability hierarchy.
c) L1 transfer is constrained by processability. This implies that L1 forms can be transferred to the L2 only when it can be processed in the developing L2 system. In other words, this entails an operationalised 'partial transfer' position (cf. Pienemann et al. 2005).
d) Task variation is constrained by the processability hierarchy. This claim results in the 'Steadiness Hypothesis' which predicts that a specific interlanguage will consistently be placed at one and the same stage of development in different tasks.
e) Both first and second language acquisition are constrained by the processability hierarchy. Nevertheless, both types of acquisition may be associated with fundamentally different developmental trajectories.
f) Bilingual language development can be compared across different languages on a universal scale using the processability hierarchy inherent in PT.
g) The teachability of language is constrained by processability.

These claims are based, amongst others, on the following key constructs: (1) The processability hierarchy, and (2) Hypothesis Space.

The *processability hierarchy* derives from a universal set of processing resources that is modelled using LFG (Bresnan 2001). In Pienemann (1998) the hierarchy was based on the notion of transfer of grammatical information within constituent structure. In the extended version of PT (Pienemann et al. 2005) the processability hierarchy also includes the relationship between conceptual structure and surface grammatical structure, which is also modelled using LFG.

A simplified account of the processability hierarchy (with a focus on constituent structure) is given in Figure 5.2 where three example constituent-structures are listed in the left-hand column. The second

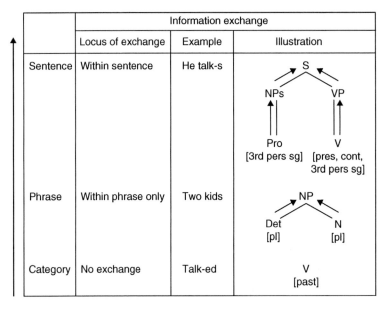

	Information exchange		
	Locus of exchange	Example	Illustration
Sentence	Within sentence	He talk-s	
Phrase	Within phrase only	Two kids	
Category	No exchange	Talk-ed	

Figure 5.2 A simplified account of the processability hierarchy

column specifies the type of information transfer possible at each stage. ESL morphological structures are given in the next column to exemplify the types of structures possible at each stage, and the information transfer involved in the generation of these structures is illustrated in the column on the right-hand side. For instance, for the noun phrase 'two kids' (for example, in the sentence 'he has two kids') the information 'plural' has to be exchanged between the determiner and the noun. (In other words, this information does not need to be exchanged with any other constituent in the sentence.)

The notion 'Hypothesis Space' was mentioned above in the context of developmental trajectories (cf. Figure 5.1). The structures that are processable at any given stage are constrained by the available processing resources. As can be seen in Figure 5.2, at the stage 'phrase', grammatical information can be exchanged only within phrases, not beyond the phrasal boundary. Subject-verb agreement cannot be processed at the stage 'phrase' because this structure requires grammatical information to be exchanged beyond the phrasal boundary – as illustrated in Figure 5.2. In other words, processing resources define and constrain the range of possible production grammars for every level.

At the same time, these constraints leave sufficient leeway for learners to find different solutions to structural learning problems. I illustrated this above with the example of the position of auxiliaries in English Wh-questions. This position requires processing procedures at the sentence level in the hierarchy. L2 learners can nevertheless produce Wh-questions before these procedures are operative. When they attempt to do this, learners have four structural options that avoid the placement of the auxiliary in second position. The options available are all processable using the resources available at the previous stage, and the number of options is limited because of the limited resources that are available. The fact that learners need to circumnavigate a structural problem (here Aux-second) is caused by the constraints inherent in the hierarchy. In this way, possible developmental trajectories are constrained by the processability hierarchy.

As stated in the list of 'claims' above, PT also implies a claim about the effect of teaching on language acquisition: '...the teachability of language is constrained by processability'. I made this point quite a few years ago (Pienemann 1984) and integrated this claim into the formal framework of PT. Essentially, the Teachability Hypothesis boils down to the claim that developmental stages cannot be skipped through formal intervention. This hypothesis has been supported by a number of empirical studies (Pienemann 1984; Ellis 1989; Boss 1996; Dyson 1996; Mansouri and Duffy 2005) which also demonstrated that within the confines of Hypothesis Space formal intervention can promote acquisition.

PT mechanisms

PT is based on four psycholinguistics mechanisms which are summarised below: (1) transfer of grammatical information, (2) lexically driven grammar (3) lexical mapping, and (4) the TOPIC Hypothesis.

As mentioned above, the original version of PT focused on constituent structure and the *transfer of grammatical information* within it, using feature unification. The modelling of feature unification, as envisaged in this approach, is illustrated in Figure 5.3. In the sentence 'Peter sees a dog', the insertion of the verbal affix '-s' relies on information contained in the subject-noun phrase, namely the features PERS(ON) and NUM(BER) and their values PERS=3 and NUM=SG. These features are unified in S as shown in Figure 5.3. In other words, the need to store grammatical information on PERS and NUM during sentence generation illustrates the non-linearity of this morphological process.

In the design of PT, the point of unification is related to a hierarchy of processability that reflects the time course of real-time processing as detailed in Levelt (1989). In this way a range of morphological and syntactic processes can be aligned with a universal hierarchy of processability yielding developmental trajectories for the given target languages,

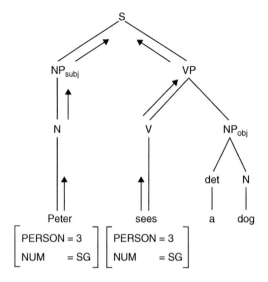

Figure 5.3   Feature unification in the S-procedures

as shown in several chapters of Pienemann (2005). The hierarchy that results from a comparison of the points of feature unification can be illustrated on the basis of Figure 5.2, which shows that the example structures illustrated in Figure 5.2 can be ordered as follows:

1. no exchange of grammatical information (= no unification of features),
2. exchange of grammatical information within the phrase,
3. exchange of grammatical information within the sentence.

Once one applies this hierarchy to ESL morphology, the following developmental trajectory can be predicted:

1. past -ed,
2. plural -s,
3. third person -s.

In order to appreciate the universal nature of PT it is crucial to consider that the hierarchy illustrated in Figure 5.2 is not language-specific and that, in principle, it applies to the transfer of grammatical information in any language. In contrast, the examples that were given for ESL morphology utilise this hierarchy and apply it to one specific target language. The application of the full processability hierarchy to the syntax and morphology of specific languages will, of course, involve more detail of the LFG formalism.

A *lexically driven grammar* (mechanism no. 2) stores grammatical information in the lexicon. For instance, the lexical entry for 'walked' is marked for past tense and it lists the core argument of the verb as 'agent'. This lexical information is required in the assembly of the sentence. The lexically driven nature of sentence generation is an integral part of Levelt's approach and is backed up by extensive empirical evidence. LFG also encodes syntactic properties primarily in the lexicon (cf. Schwarze 2002: 148–9). This makes LFG particularly suitable for the study of dynamic linguistic systems such as developing learner grammars, because LFG affords a formal account of the linguistic dynamics present in developing learner grammars.

The lexically driven nature of sentence generation is supported by a wide range of psycholinguistic empirical evidence including research on slips of the tongue and online experiments (cf. Levelt 1989), and was demonstrated again recently in experimental work on sentence production by Pickering et al. (2002) which shows that 'constituent structure is formulated in one stage' and thus supports the architecture of LFG.

Pienemann (1998) showed that every level of the PT hierarchy-processing procedures can be captured through feature unification in LFG, which in turn shares key characteristics with Kempen and Hoenkamp's (1987) procedural account of language generation.

The third PT mechanism, *lexical mapping*, is based on Lexical Mapping Theory which is a component of LFG (cf. Bresnan 2001). LFG has three independent and parallel levels of representation as shown in Figure 5.4: a(rgument) structure, f(unctional) structure and c(onstituent) structure. A-structure is universal. The component parts of f-structure and c-structure are also universal, whereas the specific form of the latter two are language-specific.

As indicated in Figure 5.4, lexical mapping refers to the mapping of argument structure onto functional structure. In PT the default mapping principle is *unmarked alignment* which is based on the one-to-one mapping of semantic roles onto grammatical functions. Naturally, mature languages allow for a much wider range of relationships between argument structure and functional structure (including passives, topicalisation, and so on), and these develop step-wise in SLA. Principles of lexical mapping can account for these developmental processes.

In other words, *unmarked alignment* is the initial state of L2 development. It is based on the one-to-one mapping of the three parallel levels of representation onto each other. Unmarked alignment results in canonical

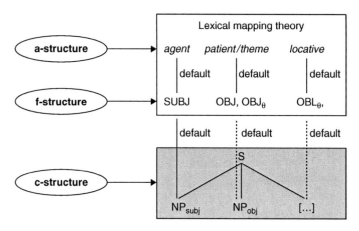

Figure 5.4   Unmarked alignment in LFG
Source: Pienemann, Di Biase and Kawaguchi 2005.

word order. For ESL this is SVO. *Unmarked alignment* simplifies language processing for the learner who, at this stage, will analyse the first noun-phrase as the agent. This way, canonical word order avoids any kind of transfer of grammatical information during language processing.

It follows from the *unmarked alignment hypothesis* that L2 learners will not have access to L2-specific a-structures for predicates. In other words, in cases where L1 and L2 predicates have different a-structures one can predict that L2 learners will initially have to map arguments canonically onto the LMT hierarchy of core grammatical functions. This is illustrated in (1), an example taken from Kawguchi's (2005) work on Japanese L2 acquisition. In (1) an L2 learner canonically maps the participants in the event, where his lexical learning is incomplete and generates the wrong a-structure for the predicate.

(1)   * *okaasan-wa kodomo-o ryoorisimasu*
      mother-NOM child-ACC cook-PRES.POL
      Literally: 'Mother cooks the child'
      (Intended. 'Mother cooks [something] for the child')

The Japanese L2 learner attempts to designate two participants in the 'cooking' event: 'agent' and 'beneficiary'. So he creates an a-structure where the initial argument is canonically mapped onto SUBJ and the second argument onto OBJ. However, Kawaguchi points out that the Japanese verb *ryoorisuru* ('to cook') designates 'agent' and 'patient' (not 'beneficiary').[1]

In other words, PT implies that SLA starts with a linear relationship between argument structure and functional structure and that changes of this linear relationship will require additional processing resources which will be acquired later. Hence the <u>unmarked alignment hypothesis</u> implies a developmental prediction for L2 structures that affect the relationship between a-structure and f-structure. One example is the passive.

In the passive the relationship between argument roles and syntactic functions may be altered, as can be seen in the supression of argument roles and altered function-assignment. These alterations for passives are illustrated in examples (2)–(5).

(2) Peter sees a dog.

(3) see   <experiencer, theme>

         | |

      SUBJ OBJ

(4) A dog is seen by Peter.

(5) seen   <experiencer, theme>

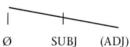

   Ø   SUBJ (ADJ)

Sentences (2) and (4) describe the same event involving two participants. The difference between the two is that in (4) the constituent <u>a dog</u> that is OBJ in (2) is promoted to SUBJ, and the constituent <u>Peter</u> that is SUBJ in (2) is defocused and realised as ADJ.

These alterations of the relationship between argument roles and syntactic functions constitute a deviation from <u>unmarked alignment</u>. Kawaguchi (2005) argues that in order for this type of marked alignment to be possible, the functional destination of an NP can be established only by assembling information about the constituents and by assembling them at the S-node. 'The identification of the phrases' grammatical functions and their functional assignments in passive, causative and benefactive constructions requires that the learner unify information from different sources: the V and the N phrases. This calls for an interphrasal process' (Kawaguchi 2005). In other words, Kawaguchi shows that in Japanese the passive is based on a non-linear relationship between a-structure and f-structure and that this construction requires the S-procedure, that is, the highest level in the processability hierarchy which is illustrated in Figure 5.2.[2] (The reader needs to bear in mind here that Figure 5.2 is merely a simplified illustration of the processability hierarchy which consists of six levels in Pienemann (1998), and is extended further in Pienemann et al. (2005).

As I pointed out above, <u>unmarked alignment</u> ties together in a linear way the three parallel levels of representation, argument structure, functional structure and constituent structure. Lexical Mapping Theory specifies the relationship between a-structure and f-structure, and as I illustrated above, PT derives developmental predictions from the language-specific relationship between a-structure and f-structure using Lexical Mapping Theory. Similar predictions can also be derived from the relationship between f-structure and c-structure. One set of such predictions is 'packaged' in the *TOPIC Hypothesis*, the fourth PT mechanism. To account for developmental dynamics in the relationship between f-structure and c-structure Pienemann et al. (2005) propose the TOPIC hypothesis as in (6).

(6) *The TOPIC hypothesis.*

In second language acquisition learners will initially not differentiate between SUBJ and other discourse functions (for example, TOP). The addition of an XP to a canonical string will trigger a differentiation of TOP and SUBJ which first extends to non-arguments and successively to core arguments, thus causing further structural consequences.

The mapping principles involved in the TOPIC Hypothesis and their structural outcomes are summarised in Table 5.2.

Table 5.2 The topic hypothesis

Discourse principle	c- to f- mapping	Structural outcomes
Topicalisation of core arguments	TOP = OBJ	The TOP function is assigned to a *core* argument other than SUBJ
↑	↑	↑
XP adjunction	TOP = ADJ	Initial constituent is a circumstantial adjunct or a FOCUS Wh-word. TOPIC is differentiated from SUBJECT
↑	↑	↑
Canonical Order	SUBJ = default TOP	TOPIC and SUBJECT are not differentiated

Studying the effect of IL grammar on expressiveness

In this section I will present some preliminary thoughts about the contribution that PT can make to the study of the interface between the learner's developmental grammar and its effect on discourse and interaction. Our basic approach to exploring the grammar–discourse interface follows from the logic entailed in PT: The L2 grammar is constrained by processing and other factors, and these constraints on L2 grammar also constrain L2 discourse and interaction. This interlocking of constraints at different levels became apparent in the Unmarked Alignment Hypothesis and the TOPIC Hypothesis. Both hypotheses describe sets of constraints that operate on the relationship between argument structure, functional structure, and constituent structure.

These hypotheses and the overall PT framework imply that at the initial state of L2 acquisition learners have no choice other than to produce sentences using canonical word order (SVO for ESL), and that these constraints are relaxed in a systematic manner as the acquisition process proceeds. This means that at the initial state learners lack the grammatical means to express information that is structured in a non-linear way. For instance, at this stage learners do not have the freedom to structure information according to 'given' and 'new' information. Instead, the agent-subject always needs to appear as the first constituent.

The effect of Unmarked Alignment is demonstrated in examples (7)–(11) below:

Non-linear alignment	Unmarked Alignment
(7a) Jim was visited by his girlfriend. *Patient agent*	(7b) Jim's girlfriend visited Jim. *agent theme*
(8a) In Italy we eat pizza. *Locative agent theme*	(8b) We eat pizza in Italy. *agent theme locative*
(9a) What did he buy? *Theme agent*	(9b) He buy what? *agent theme*
(10a) Peter I like a lot, but ... *Theme agent*	(10b) I like Peter a lot, but ... *agent theme*
(11a) I had my car fixed. *(+ causative)*	(11b) Somebody fixed my car. *(- causative)*

The propositions contained in examples (7)–(10) are the same in the non-linear and in the linear version of the corresponding sentences. The key difference between the pairs of sentences is their focus. For instance, in (7a) the focus is on 'Jim', whereas in (7b) it is on 'Jim's girlfriend'. In conversation, the focus in (7a) was created by a previous mention of 'Jim'.

(12) A: 'Why is Jim smiling?'
      B: '[He] was visited by his girlfriend.'

Pronominalising the previous mention of the referent 'Jim' yields cohesion in the corresponding utterances, and this makes them easier to process than dyadic discourse that lacks cohesion (cf. Levelt 1989). In other words, Unmarked Alignment prevents the learner/speaker from shifting focus through passivisation, thus creating chains of reference that are harder to trace than those in cohesive discourse.

Topicalising the locative and the theme has a similar effect on focus to the effect of the passive. What these structures have in common is to bring arguments other than the agent into focus position. Again, at the initial state L2 learners are unable to process these focusing mechanisms, and this limits their expressiveness.

(13a) A: 'Potato chips are very popular here.'
       B: 'In Italy we eat pizza.'

(13b) A: 'Potato chips are very popular here.'
       B: 'We eat pizza in Italy.'

Examples (13a) and (13b) illustrate this effect. In (13a) the locative is in focus position. Placing the locative in focus position gives it prominence in the utterance, and this prominence serves to mark the contrast with the locative in the previous utterance ('here'). The contrast of the locatives constitutes a key aspect of the message conveyed by B in (13a). Therefore placing the focus on the contrasting locative supports the comprehensibility of B's message. Having the locative in an unmarked position, the contrast between the locatives needs to be inferred from the content of the message. This increases the processing demand on the listener.

A similar limitation in the expressiveness of L2 learners is apparent in implicit causatives, as shown in examples (11a) and (11b). Again, the 'a-version' of the example is non-linear and developmentally late, whereas the 'b-version' is linear and developmentally early. Obviously, the key difference between the two examples is the presence and absence of causation.

All these examples show that an underdeveloped grammar limits expressiveness. A limitation of expressiveness can also be found at the level of interlanguage variation (cf. section 2 above). The reader will recall that at every level of development the learner can choose different solutions of developmental problems – yielding different interlanguage varieties. Figure 5.5 illustrates this phenomenon with Wh-questions (level 5) as a target structure. The example given in Figure 5.5 is 'Where do they live?', and two early variants of Wh-questions are 'Where live?' and 'Where they live?' In the first variant all propositions that can be retrieved from the context have been left out, whereas in the second variant no 'redundant' information has been left out, and the sentence is based on the second level of the TOPIC Hypothesis with XP-adjunction. Both variants appear at the same developmental level. However, they limit expressiveness to different degrees, as can be seen in examples (14a) and (14b).

(14a)   A: Jane went to pick up her kids from their friends' place.
        B: Where live?
        A: Who? Are you asking about Jane or the friends?

(14b)   A: Jane went to pick up her kids from their friends' place.
        B: Where they live?
        A: In Chiswick.

The restrictive simplification present in (14a) creates referential ambiguity because speaker A introduced three referents, and speaker B does not establish overt reference to any of the referents. This ambiguity is avoided in (14b) where overt reference is made to 'their friends' through pronominalisation using the more expressive IL variant.

These more than brief and preliminary thoughts on the effect of interlanguage grammar on expressiveness have illustrated two sources of constraints on expressiveness: (1) restrictive simplification, and (2) constraints on the alignment of argument structure, functional structure and constituent structure. These two sources of constraints on expressiveness can be modelled systematically within PT, as illustrated in Figure 5.6, where each of the two sets of constraints relates to one of the two dimensions of Hypothesis Space. In other words, PT provides a dynamic developmental framework that details the structural

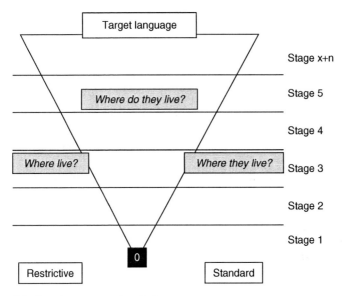

Figure 5.5 Development and variation

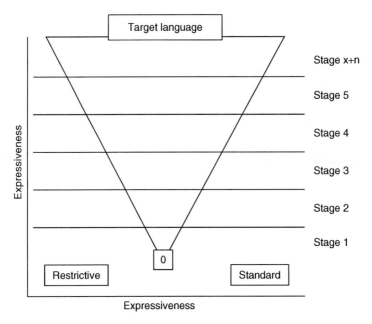

Figure 5.6 Development, variation and expressiveness

preconditions of constraints on IL expressiveness for all well-defined points within Hypothesis Space.

What is not well understood is the impact that constraints on IL expressiveness have on discourse and interaction. Is restrictive simplification more likely to lead to communication breakdown than developmental simplification? Is comprehensibility a function of IL variation and development and if so, is proficiency rating related to comprehensibility? Addressing these issues goes beyond the scope of this chapter. However, this chapter may have served the purpose of identifying these issues. A treatment that follows the logic outlined in this section would need to be based on a framework that integrates PT and an operationalisable model of L2 discourse and interaction.

Discussion

As I showed above, PT is designed to explain L2 developmental trajectories as well as the way in which the learner discovers L2 forms. In order to achieve these objectives, PT contains a universal linguistic component, a language-processing component and an input component. These components interact in such a way that the input and the universal linguistic component serve as the basis for the linguistic 'discovery' process which is constrained by the available processing resources. In other words, the view of language learning that is inherent in PT is determined by the architecture of PT.

At the beginning of this chapter I contrasted this view with that of traditional learnability theory which does not contain a processing component. The reader will recall that learnability theory attempts to specify how a learner develops from an initial state to the target grammar with the available input and the given learning device. In the rationalist tradition most of the 'discovery' process is seen to exist in a very rich initial state that contains most of the basic information that is to be discovered, and the input serves as a mere trigger for that process.

In contrast, PT adds to this formula a (human) language-processing component that constrains the initial state. The effect is that in the PT scenario one needs to make far fewer assumptions about the initial state. In other words, one can do with a greatly reduced initial state.

This 'trading relationship' between the initial state and other components of accounts of language learning was also noticed by Pinker (1979). For instance, interactionists usually do not subscribe to a rationalist perspective. Hence, they will not assume that syntax is an autonomous component of language and that most of the fundamental ideas about syntax are innate (that is, given in the initial state). Instead, they will place more emphasis on the relationship between linguistic forms and their function in interaction, and they will place more emphasis on inferential processes that the learner utilises to discover such form-function relationships. These differences in focus are deeply entrenched in the epistemological assumptions that underlie the rationalist, empiricist and other perspectives on learning.

The interdependence between the specific foci of theories of language learning and their orientation in the philosophy of science has been noted by many scholars (cf. Pienemann 1998: 14–37). The editors of this volume asked the authors to address the question whether it is '... possible to produce a conceptualisation of "learning" to which members of different schools of SLA will be able to subscribe'. In my view the answer is 'unlikely in the foreseeable future', and this is not a situation that is in any way negative. I would like to advance three reasons for this view:

1. The different epistemological stances of theories of language learning *require* different conceptualisations of 'learning'. For instance, rationalist views of learning logically require the assumption of innate linguistic knowledge, and this view is irreconcilable with the empiricist view that linguistic knowledge is inferred by the learner from input and interaction.
2. Incorporating new variables into approaches to language learning is not merely a matter of policy. For instance, the integration of a language-processing component into PT required this component to be made explicit and compatible with the chosen theory of grammar, LFG, in order to be able to make precise predictions for the acquisition of typologically different L2s. This requirement makes the integration of the syntax-pragmatics interface a very major undertaking in the extension of PT – as was also apparent in my outline of the possible integration of discourse and interaction. Integrating all major areas of language to an operationalisable point would be a massive task, bigger than anything that has ever been attempted in the history of SLA.
3. The fact that epistemological stances of some theories of language learning are irreconcilable is not in any way negative or regrettable, because the different epistemologies permit the creation of inherently different theories that need to be refined and tested within the confines of the chosen epistemological approach. It is not the failure

of one theory that determines the adequacy of its rival. Instead, the internal consistency of an approach and its ability to account for a wide range of phenomena in SLA determine its explanatory power – or its failure. Therefore the presence of fundamentally different approaches to SLA shows the strength of the field – and is to be welcomed.

The co-existence of radically different approaches to language learning does not preclude a clear view on the relationship between theory and data that may be shared by several approaches. In my view a theory of SLA needs to make testable predictions on phenomena that are relevant for SLA. Within the PT framework an explicit and operationalisable relationship between theory and data is essential. PT makes precise predictions for developmental grammars. Above I summarised the PT approach to distributional analysis in L2 corpora. This approach permits predictions made by the theory to be tested in suitable L2 corpora.

Notes

1. In fact, the beneficiary role would need to be expressed as OBJ_0 requiring dative case marker, and in addition the verb would require benefactive auxiliary. This construction is acquired much later.
2. Pienemann et al. (2005) point out that for an accurate location of the passive within the processability hierarchy one needs to distinguish between different types of passives which are not discussed here.

6
Vocabulary Learning in a Second Language: Familiar Answers to New Questions

Irina Elgort and Paul Nation

Introduction

Words and multi-word units are the building blocks of linguistic communication. Lexical errors are tolerated to a lesser degree than other types of errors by both native and non-native speakers, and vocabulary knowledge plays a critical role in text comprehension, in L1 or L2 (Hu and Nation 2000; Nation 2006). Over the last two decades, L2 vocabulary research has grown significantly across a range of topics, from teaching and learning vocabulary to measuring vocabulary knowledge, from research on acquisition of individual words to organisational and functional aspects of the bilingual lexicon (Dijkstra and Van Heuven 2002; N. Ellis 1994; Hulstijn 2002; Kroll and De Groot 2005; Nation 2001; Read 2000; Schmitt 2000; Wesche and Paribakht 1996). The complexity of the field is also reflected in the multidisciplinary nature of these investigations, with researchers from the fields of linguistics, psychology, education, pragmatics and computer science contributing to our knowledge about L2 vocabulary acquisition and use.

Conceptualisations of *vocabulary learning* are fundamental to our understanding of linguistic development both in L1 and L2. However, as Read (2004: 224) points out, '[w]hether we focus on individual lexical items or the mental lexicon as a whole, we are setting out to describe something that is inherently ill-defined, multidimensional, variable and thus resistant to neat classification'. Multiple conceptualisations of second-language vocabulary acquisition (SLVA) are therefore inevitable and necessary to mirror the complexity of the field (Larsen-Freeman 2007). The authors' position on SLVA sits within cognitive SLA, focusing on the changes that take place in the mind of the learner, with evidence of learning gathered using psycholinguistic behavioural research methods. The findings of this research are then used to inform teaching and learning approaches.

In this chapter, we first address conceptualisations of what it means to *know a word* and how this knowledge can be attained and assessed; this is not to say that the choice of 'word' as a unit of description or learning is uncontroversial. We then consider vocabulary acquisition as a *process* that may take place implicitly and explicitly, incidentally and deliberately, in a natural or structured manner, in foreign or second-language settings.

Conceptualisations of L2 vocabulary knowledge and learning

What does it mean to know a word in L2?

Daller et al. (2007: 4) suggest that 'perhaps the most basic, catch-all definition [of knowing a word] would be simple, passive, word recognition: the learner recognises the form of a word and that it is a word rather than a meaningless jumble of symbols'. For example, when presented with a letter-string *graceful* or *geometry* the reader is able to recognise them as words, as opposed to *gracetul* or *geobetry*, which are not. Albeit this kind of recognition is a necessary condition of vocabulary knowledge, it addresses only a small fraction of what is involved in knowing a word in another language. At the very least, we must concede that another key aspect of a word's knowledge is meaning. For example, the letter-string *graceful* carries the meaning of 'elegant' or 'beautiful', while the letter-string *geometry* may be associated with 'a branch of mathematics'. Hulstijn (2002) argues that lexical units have a special status among linguistic phenomena because they represent a more or less stable mapping between form and meaning, combining lower-order formal representations (phonemes and graphemes) with higher-order cognitive representations of meaning, with pragmatics and discourse aspects situated at the highest level. Theoretical and computational models of SLVA commonly distinguish between *lexical representations* of a word (including phonological, orthographic and semantic representations), and *conceptual representations* (extralinguistic knowledge about the world).

L2 lexical competence can be conceptualised in terms of quality of representational knowledge (partial/precise; deep/surface) (Henriksen 1999). For example, knowing that *geometry* has something to do with mathematics is not the same as knowing that *geometry* deals with 'the properties and relations of points, lines, angles, surfaces and solids'. Other aspects of quality include knowing the special purpose or peripheral meanings of a word and its collocations, for example an L2 speaker who knows that *graceful* usually describes a person or movement may not be aware of the collocation *graceful degradation* used commonly in relation to computer systems. In addition, Jiang (2004: 103) suggests that knowing an L2 word includes 'semantic differences from its L1 translation and other semantically related L2 words'. Furthermore, knowing a word can be conceptualised as having pragmatic knowledge, that is, sensitivity to linguistic and communicative context, and sociocultural competence, that is, ability to situate a word's knowledge in the broader knowledge about the world and about attitudes, beliefs and behaviours practised by members of the target-language community. Lantolf and Thorne (2006: 5) argue that 'learning a new language is about much more than acquiring new signifiers for already given signifieds (for example, the Spanish word for 'fork' is *tenedor*). It is about acquiring new conceptual knowledge and/or modifying already existing knowledge as a way of re-mediating one's interaction with the world and with one's own psychological functioning.'

What is more, there are further aspects to knowing a word than representational knowledge of form and meaning, and their cross-mapping. Jiang (2004: 101–2), for example, maintains that 'before the word becomes a part of one's automatic linguistic competence, it has to be recognised as a word, its morphosyntactic and semantic properties have to be learned, and it has to be integrated into one's mental lexicon so that it can be retrieved automatically when needed'. Jiang's account of L2 vocabulary competency comprises not only representational but also procedural or functional knowledge. This ability to retrieve a word automatically in comprehension and production (aka functional knowledge) is another facet of the complex picture representing what it means to know a word (Segalowitz 2000).

In terms of functional knowledge, it is useful to further distinguish between *receptive* knowledge (ability to use a word in listening or reading) and *productive* knowledge (ability to use a word in speaking or writing). Productive vocabulary develops more slowly than receptive vocabulary, both in L1 and L2, and at any given time a person's passive lexicon is larger than her/his active lexicon. However, there are also exceptions to this rule: a child or an adult L2 speaker, for example, may be able to use the word *quay* in a conversation (productive use), but fail to recognise its written form (receptive use), if this word was acquired conversationally.

Describing and measuring L2 vocabulary knowledge

The complexity of the SLVA domain is reflected in multiple ways of describing and measuring L2 vocabulary knowledge. In this context, it is common to distinguish between the breadth, depth and fluency dimensions (Daller et al. 2007: 7–9). Lexical breadth is understood as the overall size of a learner's vocabulary, with little attention paid to the quality of this knowledge. In contrast, lexical depth (or quality) refers to how well a word is known in terms of its meaning, its formal (orthographic and phonological), morphological, syntactic, collocational and pragmatic characteristics, and in terms of how well it is integrated into the mental lexicon of an L2 user (Read 2004: 211–2). Finally, Daller et al. (2007) explain that lexical fluency refers to how readily and easily a learner is able to access the word, receptively (in reading or listening) or productively (in speaking or writing).

While measuring vocabulary size of L2 learners is something that is more or less routinely and reliably done, measuring the quality or depth of knowledge and lexical fluency are less straightforward. The challenge here is to select or devise measures that are appropriate for investigating specific aspects of word knowledge, for example the quality of receptive and productive knowledge, implicit and explicit knowledge, and fluency of access to lexical knowledge.

There is a growing agreement among vocabulary researchers that a multiple measure approach is the way forward in assessing the quality of lexical knowledge (Read 2000). This can be achieved, for example, by supplementing traditional vocabulary tests (such as Wesche and Paribakht's 1996 *Vocabulary Knowledge Scale*) that present words in isolation or in very limited contexts, with testing vocabulary knowledge *in context* and *in use* (Read 2000, 2004). Measures of lexical richness in writing or assessment of lexical diversity and style go some way towards addressing these aspects of lexical knowledge. Digital language corpora and tools developed for their analysis enable assessment researchers to use contextual information to create tests that better reflect the register of various target L2 contexts, such as technical, academic or business vocabularies (Coxhead 2000). More relevant vocabulary size tests can be created using these resources.

What does it mean to learn a word in L2?

The multidimensional nature of L2 vocabulary knowledge is also reflected in multiple conceptualisations of what it means to learn a word in L2. At the end of the last millennium, Long (1997: 319) set the following SLA research agenda:

> The goal of research on SLA, qualitative or quantitative, inside or outside the classroom, in the laboratory or on the street, is to understand how changes in that internal mental representation are achieved, why they sometimes appear to cease (so-called 'fossilisation'), and which learner, linguistic, and social factors (and where relevant, which instructional practices) affect and effect the process.

In SLVA, this agenda brings attention to the nature of changes that occur in representational knowledge, both in terms of individual word representations and in the organisational structure of the bilingual lexicon (for example, integration of the new representations into existing knowledge). In addition, conceptualisations of L2 vocabulary learning need to account for the development of functional knowledge that enables learners to use L2 words in comprehension and production.

Furthermore, following Long's conceptualisation of learning, *learner-external* and *learner-internal* conditions that affect learning need to be factored in when conceptualising SLVA as a process. External conditions refer to linguistic and extra-linguistic contexts in which the target language is learned, including whether or not learning takes place in the target-language community, and whether L2 is learned independently or through instructional interventions. Internal factors refer to individual differences, including available cognitive resources (for example memory span, phonological memory) and cognitive development at the time of L2 learning (children vs adults), as well as attitudes and motivation.

L2 vocabulary learning as development of representational knowledge

Evidence gathered in studies with bilinguals suggests that L1 and L2 lexical representations are integrated in the memory structures, and that bilinguals access lexical codes in a non-selective way (Dijkstra and Van Heuven 2002; see also Kroll et al. 2005 for an overview). However, it is possible that, within a common linguistic competence system, each language of the bilingual is represented by a separate sub-system (Dijkstra and Van Heuven, 2002; Grosjean 1997). These lexical sub-systems are connected to a single language non-specific conceptual system represented in the extralinguistic memory. Within this architecture, lexical representations are stored separately from conceptual representations (Paradis 2007).

N. Ellis (1994) further suggests (citing evidence from studies with amnesic participants, vocabulary development studies and memory studies in L1 and L2) that formal-lexical representations and access to these representations (the recognition and production aspects of vocabulary learning) are mostly acquired implicitly through repeated exposure to and use of the language (see also Ellis 2002b). The meaning aspects (or conceptual representations) and the mapping of the surface form (that is, sound and orthographic patterns) to the semantic and conceptual representations, on the other hand, can be and often are learned explicitly, for example, by noticing the referent of a word or engaging in learning activities that promote deep (elaborative, semantic) processing. In a similar vein, Hulstijn (2002: 202) argues that although it may be possible to explicitly learn some of the higher-order representations of meaning, lower-order linguistic features, such as formal-lexical representations, can only be processed and acquired implicitly, through exposure to perceptual input. However, we should not equate implicit learning with unintentional (incidental) usage-based learning. In his discussion of implicit and explicit learning, Hulstijn argues that implicit learning takes place every time information is processed (through hearing or seeing), which includes deliberate learning.

Some bilingual studies suggest that there may be a developmental progression in the way new L2 words are stored and accessed, in particular, in the way their meanings are accessed by L2 learners in production (for example, Jiang 2000; Kroll et al. 2002). To account for these differences, Kroll and Stewart (1994) proposed that initially bilinguals may map a newly-learned L2 word onto its L1 translation, which is then used to access meaning, but that, as their L2 proficiency develops, so do direct links between L2 lexical and conceptual representations. Support for this developmental view comes primarily from behavioural data gathered in translation studies (Kroll and Stewart 1994; Talamas et al. 1999). Talamas et al. (1999), for example, examined this prediction using a translation recognition task with less and more fluent Spanish–English and English–Spanish bilinguals. The results showed that response times of less fluent bilinguals were affected by the form-related false translations, while for more fluent bilinguals, response times were affected by the semantically related false translations (in both cases the effect was that of inhibition), suggesting that proficient bilinguals are able to directly access L2 meanings, while for less proficient bilinguals L2 forms may be linked to L1 translation equivalents. This developmental progression is upheld theoretically in the work of Paradis (2007), and represented computationally in the *Unified Model* of L1 and L2 acquisition proposed by MacWhinney. In this model initial stages of L2 word learning are represented by 'transferring the L1 conceptual world en masse to L2. When learners first acquire a new L2 form, such as *silla* in Spanish, they treat this form as simply another way of saying *chair*. This means that initially the L2 system has no separate conceptual structure and that its formal structure relies on the structure of L1' (MacWhinney 2008: 348). MacWhinney conceptualises lexical development as the process of L2 learners reducing their reliance on L1 by building a new system of L2 representations where L2 lexical representations are connected directly to conceptual representations.

A compatible developmental view of SLVA is put forward by Jiang (2000, 2002, 2004), who suggests that L2 word acquisition proceeds in three stages. During the first stage a new lexical entry is created that initially contains only formal-lexical information (orthographic or phonological), while semantic, syntactic and morphological information are stored outside the lexical entry of the new word (for example as part of the learner's general or episodic memory), and cannot be accessed automatically. Jiang (2000: 51) referred to this stage of acquisition as the *word association stage*, because at this stage the use of L2 words is likely to involve activation of L2–L1 links and their L1 translation equivalents, in order to access semantic and grammatical information that is absent from the newly created L2 lexical entries. At the next stage a much stronger link develops between the L2 word and information in the corresponding L1 lemma (containing semantic and syntactic information), which may even get copied into the L2 lexical entry. This stage is referred to as the *L1 lemma mediation stage*. The connections between L2 words and conceptual representations at this stage of acquisition are still quite weak. Access to conceptual information is primarily mediated by the lemmas of L1 translation equivalents, but some direct connections through the copied L1 lemma may also be established at this stage. Finally, at the third and final stage of L2 word acquisition, which occurs after considerable exposure to 'contextualised input' and use of the new word, original semantic, syntactic and morphological information components are created for the L2 word, and its structure becomes essentially indistinguishable from that of an L1 lexical entry.

L2 vocabulary learning as development of automaticity and autonomy

Another important developmental component of SLVA is functional knowledge, which underpins fluency. It is useful to distinguish between cognitive fluency and performance fluency, where cognitive fluency 'refers to the efficiency of the operation of the cognitive mechanisms underlying performance' and reflects 'the balance that is struck between automatic and attention-based processing' (Segalowitz 2000: 202). Performance fluency, on the other hand, refers to 'the observable speed, fluidity, and accuracy of the original performance [...], for example, as observed in the act of reading, speaking, or listening' (ibid: 202). Performance fluency can increase as a result of a simple speed-up of both controlled and automatic processes while retaining the overall balance of the involvement of these two types of processes in a cognitive task. To determine whether there has been a qualitative change in the nature of a particular cognitive operation, Segalowitz and Segalowitz (1993) proposed using a coefficient of variability (CV). CV is calculated by dividing the standard deviation (SD) of response time (RT) by the mean latency. Participants' RTs to experimental stimuli are commonly used in psychological studies as a dependent variable that measures performance. CV, on the other hand, indicates 'variability for a given level of response latency' (Guilford 1942, in Segalowitz and Segalowitz 1993). The CV is reduced as a result of the processing system becoming more stable, as the reliance on more variable controlled supervisory mechanisms is reduced, rendering performance more automatic. Using CV as a measure of individual differences in a semantic judgement task, Segalowitz and colleagues (Phillips et al. 2004) demonstrate that performance of highly proficient bilinguals is faster and more automatic than that of less proficient participants. This was corroborated by the finding that highly proficient bilinguals exhibited higher processing efficiency in neurological terms, when N400 ERP (event-related potentials) was used to measure their electrical brain activity. Thus, acquisition of functional knowledge of L2 vocabulary can be conceptualised as the development of automaticy in accessing and processing representations of L2 vocabulary items by the learner.

L2 learning has also been conceptualised as development of L2 *autonomy*, that is, ability to suppress interference from L1 and operate mostly within the target language in a fluent and coherent way. Empirical evidence shows that both languages of bilinguals are active when they process information in L2 (or L1, for that matter), regardless of their proficiency. However, proficient bilinguals appear to be more successful in avoiding interference from the non-target language than less proficient bilinguals (Bobb et al. 2008). One way to explain this autonomy is to suggest that L1 is inhibited using some cognitive control mechanism to enable L2 production (see Kroll et al. 2006, for a review), and that these mechanisms are better developed in proficient bilinguals.

It is important to point out that research into acquisition of L2 lexical and conceptual representations and their organisation in the memory structures of bilinguals is ongoing. New evidence is being generated using a range of approaches, including behavioural, neuro-cognitive, computational and theoretical modelling techniques. As a result of these ongoing efforts some aspects are becoming much clearer, but there are still many gaps in our knowledge in this area that need further research. For example, the field is now more or less in agreement that L2 and L1 lexical representations are stored and integrated within the same memory structures, and that access to lexical representations is language non-selective, that is, all languages of the bilingual are activated (at least initially) in comprehension and production, even when only one of the languages is required. However, significantly less is known about the mechanisms that enable bilinguals to achieve fluent performance in reading or speaking in the target language (whether in L1 or L2) without interference from other languages of the bilingual. More data is also needed to understand how bilinguals develop L2 lexical competence. Although some studies have shown that the knowledge of L2 words may be mediated through their L1 translation equivalents during early stages of L2 acquisition, it is not clear at what level of L2 proficiency this mediation ceases, and whether it is an inevitable by-product of L2 vocabulary acquisition or whether it is caused by particular ways of learning L2 words.

Conditions that affect L2 vocabulary learning

The process and outcomes of L2 vocabulary learning are affected by a number of non-linguistic factors, including learner-internal factors, such as motivation, attitudes and ability, and learner-external factors, for example cultural contexts and educational settings (Gardner 2006). Motivation is one of the key factors in L2 acquisition; it affects learning outcomes (Dörnyei 2003; Gardner 2006) and the rate of attrition (Pavlenko 2005). Laufer and Hulstijn (2001) suggest that motivation influences the retention of unfamiliar words in incidental learning tasks. This influence can be either moderate or strong, depending on whether motivation is extrinsic (imposed by an external agent, such as the teacher) or intrinsic (self-imposed by the learner). Tseng and Schmitt (2008: 360) argue that motivation is a dynamic phenomenon, and that L2 learners need to sustain their motivation in order to keep increasing the size of their vocabularies and improving the quality of their knowledge. In their model of *motivated vocabulary learning*, they detail the role of motivation at various stages of lexical development and propose that initial motivation and self-regulation, metacognitive control of vocabulary learning tactics, and postlearning evaluation are important components of successful SLVA.

Individual differences in terms of attentional and cognitive resources also affect the success of SLVA, because L2 acquisition and processing require greater allocation of these resources than L1 (Kroll and Linck 2007). Learners who achieve high L2 proficiency tend to have better memory spans (Atkins and Baddeley 1998). Bilingual studies that focus on the role of working memory in L2 processing in naturalistic and laboratory settings show that greater memory span is, most likely, beneficial in L2 performance (see Michael and Gollan 2005: 400–3, for a review). Working memory capacity contributes to a learner's ability to suppress L1 in L2 processing or production, especially at early stages of L2 acquisition (Kroll et al. 2002; Michael and Gollan 2005). Phonological memory skills and capacity are also linked to vocabulary development in L1 and L2 (Gathercole and Pickering 1999). More experienced language learners (such as polyglots) demonstrate better developed phonological memory skills, which makes them more receptive to the phonological aspects of new foreign-language vocabulary items, and facilitates the learning of these items (De Groot and Van Hell 2005).

Learner-internal factors often interact with learner-external factors in language learning, jointly influencing learning outcomes (Gardner 2006). Research by Kroll and colleagues shows that the positive effect of the study-abroad experience (as compared to classroom learning) on L2 learners' willingness to communicate and on their ability to reduce lexical interference from L1 is modulated by learners' available working memory resources (Kroll and Linck 2007; Tokowicz et al. 2004). Kroll and Linck (2007: 260) argue that 'study abroad experience and greater memory resources each provided benefits to the learners, but the combination of the two was especially valuable'.

Incidental usage-based learning

Conceptualisations of L2 lexical development differ significantly in relation to the role of naturalistic usage-based learning and deliberate learning. Some researchers have argued that L2 vocabulary is acquired through exposure to input (Krashen 1989) and meaning-focused instruction (DeKeyser 1998), and that deliberate learning of vocabulary is not useful. Others (including ourselves) maintain that successful SLVA requires higher levels of language awareness, form-focused instruction and explicit learning than L1 vocabulary acquisition (N. Ellis 2008; Laufer 2006; Nation 2001). L1 vocabulary development starts around the age of one. Most vocabulary is learned by children incidentally, with only a relatively small proportion of L1 words learned in a deliberate manner, for example through pointing and naming. School-age children continue to learn about 1,000 new L1 words a year. In L2 contexts, however, incidental learning of vocabulary from reading, listening or interaction does not appear to result in vocabulary sizes, or quality of lexical knowledge, similar to those in L1.

Cobb and Horst (2004: 16–17) outline a number of factors that render incidental learning from context insufficient for acquiring L2 lexicons. First, L2 learners who learn primarily from informal spoken interactions are unlikely to ever meet a large proportion of the lexicon, because only a relatively small number of words are used in everyday spoken discourse (at least, in English). Estimates vary, but roughly 2,000 word families provide approximately 95% coverage in spoken discourse (Adolphs and Schmitt 2004). Furthermore, even for those L2 learners who have to read a lot (for example university students), vocabulary acquisition through exposure to texts is slow and uncertain. Cobb and Horst refer to research by Nagy and Herman (1987) in the L1, which indicates that the likelihood of an L1 learner later recognising the meaning of a new word after encountering it once incidentally in reading is 0.7%. For L2 readers the probability of word learning from reading is even lower. Research shows that learning is best accomplished in the contexts where most of the running words are known; 95 to 98% of words have to be familiar to the reader in order for him/her to be able to learn new words incidentally from listening or reading (Hu and Nation 2000). For non-simplified written English texts, 98% running words coverage is achievable with the knowledge of about 8,000 to 9,000 words (Nation 2006). This is realistic for L1 school-age learners who are meeting new words in level-appropriate texts in their native language, but is unlikely to be the case for L2 learners.

Laufer (2005: 226–7) also argues that access to input is not enough to develop L2 lexical competence. She cites empirical evidence showing that L2 learners ignore unfamiliar words whose meaning is difficult to guess from context, and often fail to retain words they have guessed, because words that are easy to guess are also easy to forget. Furthermore, only partial (and sometimes incorrect) meaning is often initially discerned from context, with the desired degree of accuracy and depth of knowledge taking a long time to achieve. In an input-impoverished language-learning situation, such as foreign language learning, such incomplete or inaccurate learning may lead to fossilisation.

Jiang (2004) further argues that, without sufficient reasons for restructuring, contextualised exposure to L2 may reinforce the link between the L1 lemma and the L2 lexical entry, making it more automatised and leading to fossilisation at the L1 lemma-mediation stage. In order for the semantic restructuring to occur, two conditions need to be true: L2 learners need to identify that there is a mismatch (for example, when using the word incorrectly and generating an error); and they need to have information on how the L2 word is semantically different from its L1 translation equivalent. This is less likely to happen in a foreign-language learning situation because of limited opportunities to encounter new words in powerful contexts needed to reveal the subtle differences between L1 and L2 meanings. Jiang (2004: 121) suggests that instructional intervention is needed to help L2 learners 'overcome plateaus in semantic development'. He also argues that this intervention can benefit from the 'old wisdom of contrastive analysis' (ibid: 122), which focuses on systemic differences between L1 and L2. For example, it is useful to point out to an English speaker learning Chinese that the naming of concrete objects in Chinese commonly follows functional principles, while in English it is generally based on their shapes; or to an English speaker learning Korean that spatial relationships in Korean are conceptualised based on the distinction between *tight-fitting* and *loose-fitting*, while in English the focus is on the concepts of containment and support (*in, on*) (Tomasello 2003).

This evidence based on text analysis, learning attributes and constraints, and the nature of L2 vocabulary knowledge, indicate that incidental usage-based learning from context or interactions needs a boost from form-focused deliberate learning for L2 lexical development to be successful.

Deliberate learning

An observation that the majority of the words we know in our first language are acquired incidentally does not imply that we *cannot* acquire new words intentionally. Deliberate learning of L2 words is efficient and convenient. There is plenty of evidence that deliberate learning approaches which incorporate rehearsal and memorisation techniques (for example, keyword mnemonics, semantic mapping) improve retention of vocabulary items. Nation (2001) suggests that people are able to memorise between 30 and 100 new words (L2–L1 associations) per hour from bilingual word pairs. Deliberate learning therefore can be used to quickly learn the 2,000 most frequent word families in English, or at more advanced stages, to advance the knowledge of words that have been first encountered incidentally (Hunt and Beglar 2005). The first 2,000 word-families provide up to 90% coverage in non-academic texts (Nation 2001), while a further 570 word families on the Academic Word List (Coxhead 2000) provide 90% running word coverage in academic texts. By learning a relatively small number of words, therefore, a beginner gets a head start in understanding and communicating in English.

Such techniques as flash-cards, word lists or vocabulary notebooks are accessible and easy to use; no external help is required and learning can be done anytime, anywhere. These techniques can be used even by advanced learners for practicing receptive (form-to-meaning) and productive (meaning-to-form) recall (Nation 2001). This approach is useful for increasing learning rate and accuracy of the L2 word knowledge, preventing stabilisation of lexical development at early acquisition stages. Once a new word or a multi-word unit has been noticed in context, deliberate learning can be used to practice its retrieval and improve retention. Deliberate learning is also appropriate when speedy acquisition of specialised or technical vocabularies is needed, for example when engaging in business negotiations with a foreign company or enrolling for a university degree in a foreign country. Although technical words are usually low-frequency in general-purpose communication, within a particular subject area they are used much more frequently (20 or 30% of the running words in written texts), contributing significantly to the overall understanding of discipline-specific communication (see Nation 2001: 17–21, for an overview).

The catch is, however, that conceptualisations of learning adopted in many applied linguistic studies of deliberate L2 vocabulary learning are quite narrow, focusing on the learner's ability to retrieve form and/or meaning of the target L2 words in tasks that involve highly controlled word use (for example, cued or free recall, translation, or sentence cloze tests). Although these studies show that learners are able to memorise large numbers of words using such learning techniques as bilingual word pairs, word lists or word cards, they provide little evidence about the kind of knowledge that L2 users need to access these words fluently, in comprehension or production.

Since implicit linguistic competence is harder to achieve through naturalistic learning from context in L2, compared to L1, can deliberate paired-associate learning of L2 words provide a way of acquiring this competence? This question was investigated in a series of behavioural laboratory experiments (Elgort 2007; Elgort 2011 in press), which aimed to establish what kind of knowledge is being gained as a result of deliberate learning, in particular learning L2 (English) vocabulary from word cards using repeated passive (form-to-meaning) and active (meaning-to-form) retrieval. Learning in this study was conceptualised as the establishment of lexical representations for the new L2 vocabulary items, their integration with existing L2 formal-lexical and lexical-semantic representations, and their availability for automatic access by the learners. Lexical (both formal and semantic) representations in the memory are considered to be a part of the neurofunctional system of implicit linguistic competence (Paradis 2007). The results of the experiments showed that both formal-lexical and lexical-semantic representations of the deliberately-learned L2 vocabulary items were established and integrated with the lexical representations of known L2 words, and that these newly-established representations were available for fluent online access. That is, deliberately learned L2 vocabulary directly entered implicit knowledge as well as explicit knowledge.

These results have important implications for teaching and learning vocabulary because they demonstrate that deliberate paired-associate learning in the style of the behaviourist tradition is not only an efficient but also a very effective way of L2 vocabulary acquisition, because this type of learning results in the kind of knowledge that is characteristic of known words in both L1 and L2. However, the experiment focusing on the lexical-semantic representations revealed that the quality of these representations for the deliberately-learned items and their integration into the existing memory structures were not as robust as those that exist for known L2 words. This suggests that deliberate learning needs to be supplemented by other types of learning (for example, repeated exposure to new vocabulary in a variety of meaningful contexts; learning that encourages deep processing of meaning), in order to create richer knowledge of the new L2 words and encourage further integration of their meanings with existing semantic and conceptual representations.

Conditions that promote L2 vocabulary learning: Applied linguistic perspective

Among external and internal conditions that influence SLVA, certain factors that promote better learning can be facilitated using instructional approaches. These factors can be grouped under the headings of *motivation; repetition; balanced opportunities for learning* (the *four strands*, Nation 2007); *thoughtful processing* (noticing, retrieval, deep processing, generative use); and *meaningful syntagmatic relationship* (learning words together in thematic clusters, for example *conditions, apply, frequently*).

The *four strands* framework (Nation 2007) warrants a more detailed overview, because it combines a number of conceptualisations of L2 vocabulary learning from different SLA research perspectives into a framework that informs the design of L2 courses (Nation 2007). The main tenet of the framework is that roughly equal amounts of time should be devoted in a language course to four strands (or sets of learning conditions): meaning-focused input, meaning-focused output, language-focused learning, and fluency development. The first two strands emphasise the role of meaningful comprehensible input (Krashen 1985) and opportunities to develop more precise knowledge through production (Swain 2005). The meaning-focused input strand is realised through listening and reading opportunities, while the meaning-focused output strand needs to offer speaking and writing opportunities. In both of these strands, focus on the message is important to make learning interesting and engaging. In reading, listening, writing and speaking activities of these two strands, familiar language should be used. For example, reading materials must have 95 to 98% familiar words. These two strands should provide large quantities of comprehensible input and plenty of opportunities for output.

The strand of language-focused learning relies primarily on deliberate learning and language-focused (or form-focused) instruction. L2 features that are the focus of learning in this strand should also frequently occur in the other three strands. Finally, the fluency development strand is about helping learners make the best use of what they already know. This strand provides opportunities to practice receptive and productive L2 word knowledge, improving automaticity and fluency of access to and control over the existing knowledge. Activities in this strand should use known vocabulary, encourage focus on receiving and conveying messages, facilitate faster and smoother performance and, as with the first two strands, use large volumes of input and output. The 'four strands' framework is a useful tool for language teaching and curriculum development because it translates SLVA research findings into pedagogical principles and offers ideas on teaching practice. Nation (2007: 10) suggests that the framework makes it possible 'to make innovative changes such as using computer-assisted language learning, having a negotiated syllabus, making maximum use of the target language, or taking an experience approach to learning'. While classroom-based instructed SLA continues to be one of the predominant modes of L2 learning, the four strands framework challenges teaching innovation to be grounded in SLVA research.

Conclusion

To enable better understanding of specific aspects of the multifaceted construct that is L2 lexical development, we need to spotlight some facets, inevitably leaving others in the dark. In this chapter we have adopted a cognitive psycholinguistic view of L2 vocabulary learning and teaching, which is primarily interested in changes that occur in the individual cognitive state and factors that affect these changes. Representational and functional knowledge have been the focus of our discussion. We have argued that, in L2, the likelihood of learners reaching higher levels of lexical development is increased if they engage in deliberate and language-focused learning in addition to incidental usage-based learning. The proposed deliberate learning approaches are not new; they were used in the past when behaviourist theories and principles of contrastive analysis informed L2 pedagogies, but were mostly discarded when the communicative view of teaching and learning became predominant in applied linguistics. Although it is important to acknowledge past problematic interpretations and applications of these theories, their conceptualisations of learning can and should be used to construct more balanced learning and teaching approaches, such as the 'four strands' framework. Conversely, deliberate learning, language focus and classroom interactions do not provide sufficient opportunities for learners to develop the pragmatic and sociocultural knowledge needed to understand and use L2 vocabulary successfully. These knowledge aspects benefit from interaction with members of the target-language community, and exposure to real language use. Different conceptualisations of vocabulary learning may well be more appropriate for these goals.

7
Conceptual Changes and Methodological Challenges: On Language and Learning from a Conversation Analytic Perspective on SLA

Simona Pekarek Doehler

Introduction

The last two decades have been witness to the increasing influence, across several disciplines in the human sciences, of research that challenges established conceptions of learning and of language. Within socioculturally and socio-interactionally oriented research, attention has shifted away from an understanding of language learning/acquisition as an intra-psychological, cognitive process enclosed in the mind of the individual, toward a concern with how learning is anchored and configured in and through the social practices the learner engages in. This rethinking has partially gone hand-in-hand with a reconceptualisation of language: usage-based approaches to language have refuted a static, context-independent notion of linguistic knowledge, insisting on its adaptative, dynamic character. These reconceptualisations broaden the scope of thinking about language and learning, and open new possibilities for how we go about documenting learning.

Within the field of SLA, conversation analytic research has played a major role in these developments. Ethnomethodological conversation analysis (CA) provides a conceptual and analytic apparatus that has been put to use in an important body of empirical studies across the last two decades, helping us to understand the detailed unfolding of L2 communicative practices and learning activities. Also, CA work on SLA (henceforward: CA-SLA) has provided important impulses

106 *Simona Pekarek Doehler*

for rethinking dominant conceptions of learning, meeting in several regards sociocultural theory (Lantolf and Thorne 2006) as well as ecological (Kramsch 2002) and sociocognitive approaches (Atkinson et al. 2007) to SLA. Based on the immense impact of Firth and Wagner's (1997: 286) seminal position chapter calling for a 'significantly enhanced awareness of the contextual and interactional dimensions of language use', CA-SLA has forged a notion of learning as 'learning-in-action' (Firth and Wagner 2007): learning is seen as a sociocognitive process that is embedded in the context of locally accomplished social practices. Learning a language is not the mere internalisation of linguistic knowledge that can then be simply put to use, rather it consists of the continuous adaptation of linguistic and other semiotic resources in response to locally emergent communicative needs. It involves the routinisation of patterns of language-use-for-action through repeated participation in social activities. Such a conception rests on an understanding of social interaction as the bedrock of human linguistic and more generally social and mental functioning (cf. Garfinkel 1967; Schegloff 1991, 2006), and hence as the starting point for the study of second language learning.

The quoted developments bear testimony to a paradigm shift in contemporary thinking about language and language development, profoundly calling into question any ontological separation between language development and language use (Firth and Wagner 1997, 2007; Markee and Kasper 2004; Wagner and Gardner 2004; see also, from different horizons, Atkinson et al. 2007; Ellis 2003; Hopper 1998; Tomasello 2003). CA's current empirical contribution to this shift lies in documenting how language development, as part of interactional development, is inscribed in the micro-details of communicative practice.

Despite the intense conceptual discussions that the field has generated recently, CA-SLA's understanding of language has mostly remained implicit (but see Markee 2008). This is why, in this chapter, I wish to pay specific attention to what CA, and in particular CA as applied to L2 talk, can contribute to our understanding of language, and how this understanding relates to a reconceptualised notion of language learning.

This chapter first exposes the conceptions of learning and of language that emanate from CA-SLA, briefly sketching their relation to other research traditions. The chapter then addresses the methodological challenges that result from these conceptions when it comes to documenting learning, and discusses the empirical evidence for learning that is provided by current work in CA-SLA in terms of both interactional and linguistic L2 development. The chapter concludes by outlining some parameters as regards a future CA-SLA research agenda.

Learning as learning-in-action

CA-SLA's conception of learning

In their introduction to the 88/4, 2004 issue of *The Modern Language Journal*, Markee and Kasper (2004: 496) state the following:

> Learning behaviors may usefully be understood as a conversational process that observably occurs in the intersubjective space between participants, not just in the mind/brain of individuals.

Such a view does not deny that our capacities/aptitudes have an individual or even biologically determined dimension, but it stresses that they function and are shaped within the micro-details of everyday communicative practices and the social agents' local interpretive processes (for example, Firth and Wagner 1997, 2007; Kasper 2004, 2009). Learning is seen as rooted in the moment-by-moment deployment of socioculturally elaborated, locally accomplished and – most typically – interactionally organised courses of practical activities, such as telling a story, discussing an event, negotiating a mutual understanding, but also reading or writing. Factors such as motivation, learning strategies, and cognitive processing are seen as being configured in response to social practices – and as analysable in terms of how they are observably enacted within these practices. As a consequence, learning behaviours are not interpreted as the pure result of previous knowledge, stable individual traits or learner types; rather, learners behave in situated ways, depending on how they interpret the situation at hand through the course of its accomplishment. Therefore, learning a language involves a continuous process of adaptation of patterns of language-use-for-action in response to locally emergent communicative needs, and the routinisation of these patterns through repeated participation in social activities. The resulting competencies are adaptive, flexible and sensitive to the contingencies of use. This is what is captured by the notions of *learning-in-action* (Firth and Wagner 2007) and *competence-in-action* (Pekarek Doehler 2006b).

The situated dimension of learning has been highlighted by socially-oriented studies of cognitive functioning and development, in particular theories of situated learning (Lave and Wenger 1991) and ethnomethodological analysis of practical cognition (cf. infra). Within socially-oriented SLA research, empirical support for such a view is provided by work which shows that linguistic and interactional competence is highly context-sensitive and co-constructible (Atkinson et al. 2007; Donato 1994; Firth and Wagner 2007; Hall 1995; Hellermann 2007, 2008; Markee and Seo 2009; Pekarek Doehler 2006b; Young and Miller 2004, inter alia).

Situated cognition

Situated cognition and its observability

The CA notion of learning builds on a notion of cognition as socially situated, distributed and hence inextricably intertwined with action/ interaction (cf. Schegloff 1991). A central correlate of such an understanding, which has crucial implication on how we go about documenting learning, is that cognition is not tucked away in a black box, but is deployed and made publicly available in interaction (see also Seedhouse and Walsh, this volume); as a consequence, it becomes at least partially observable for the researcher. The publicly accountable nature of social cognition has been stressed early on by Garfinkel (1967) in his ethnomethodological work on practical reasoning.[1] Garfinkel sees the relation between cognition and social organisation as being 'accountable', that is, observable and reportable: participants employ interactional procedures in a way that they are recognisable as doing such and such a thing.

The notion of *methods* plays a crucial role in this. Methods, in the ethnomethodological sense of the term, are instruments for accomplishing intersubjectivity and for establishing and maintaining social order; they are systematic procedures (of turn-taking, repairing, opening or closing conversation, and so on) by which members organise their behaviour in a mutually understandable way – and they use language as a central resource to do so. As such, 'methods' are part of a practical reasoning that defines human cognition as a situated process enacted through social activities. We have suggested earlier (Mondada and Pekarek Doehler 2004: 503) that these methods play a key role in situated learning; they are part of the competence that allows members to participate in social interactions (cf. Garfinkel 1967), including learning activities. At the same time, they are the very object of developing the ability to interact in a (second) language.

The publicly accountable nature of processes such as reasoning and understanding is a central issue for our purpose here, as it implies the possibility of analysing jointly accomplished activities as micro-moments of socially situated cognition (Kasper 2009; Markee and Seo 2009; Mori and Hasegawa 2009; Schegloff 1991). It implies that at least part of the process of learning is analysable as embodied in the details of social interaction, through such pervasive elements as repair, hesitation, repetition, turn-taking and sequential organisation, but also gaze, gesture, body orientation and the manipulation of objects.

This is shown in extract (1), where three students, Anila, Ebru and Natascha, are involved in group-work in a French L2 lower-intermediate classroom. The extract starts with the researcher (who participates in the teaching) joining the group and asking (l. 1) 'what do you want to say', to which Anila responds (l. 2) that she wants to express more than 'to love' (non-verbal behaviour appears on a separate line, following the translation; its onset is marked by + within the speaker's turn).

Extract 1

```
001 R:  qu'est-ce que tu veux dire.
        what do       you want to say

002 A:  +/ply/ que elle aime,  (.)  /ply/  que aime.
        more   than she loves        more  than loves

003 (1.5)

004 R:  h::m ehm tu peux m'expliquer la situation?
             can you explain the situation to me

005 A:  ehm tz (...) +>mais nous achetons une petit cadeau, une
                     but  we   buy        a little present  a
ani                   +reads her notes

006     CD de chansons bollywood=parce< +que elle aim:e ça très?
        CD of bollywood songs   because  she  loves that very
ani                                      +looks at Res

007 R:  parce qu'elle aime ça beaucoup.
        because she likes that very much

008 A:  +ai- b- okay.
all     +bend over their sheets to write

009 R:  on peut dire elle adore  +ça. [adorer
        you can say  she  adores this to adore
ani                               +lifts gaze to Res

010 A:                               [+ah adore+
ani                                   +nods
res                                          +Res leaves the group

011 E:  parce que
        because
```

```
012 N:  elle

013 E:  +adore
        adores
ebr     +looks at Ani

014     (..)

015 E:  elle adore?
        she  adores

016 A:  elle adore.
        she  adores

017 E:  +(hm?)
ebr     +looks at Anila
ani     +nods

018 +(3.8)
all     +bent over their respective sheets, writing
```
(CODI WSB -Tschu-181105-TG-s 12Sec-1)

The excerpt shows how learning-related cognitive processes are
embodied in the multimodal enactment of talk (for an analysis of the
co-construction processes in this excerpt, see Steinbach Kohler 2008).[2]
After declaring what she is searching for (l.1–2), Anila provides a first
possible wording (l. 6: *elle aima ça très* 'she loves that very'), which is not
target-language-like. Her rising intonation on *très* (l. 6), together with
her gazing toward the researcher, can be interpreted as soliciting help.
The researcher then proposes an alternative wording (l. 7), thereby
displaying her understanding of Anila's turn (and possibly gaze) as
searching for help. Taken together, lines 6 and 7 show a self-initiated
other-repair (cf. Schegloff et al. 1977). The candidate solution proposed
by the teacher is ratified by Anila's *okay* (l. 8), and the students' bending
down to write (see also l. 18) functions as a classroom-bound practice
which consecrates the 'correct' linguistic form as it is jointly accepted
by the participants.
    At this very moment, the researcher presents an alternative wording,
namely 'to adore' (l. 9). Anila again both verbally (by means of the change
of state token 'ah' and repetition) and physically (nodding) enacts her
recognition and acceptance of this alternative wording. The researcher's
subsequent physical moving away from the group (l. 10) indicates her
understanding of the communicative obstacle as being solved.
    The participant's cognitive orientation toward language (and pos-
sibly learning) is organised through the sequential deployment of turns

at talk. This deployment demonstrably reflects and enacts processes that can be cast in cognitive terms as 'attention focus', 'noticing', or 'understanding'. The noticing of the gap, the providing of a candidate solution, and its acceptance are interactionally occasioned. The interactional and the cognitive work deployed by the co-participants are inextricably intertwined.

In the following lines, a reconfiguration of the roles of expert and novice is embodied through talk and gaze. At l. 11, Ebru returns to the group's micro task: formulating why the group will buy a CD. Ebru orients his gaze toward Anila at the very moment of producing the verb *adore* (1. 13), possibly in order to solicit Anila's acknowledgement of the form, and then repeats *elle adore*, this time with rising intonation (1. 15), thereby more clearly displaying a call for ratification. Anila, in l. 16, fully assumes the role of expert by confirming Ebru's wording, while clearly articulating every syllable of *adore*. Subsequently, a final checking is done by means of gaze between Ebru and Anila, which is then treated as confirmation of the wording *elle adore*, as shown by the students writing on their sheets (l. 18).

Clearly, the participants' understanding of the 'correctness' of linguistic forms, as well as their conduct as 'experts' or as 'learners', are configured locally, through the moment-to-moment unfolding of the situation. Extract (1) demonstrates how socially contingent, mutually occasioned cognitive processes emerge out of the course of interaction. We observe a cognition in action that is organised through the sequential deployment of turns at talk, and embodied through gaze, prosody, body movements and verbal behaviour (cf. Mori and Hasegawa 2009; Olsher 2004).

Whether, in extract (1), learning is taking place is an open question: what we see are micro-moments of potential learning as observable through a sequentially contingent cognition in action. Evidence for learning, however, is provided by what Anila does exactly one month later in the same classroom, with the same researcher (cf. extract 2).

Situated cognition and evidence for learning

In extract (2), the group is discussing with the researcher what kinds of clothing they like:

Extract 2

```
001 R: et pour toi anila?
       and for you Anila
```

```
002 A:   <eh j'achète eh: °ähm°>=mais >j'a-=
              I buy              but    I
picture       #1                #2     #3
003 A:   =j'aDOre les vêtements s-=sportifs,<
              I adore   clothing   (that is)  casual
picture       #4
004 R:   mhm
005 A:   et aussi (.) un peu élégants.
          and also   a  bit  elegant
006 R:   mhm?
```
(CODI WBS – tschu-211205, 13'07-13'18)

#1
1. 002 *j'achète*
~~Anila gazes into the void~~
(researcher is to the very left,
kneeling)

7.1   Extract 2 photo 1

#2
1. 002 *mais*
Anila closes her eyes, keeps
posture

7.2   Extract 2 photo 2

#3
1. 002 *j'a-*
Anila leans forward, gazes at researcher

7.3   Extract 2 photo 3

#4
l. 003 *j'aDOre*
Anila leans further forward, gazes at researcher

7.4   Extract 2 photo 4

Anila's re-use of the verb *adore* (l. 3), one month later, can be taken as evidence for learning: a linguistic item that had been worked on inter-actionally earlier, and which proved problematic at that time, is now re-used in a contextualised way within a new communicative environment. But on what grounds can we claim that this learning is grounded exactly in what we have seen Anila do one month earlier (extract 1)? A close look at the linguistic, prosodic and bodily resources used by Anila can shed light on this question.

Anila's turn (l.2) starts off with slow pace, including a series of hesitation marks. It shows an online revision of the initial *j'achète* 'I buy' to yield *j'adore* 'I adore'. The *adore* is highlighted by several means: speeding up of talk, increase of volume, fixing of Anila's gaze on the researcher, and progressive leaning forward towards the researcher. This is illustrated in pictures 1 to 4.

Through her detailed temporal coordination between talk, gaze and body, Anila not only displays her knowledge of the verb, but tags it as a particularly noteworthy item *for this specific interlocutor*. It is as if she was enacting 'look, I know that word which you taught me a while ago'. From an emic perspective, we witness how a previous moment of interaction is treated as a moment of learning, and how the present interlocutor is treated as a person designed to witness that learning. A shared interactional history is invoked, and Anila's understanding of her learning as being contingent on that history is publicly displayed (for similar observations, see Markee and Seo 2009).

Taken together, extracts (1) and (2) show how, throughout the micro-details of talk-in-interaction, embodied and socially situated cognition and learning-in-action can be documented. Such observations feed into a praxeological understanding of cognition and learning as deployed, structured and publicly accountable in and through social interaction.

Implications for studying SLA

One highly significant observation with regard to this situatedness of learning in the course of practical activities is that language learning practices are embedded within patterns of participation (Mori 2004), interactionally configured and exhibited social identities (Kasper 2004), and organisational structures of talk-in-interaction both in the classroom (Hellermann 2008; Mondada and Pekarek Doehler 2004; Pekarek Doehler and Ziegler 2007; Seedhouse 2004) and in naturally occurring conversation (see the chapters in Gardner and Wagner 2004): all of these shape participants' learning activities and linguistic resources, while being at the same time structured by them. Language competence cannot therefore be seen as independent of the social-interactional dimensions of language practice, nor can the process of learning be so viewed.

Another empirical correlate of this conception of learning, as shown in extracts (1) and (2), is the fact that participants themselves exhibit orientation towards (and ongoing assessment of) each other's language expertise (Firth 2009; Kasper 2009) or cognitive states (Mori and Hasegawa 2009), and towards learning opportunities whose construction they contribute to (Firth and Wagner 2007; Mondada and Pekarek Doehler 2004; Mori 2004; Pekarek Doehler 2002). Such evidence opens one interesting window onto the *process* of learning, helping us to understand what learning is for the learner and his or her co-participants.

Language as language-in-action

CA-SLA's conception of language

Such a notion of learning, and of its embeddedness in action, implies a specific understanding of language. Emanating originally from sociology, CA's primary concern is with social practice and not with language forms (Sacks 1992, vol. I: 622). Also, until recently, CA-SLA has not paid systematic attention to the specifics of linguistic structure, taking activity rather than language form as the point of departure for analysis. Yet, in looking at the details of language as a resource for interaction, CA-SLA has the potential to bring to bear new insights on the development of L2 grammar, as part of the development of L2 interactional competence.

From the classic CA chapters, grammar – broadly understood as the resources provided by the linguistic system, including lexicon, morphology, syntax, phonology and prosody – is treated as a (if not *the*) central resource allowing participants to coordinate their actions: it is central for turn-taking through the fact that participants orient toward the syntactic organisation of utterances in order to anticipate possible transition relevance points (Sacks et al. 1974); and it is central for the social coordination of activities by organising projection, allowing participants to anticipate, on the basis of sequentially prior segments of talk, sequentially subsequent segments of talk (Schegloff 1996).

A central consequence of this embeddedness of language in (inter) action bears on the very nature of linguistic patterns or constructions. As language is a central tool for the coordination of the temporal and sequential unfolding of actions, its structures cannot but be continually adapted to the contingencies of social (inter)actions (Auer 2009; Schegloff 1996). This point has persuasively been documented in Goodwin's (1979) early CA analysis of how the construction of a single sentence is formatted in real time in response to local contingencies, such as recipient reactions or their absence. It has also been evidenced in Lerner's (1991) work on utterance co-construction, where a second speaker completes a syntactic trajectory initiated by a first speaker, and thereby accomplishes locally relevant interactional work such as displaying alignment. Such observations can be interpreted as providing evidence for the distributed nature of grammar (Pekarek Doehler, in press): language is a shared resource for action, distributed among speakers, whose structures and functioning are inextricably embedded in its natural habitat, that is, the moment-to-moment deployment of talk-in-progress.

On the basis of such observations, current work in CA-SLA proposes a praxeological and dialogic conception of language, whose most explicit formulations understand language and social activity as mutually constitutive (Firth and Wagner 1997, 2007; Mondada and Pekarek Doehler 2004; Wagner and Gardner 2004): the structures of language are used as a resource for organising and coordinating actions and are in turn shaped in response to this organisation: the linguistic system is fundamentally made not simply to say things, but to accomplish social activities.

This, of course, is a crucial point, as it radically challenges received conceptions of language within and outside of SLA. It is, however, a point that is corroborated by compelling evidence from a growing body of research emanating from different research traditions. Most importantly, in the field of interactional linguistics, numerous studies have documented that the way utterances are constructed, down to their linguistic details, is sensitive to their interactional context and more precisely to the organisation of the actions interlocutors are engaged in (Auer 2009; Ochs et al. 1996; Schegloff 1996).

This conception of language also resonates with usage-based approaches that see grammar not as a static, self-contained system, but as variable, adaptive, flexible and emergent through contextualised language use (Hopper 1998; Tomasello 2003; see also Larsen-Freeman, this volume). Despite their epistemological and methodological differences, the quoted research paradigms converge on one central issue: they radically question a stable, context-neutral notion of our linguistic knowledge as independent from language use.

Grammar as a resource for action: Evidence from L2 talk

This dynamic character of language is a consequential issue when it comes to analysing and understanding L2 learning and use. In order to illustrate its relevance for issues of L2 talk and learning, I will focus in this section on how L2 speakers use one classic construction, namely left-dislocation,[3] for accomplishing locally relevant interactional work.

Extract (3) shows a self-initiated other-repair sequence that closes with
a left-dislocation at l. 8:

Extract 3

```
001 G:  euh (..) la: (..) je pense que euh la b- (.) la b- (.)
        hum    the:      I think that um  the b-    the b-
002     la  ba- [bilance
        the ba- bilance
003 ?              [((coughing))
004 (0.4)
005 T:  pardon?
        pardon
006 G:  la bilance, (.) °la balance°?
        the bilance     the balance
007 T:  la balance oui.
        the balance yes
008 G:  la  balance (.) ça: montre (..) s- euh si    on était juste (.)
        the balance     it shows        s- um whether one was  right
009     ou pas?
        or not
```

(SPD25/26:29:13)

At l. 8, the repetition/acknowledgement of the candidate solution provided by the teacher at l. 7 is integrated by Gerd into a left-dislocated
construction, produced under a single intonation contour. The left-
dislocation allows the speaker to do two things at once: first it sets off
the NP *la balance* from the rest of the turn, thereby scaffolding its recognition as doing a ratification (that is, ratifying the teacher's *la balance*); then it recasts that item by a clitic pronoun, thereby warranting
its integration into the pursuit of the turn. The dislocated construction hence amalgamates two functions: ratification of a linguistic form,
and pursuit of the communicative project under way. In this way, l. 8
presents itself as a direct continuation of the syntactic trajectory initiated at l. 1, the two together forming *je pense que la balance ça montre si
on était juste ou pas*. Visibly, the use of the construction here responds to
interactional contingencies as they emerge from the sequential unfolding of turns and actions, allowing the speakers to minimise the disrup-
tive effect of other-repair.

A second case in point for left-dislocation as an interactional
resource is provided by extract (4), where the left-dislocation is again

instrumental in minimising disruption, but this time in the case of self-repair.

Extract 4

```
[talking about Swiss Germans' need to master standard German]
001 G: moi je trouve que  ce n'est pas nécessaire parce que: en allemand
       me  I  think  that  it isn't      necessary  because:   in German
002    (.) ou en Allemagne on peut aussi parler suisse allemand,
           or in Germany    one can  also  speak swiss german
003    et  les autres ils: (2.2) on les comprend. (.) quand même.
       and the others they       we understand them    anyway
```

(SPD 19 «les autres»; Pekarek Doehler, in press)

At line 3, Gerôme starts off a turn construction unit as a left-dislocated format where *les autres* 'the others' is co-indexed by the subsequent subject clitic *ils* 'they'. However, after a 2.2 second pause, the
plan is revised. The left detached constituent remains available for a
second, yet grammatically different, exploitation: *les autres* is now co-
indexed by the object clitic *les* 'them'. The self-repair is built so as to
minimise disruption: there is no cut-off, reformulation signal or up/
down-step of pitch. The left-dislocation itself is instrumental in this
minimisation, as it allows the speaker to restart a syntactic trajectory
with a proform that is continuous, both syntactically and pragmat-
ically, with the lexical NP in the precedingly abandoned structure,
while proffering a retrospective re-analysis of the grammatical function of that NP (for a more detailed discussions of such revisions see
Pekarek Doehler, in press). Again, the left-dislocation is a resource for
dealing with the contingencies of talk-in-interaction. Also note that
the initial NP+clitic cluster allows the speaker to 'buy time' while
searching for his or her wording (see the 2.2-second pause), without being interrupted by the co-participant(s). Such occurrences of
left-dislocated constructions suggest that speakers use grammar as a
central resource for organising talk, and particularly L2 talk (where
hesitations are frequent), and hence as a key component of their (L2)
interactional competence.

Excerpts (3) and (4) present micro-phenomena bearing witness to the
locally contingent nature of the linguistic system: grammatical constructions are used and sometimes moulded for all practical purposes,
in response to local interactional needs, such as overcoming hesitations and minimising the disruptiveness of repair, thereby maximis-
ing the progressivity of talk. More importantly, for our purpose here,

such evidence suggests that a central business for the L2 speaker is to develop a grammar that can serve as a resource for dealing with the specifics of L2 talk-in-interaction. Clearly, such adaptative uses of syntactic resources by the participants cannot be accounted for in terms of sentence-level grammar, nor in terms of approximation to target-language norms. Yet, they are an integral part of learners' developing interactional competence. Therefore, they call for a microanalysis of grammar as it is deployed in interaction.

Implications for studying SLA

By empirically documenting the embeddedness of speakers' developing L2 grammar in the micro-details of social interaction, CA-SLA brings to bear on SLA research a new view of language that has several critical implications.

First, it implies that language form is analysable in the first place as a contextualised solution to an interactional problem – part of members' 'methods' of dealing with the issues of everyday life/talk. This may, and regularly does, imply issues of grammatical appropriateness, and proximity to target language, but it also may, and regularly does, imply the use of transitional, alternative grammatical formats that are communicatively efficient and may serve as stepping-stones into more target-like constructions. Moreover, it may, and regularly does, imply the use of target-language constructions in a way that is instrumental in dealing with the specifics of (second language) talk-in-interaction. In this sense, language learning can be seen as a central part of the elaboration of contextually sensitive methods for 'doing things' (cf. Hellermann 2008; Mondada and Pekarek Doehler 2004).

Second, it suggests that language is not simply applied in action, but is emergent from action: it is (re)shaped (that is, sedimented or changed) through each use as a response to locally configured communicative needs. This is what I mean when defining language learning as routinisation of patterns of language-use-for-action (cf. supra). Language and practice are mutually constitutive; mutatis mutandis, language learning and language use are not ontologically separate phenomena.

Finally, while this view 'establishes talk-in-interaction as the key object of study for SLA' (Markee 2008: 5) – and perhaps of language more generally – it also outlines the need to look closely at the details of how talk is produced in real time, including how grammar is recycled, infused with hesitations and recasts, and incrementally extended for all practical purposes, both as part of language-as-a-resource-for-action and as a possible trace of learning behaviours. In this sense, CA-SLA participates in a wider field of investigations which consider that it is by looking at the micro-details of language as it is used in communicative practice that we can provide new insights into both the nature of language and the process of language learning.

The methodological challenge: What is evidence for learning?

The above-mentioned re-conceptualisations of learning and of language have fundamental implications for how we go about documenting learning and what we take as empirical evidence for learning. Within the conceptual framework and on the basis of the empirical research discussed above, the analytic focus is on how learners use language in talk-in-interaction to accomplish situated activities (such as opening a conversation, disagreeing, writing collaboratively) and in which they simultaneously orient to the rules of a social practice, linguistic norms, mutual organisation of actions, and so on. As the analytic interest focuses on how people behave in their everyday practices, analyses are carried out on L2 speakers within naturally-occurring data and not, for instance, in experimental or semi-experimental settings. A central concern is with how participants themselves orient to language and to language learning (emic perspective), as well as how they treat each others as 'learners' or as 'experts'.

Based on these analytic priorities, CA-SLA sets out to understand language learning in the light of the dynamics of language use. Here exactly lies a central methodological challenge when it comes to documenting learning. What is at stake is finding ways of looking not only at language across time, but at language-in-action across time: How does the accomplishment of L2 talk-in-interaction and L2 speakers' participation in talk change across time? And how are changes in linguistic form and in other semiotic means embedded in (changes in) the accomplishment of talk and participation? It is these embedded changes that provide evidence for L2 learning.

Currently, CA studies on SLA face two major challenges. On the one hand, classic CA work, while aiming to discover the 'methods' by which members organise their conduct in mutually recognisable ways, does not address the question of how members develop these methods:

> The absence of a 'learning mechanism' creates a dilemma for L2 researchers who wish to apply CA not only to the study of L2 interaction, but to second language development. (Kasper 2009: 11)

There is no readily available conceptual or methodological apparatus that CA-SLA can draw on to investigate development over time. On the other hand, the object of study – that is, the ever-changing micro-details of social interaction – is dynamic, flexible, organic. Looking at language-in-action across time implies tracking language resources used within the same type of practice at (at least) two different moments in time – which presupposes a certain *consistency* across time of the practice being studied. Obviously, this is far from easy to achieve given CA's uncompromising insistence on naturally-occurring data. Because real-life situations are involved, control of variables can only be limited when comparing behaviour across time. Therefore, a central but tricky analytic task lies in clearly differentiating between what, in the observable change in behaviour, can be accounted for in terms of *local context-sensitivity* (that is, adaptation to a given interactional context), and what provides evidence for *change across time*, that is, learning.

Two scales of the time axis are currently being investigated. The first relates to change across larger time-spans as addressed by longitudinal (or cross-sectional) studies that are designed to capture some dimensions of the outcome (*product*) of learning – that is, a state of competence at a time X, X+1, and so on. Recently, a series of studies on interactional competence has been carried out in this vein. The second is concerned with how participants, within short time-spans, work their competencies in real time through the moment-by-moment unfolding of talk. These studies are designed to capture some dimensions of the *process* of learning, and typically focus on the learning of specific linguistic items or patterns. In what follows, I will briefly discuss some of the empirical evidence provided by these two lines of investigation.

Documenting learning I: Interactional development over time

CA-SLA has recently generated or inspired a small series of longitudinal studies directly concerned with the development of L2 interactional competence.

Possibly the most systematic investigation into interactional L2 development to date is provided by Hellermann (2008). On the basis of a research design that enabled the same dyads of adult EFL learners to be followed in class across several months and even years, Hellermann documents their developing practices of opening tasks, of telling stories, and of disengaging from an activity. For instance, openings of teacher-assigned dyadic tasks at lower levels of proficiency are typically launched directly, with little or no prefatory talk, while at more advanced levels, participants show increased use of prefatory talk before launching the task and a wider repertoire of verbal negotiations of the upcoming task. Hellermann thus documents major differences, across time, in how participants organise the sequential structure of a practice.

Cekaite (2007), in a longitudinal micro-analytic study combining the framework of language socialisation with CA methodology, follows a Kurdish immigrant child in an immersion context in a Swedish classroom. She situates the child's progress along a developmental continuum of verbal conduct moving toward fuller participation that can be observed through the child's turn-taking behaviour across three stages, ranging from silence, through inappropriate turn-taking, to correct identification of slots for turn-taking.

In a study inspired by Lave and Wenger's (1991) conceptualisation of learning as change in participation, from peripheral to full, Young and Miller (2004), again using CA methodology, show how an adult Vietnamese learner of English changes her mode of participation in weekly writing conferences with an instructor across a time-span of four weeks. The learner shows increasing interactional skills with regard to turn-taking and the sequential organisation of the practice (for example, transitioning between interactional episodes).

At the current state of research, two substantial contributions emanate from the quoted studies and a few others (for example, Brouwer and Wagner 2004; Hellermann 2007). First, they show that interactional skills related to turn-taking or the sequential organisation of a given practice are to some extent re-learned or re-calibrated in the L2, and not just automatically transferred from L1. This is a significant finding insofar as it not only adds an additional layer of complexity to SLA, but also empirically counters a conception of learning according to which communicative skills involve the simple putting-to-use of previously acquired linguistic patterns and rules, plus pragmatic and sociolinguistic knowledge. Clearly, the evidence provided by the quoted studies is based on a redefined, more holistic understanding of what the object of L2 development is. The attention paid to the details of language, however, is scant in the quoted research (for a notable exception see Ishida 2009).

Second, the quoted studies start to outline a useful methodology for documenting L2 interactional development. They show how we can track interactional development over time through longitudinal and micro-analytic research design by looking at recurrent interactional practices (such as participating in a writing conference) or micro-practices (such as opening a story). Clearly, both of these analytic focuses narrow down the concrete site of investigation to micro-moments of social interaction, but they have the advantage of zooming in on practices that show a certain consistency and comparability across time, and which allow identification of observables for analysis (for example, turn-taking, sequential organisation) which can be used as indicators of interactional development.

Documenting learning II:
The interactional configuration of linguistic patterns

When it comes to documenting the process of language learning, as it is observably configured within the detailed unfolding of talk-in-interaction, another research design is relevant. Evidence is needed that goes beyond such local mechanisms as repair or negotiation sequences, and accounts for how participants progressively, repeatedly and collectively configure their L2 resources within joint courses of activities, and how they re-use these resources within same and different environments, in more and more context-sensitive ways (that is, ways that are adapted to local interactional needs).

Several recent CA-SLA studies provide micro-analytic investigations of learning processes across short time-spans (called 'microgenesis' in Vygotskyan developmental psychology. For SLA see, for example, Donato 1994). In his account of English lingua franca telephone conversations in a workplace setting, Firth (2009) demonstrates how, during a telephone opening, participants use pace, intonation and the sequential structure of talk-in-interaction to progressively establish a synchronised rhythm of interaction. He shows that, progressively, they mutually calibrate their interactional competencies in a way that leads into a more and more fluent pursuit of a conversation which, in its beginning, was marked by slow pace and lengthy hesitations. In this study, joint interactional learning is evidenced in terms of a locally adaptive learning for all practical purposes, allowing participants to optimise their interaction in this situation, for this practical purpose, with this interlocutor.

In a recent study on French L2 classroom small-group interaction, Pekarek Doehler and Steinbach Kohler (under review) analyse how, while accomplishing the official task, students jointly work on the morphosyntactic shaping of their respective utterances online, throughout the moment-by-moment deployment of joint actions. The study documents a recurrent structure of situated learning, moving from (a) collaborative establishment of a morphosyntactic pattern, through (b) contextualised re-use of that pattern, to (c) creative re-use, that is, variation on the pattern and progressive complexification (see also extracts 1 and 2 supra). The analysis shows that each step is jointly established in response to such locally configured interactional needs as providing an answer, showing expertise, or displaying participation. One case under analysis sheds light on the *process* of construction building: it suggests that the elaboration of such morphosyntactic patterns as the word-order of *tout ça fait/coûte X* 'all this makes/costs X' and *ça fait tout* 'that's all' crucially hinges on the use of lexically-based open-slot constructions functioning as unanalysed chunks, rather than on individual items and their combination rules.

Micro-analytic studies of locally enacted, interactionally configured learning (see also Atkinson et al. 2007; Firth and Wagner 2007; Markee and Seo 2009) offer two main contributions to our understanding of the process of learning. On the one hand, they show that, for participants, working on language is not primarily a process of elaborating target-language forms; rather, it is a process of elaborating language forms for action, that is, configuring patterns of language use in order to accomplish some locally emergent interactional business, of which learning may be a collateral product. Working on a linguistic form (or on such things as intonation and rhythm) and potential learning appear as interactionally contingent processes. On the other hand, by using CA's fine-grained analytical methodology, we can uncover how participants themselves locally orient to grammar, how they treat grammar online, and how they use linguistic constructions both as stepping-stones for new constructions and as instruments for the mutual coordination of talk. And we can document how this online treatment of 'emergent L2 grammar' (Pekarek Doehler and Steinbach Kohler, under review) is inextricably embedded in the process of taking turns at talk and jointly accomplishing social actions. Here lies possibly one substantial contribution that CA-SLA can offer to current thinking about second language development, namely in providing evidence for some dimensions of the *process* of L2 grammatical development, that is, the emergence and sedimentation of patterns of language use, which has so far remained largely unexplored in SLA research (cf. Ellis 2003: 68).

Conclusion

In response to the general focus of this volume on conceptions of learning, I have set out to discuss how the concepts and methods emanating from CA research in the field of SLA can enhance our understanding of both the process and the product of SLA. I would like to conclude by summing up CA-SLA's contribution to understanding L2 learning, and by sketching some possibilities and requirements for a future CA-SLA research agenda.

While much of the earlier work in CA-SLA has been undertaken to uncover the fine-grained mechanisms of L2 talk, today CA-SLA is centrally addressing issues of L2 development. Recent work in CA-SLA has provided methodological solutions for tracking L2 interactional development (focus on micro-practices) as well as concrete analytic observables (for example, turn-taking or sequential organisation of a practice) for doing so. This is a significant contribution insofar as, until now, little has been known about L2 interactional development, despite intense calls coming for instance from education policy-makers (for example, the Common European Framework of Reference) for a better understanding of interactional competence and its development.

As to the investigation of L2 grammar, micro-analytic CA studies of how participants work on their grammar in real time show that language can usefully be analysed as a resource people use in interaction, which is prone to being patterned and re-patterned in response to locally occasioned interactional needs. This invites us not so much to ask how learners' language relates to the target language (the target-language norms being constructs in need of explanation themselves), but to describe how linguistic structure and other semiotic resources are 'occasioned' by conversational structure and conversational needs, and thereby configured and sedimented in response to these needs.

One promising future path for CA-SLA to venture on is to intensify longitudinal and possibly cross-sectional micro-analytic studies of interactional development. A prominent need in this regard is to broaden the range of observables that are taken as indicators of interactional development. Another is to broaden the range of languages and social situations (beyond educational settings) that are being studied. At a given moment, cross-linguistic as well as cross-situational comparisons may provide additional fruitful grounds for an integrated regime of investigation.

Finally, I also believe that much can be gained in understanding SLA if we pay more systematic attention to the details of how language interacts with other resources, as part of members' methods for accomplishing talk-in-interaction. Exploring the detailed inscription of language-in-action provides a basis for better understanding the complex interrelation between linguistic and interactional development over time. A close look at this interrelation may carry us one step further toward a more holistic understanding of the learning of a second language, in a way that can inform other research paradigms, but also needs to be informed by them.

Notes

1. For discussions of the relevance of the ethnomethodological conception of cognition for CA-SLA see Kasper (2009), Mondada and Pekarek Doehler (2000) and Seedhouse (2004).
2. I thank Fee Steinbach Kohler for her important help with the transcription of the data.
3. A left-dislocated construction is commonly defined as a sentence structure in which a referential element (most often a NP) is located to the left of a matrix clause containing a pronoun that is co-indexical with that element.

8
Learning a Second Language through Classroom Interaction

Paul Seedhouse and Steve Walsh

Introduction

This chapter tackles a number of the conceptual and methodological problems involved in analysing how L2 learning is related to classroom interaction from a Conversation Analysis (CA) perspective. The chapter consists of two sections: part 1 looks at socially-distributed cognition in L2 classroom interaction and part 2 at classroom interactional competence. The first part of the chapter argues that any conceptualisation of 'learning' in a classroom needs to consider the ways in which learning processes are embodied in classroom interaction. A brief introduction is provided to the CA position on socially-distributed cognition in conversation. We then develop a CA perspective on socially-distributed cognition and learning in relation to L2 classroom interaction. A data extract is analysed in relation to tracking of a learning item and in relation to learning processes.

In this chapter we do not examine learning as social integration, since that is the subject of Jenks's chapter. Rather, we argue that learning is, at least in part, a social process which is embodied in interaction. An understanding of socially-distributed cognition entails looking closely at the interplay between language, interaction and learning, making the strong case that learning is embodied in the interaction itself; any attempt to study learning must therefore begin by studying classroom interaction. In this chapter, learning is defined as a change in a socially-displayed cognitive state. It is evaluated by teachers, and by us as analysts, by examining the changes displayed by learners in their classroom talk. However, a process approach to learning an L2 by classroom interaction is also proposed.

A second strand to the view of learning proposed here argues that a micro-analytic approach to classroom interaction enables us to identify specific strategies used by teachers and learners to enhance learning. These strategies have their origins in sociocultural theories of learning and include classroom participants' ability to *scaffold* each other's contributions; their ability to offer *affordances*: opportunities for learning (evidenced, for example, by extended pauses, or fewer interruptions); teachers' and learners' competence in negotiating meaning and *appropriating* new ideas or new concepts. We argue that a CA methodology permits a fine-grained, 'up-close' analysis of these features and allows us to provide evidence that learning is taking place. We propose that teachers' and learners' ability to enhance learning processes through their online decision-making is a key element of classroom interactional competence (CIC), defined here as 'teachers' and learners' ability to use interaction as a tool for mediating and assisting learning' (Walsh 2006: 130). Using an extract of data, we consider how teachers and learners display varying levels of CIC and discuss the implications of this for gaining closer understandings of the relationship between L2 learning and interaction.

Socially-distributed cognition and L2 classroom interaction

Socially-distributed cognition in conversation

In this section a brief introduction is provided to the CA position on socially-distributed cognition (Drew 1995; Schegloff 1991) in relation to ordinary conversation. In the following section we explain the position in relation to L2 classroom interaction and demonstrate how this relates to 'learning'. CA is not able to establish the cognitive state of individuals in isolation, nor to gain a direct window into what interactants 'really mean'. What CA is able to portray and explicate, however, is the progress of intersubjectivity or socially-distributed cognition. CA aims to 'identify ways in which participants themselves orient to, display, and make sense of one another's cognitive states (among other things)' (Drew 1995: 79). Intersubjectivity is mutual understanding or interpersonal alignment, and one of the key objectives of CA is to explicate how we are able to achieve a shared understanding of each other's actions. In conversation, interactants perform social displays of their cognitive states to each other. A social display of a cognitive state may differ from an actual state, as in the case of lying. For example, A tells B he doesn't know where the money is, when in fact he does know.

The organisations of sequence, turn-taking and repair are employed by interactants in order to display to each other their social actions and cognitive state, and also to display their understandings or analyses of the previous speaker's social actions and cognitive state. These organisations are called the building blocks of intersubjectivity because interactants use them to display to one another their understanding of each others' turns, and this permits us as analysts to follow the progress of their intersubjectivity. Extract 1 illustrates how socially-distributed cognition works in ordinary conversation.

Extract 1

```
1 Marsha:    en Ilene is going to meet im:. becuz the to:p wz ripped
2            off'v iz car which is tih say someb'ddy helped th'mselfs.
3 Tony:  →   stolen.
4            (0.4)
5 Marsha:    stolen.=right out in front of my house.
6 Tony:      oh: f'r crying out loud, ...
```

(Schegloff 1996: 75)

In extract 1 line 3, Tony's turn consists of a single word. This provides both an analysis of Marsha's previous turn and a social display of Tony's cognitive state, specifically that he has understood what has happened to Marsha's car. Marsha in line 5 analyses Tony's turn as commenting retrospectively on what happened to her car, as performing a new social action of confirming understanding of Marsha's news by summarising the content in a new linguistic format, and as providing a context for her to take the sequence further. She displays her understanding of the work performed by his turn in her subsequent turn (line 5), by repeating his turn with the same intonation and adding further information on the theft.

Interactants, then, are always producing in their utterances a social display of their own cognitive state at the same time as they are displaying their understanding of a previous speaker's utterance. The production of a first turn provides an interpretative basis for the next speaker to interpret the first speaker's actions. However, it can be interpreted in this way solely by virtue of its sequential location after the first part of an adjacency pair. Any first action in interaction is an action template which creates a normative expectation for a next action and a template for interpreting it. The second action displays an interpretation of the first action and itself creates an action. This can be termed the *next-turn proof procedure* (Sacks et al. 1974: 729), which is the basic tool that analysts can use to develop an emic perspective. The next turn, then, documents an analysis of the previous turn and displays this analysis not only to the other interactants, but also to us as analysts, providing us with a proof criterion and search procedure. The point is, then, that interactants are constantly conducting a social display to each other (and to us as analysts) of their cognitive states and their understanding of each others' utterances by means of and by reference to the organisation of turn-taking, sequence and repair. The study of socially-shared cognition, then, cannot be separated from the study of interaction. This is what Schegloff (1991: 152) means by 'the embeddedness, the inextricable intertwinedness, of cognition and interaction'. CA analysis not only demonstrates *what* understandings the interactants display to each other, but also *how* they do so by normative reference to the interactional organisations. In other words, we gain access to their displays of understanding to each other in the same way that they gain this access, that is, by reference to the interactional organisations; this is what is meant by developing an emic perspective. The organisations of turn and sequence are mechanisms for displaying and checking mutual understanding, and the organisation of repair is a mechanism for repairing breakdowns in mutual understanding.

Because these organisations provide a complex framework to support mutual understanding in interaction, a single word can perform (and be designed to perform) a great deal of work in relation to socially-distributed cognition. So Tony's single word in extract 1 line 3 not only constitutes an entire turn, but it also performs three kinds of sequential work in the past, present and future. It comments retrospectively on what happened to her car, performs a new social action of confirming understanding of Marsha's news, and provides a context for Marsha to provide further information, which she does. Since the normative expectation is that a turn will perform these three kinds of sequential work, Tony can design his turn so that a single word is capable of doing so and Marsha can interpret it as doing so. The evidence that the participants are actually orienting to the system described is in the next-turn proof procedure itself.

Socially-distributed cognition and 'learning' in L2 classroom interaction

In ordinary conversation, then, Schegloff (1991: 154) suggests that 'the structures of interaction penetrate into the very warp' of cognition, so that, for example, an 'understanding-display' device (that is, the next-turn-proof-procedure) is built into the organisation of turn-taking and sequence. Processes of socially-distributed cognition are inseparable from the structures of ordinary conversation itself. In the same way, if we wish to fully understand the processes of socially-distributed cognition and 'learning' in relation to instructed L2 acquisition, it is vital to understand how L2 classroom interaction is organised, and how this differs from ordinary conversation.

Studies of institutional interaction (for example, Drew and Heritage 1992a) have focused on how the organisation of the interaction is related to the institutional aim, and on the ways in which this organisation differs from the benchmark of ordinary conversation. In contrast to conversation, participants in institutional interaction orient to some 'core goal, task or identity (or set of them) conventionally associated with the institution in question' (Drew and Heritage 1992b: 22). CA institutional discourse methodology attempts to relate not only the overall organisation of the interaction, but also individual interactional devices, to the core institutional goal. CA attempts, then, to understand the organisation of the interaction as being *rationally* derived from the core institutional goal. In the case of L2 classroom interaction, the institutional core goal is that *the teacher will teach the learners the L2*. This means that there is a reflexive relationship between pedagogy and interaction, and that interactants constantly display in their talk their analyses of the evolving relationship between pedagogy and interaction (Seedhouse 2004).

In ordinary conversation between native speakers, any utterance is a document on many levels. The utterance is a display of the learner's analysis of the prior utterance of an interactant, it performs a social action in response, and it positions the learner in a social system. It displays an understanding of the current sequential and social context, and also renews it. It performs a social display of the learner's cognitive, emotional and attitudinal states: note that this does not mean it gives a direct window into these states, as explained above. In the specific case of the L2 classroom, any utterance by the learner in L2 may perform two additional functions in addition to those already mentioned above in relation to conversation.

First, the learner's utterance may in addition be delivered in the L2, and may thereby constitute a display of his/her L2 developmental level or *learning state* as well. A learning state, in relation to L2 classroom interaction, is a cognitive state related to the acquisition of all aspects of a L2. Any utterance in L2 by a classroom learner can be taken by a teacher to be a display of a learning state. This understanding is institutionalised in various ways. In language tests (for example, IELTS), students are given scores or grades based on their spoken production during the test. In the classroom, L2 learner utterances are subject to evaluation and repair by the teacher, since they are taken to be a display of a learning state. Part of the interactional and pedagogical work undertaken by an L2 teacher is to analyse learner utterances for evidence of their learning state. The teacher may then undertake pedagogical and interactional work to transform the learning state of the learner, as we will see in lines 22–28 of extract 2 below.

Second, interactants in L2 classrooms are always displaying to one another in their talk their analyses of the current state of the evolving relationship between pedagogy and interaction. So in extract 2 below, for example, L1 displays in lines 18–19 his analysis that the current relationship between pedagogy and interaction is for him to debate with L2 which patient should receive the heart transplant. By contrast, in line 23, L1 displays his analysis that the current relationship between pedagogy and interaction is for him to repeat exactly what the teacher says.

We noted above in the case of conversation that an utterance is a social display of a cognitive state and does not necessarily correspond exactly to an actual cognitive state, as in the case of telling lies. Similarly, it is not certain that the learning state as displayed by L2 learners in interaction is necessarily their 'real' learning state. We see an example of this uncertainty in extract 2 below, where it is doubtful that the learner's correct repetition of an item (in line 14) means he has learnt it. However, the point is that teachers act on the basis that a learner's utterance is a display of their learning state (as in lines 22–29 below). This is the rationale for teacher repair work in the L2 classroom, and forms part of their professional work. In conversation and classroom interaction we have no means of verifying what an individual's actual cognitive state is. What we are doing in CA in both settings is analysing how interactants perform social displays of their cognitive state via their turns at talk, and how they analyse and act upon others' social displays of cognitive states.

A CA analysis is able to portray the learning states of an L2 learner as documented by their utterances, and to depict changes in learning states as defined above. 'Learning' is defined here as a change in learning state which moves it closer to a native-speaker standard, as illustrated in extract 2. CA analyses of learning in L2 classrooms may focus on how individual 'learning items' are learnt, using a 'tracking methodology' (Markee 2008). Alternatively, the analysis may portray learning processes in a much broader sense. In the following sections we illustrate both of these approaches in relation to a data extract.

Tracking learning items

In this section we focus on how a specific item is learnt by means of the process of interaction. In extract 2, a group of learners of mixed nationalities in New Zealand are engaged in a simulation and are discussing which of four potential recipients should receive a heart transplant. They are managing the interaction themselves (the teacher is present but not participating in the discussion) and debating the merits and demerits of the four candidates, until a problem with linguistic form impacts on communication in line 4. The 'learning item' we are examining here is phonological, namely the pronunciation of the word 'company' by L1, which is incorrect in lines 4, 6, 8, 10 and 12.

Extract 2

```
1   L3:    they live in Australia the family?

2   L1:    ( ) I don't know but they will go to Australia too. (.)

3   L3:    (1.0) okay

4   L1: →  (.) and (3.0) another one for ( ) from drug (kʌm'pɑːni)

5   L2:    sorry?

6   L1:    from drug (kʌm'pɑːni) (laughs)

7   L2:    drug

8   L1:    drug drug <d-r-u-g> (spells word) the uh drug (kʌm'pɑːni)

9   L2:    what what is (kʌm'pɑːni)?

10  L1:    (kʌm'pɑːni)

11  L2:    (kʌm'pɑːni)

12  L1:    (kʌm'pɑːni)

13  L2: →  (1.0) ah (' kʌmpəni)

14  L1:    yes (' kʌmpəni)

15  L2:    ah (.) from the drug (' kʌmpəni)

16  L1:    drug drug drug

17  L2:    yes but impossible for the parents to get ( )

18  L1:    drug (kʌm'pɑːni) know they know about this advertising

19         (.)so they will come to help this family this family(2.0)

20         you know what I mean=
```

```
21  L2:       =no=
22  L1:       =drug (kʌm'pɑːni)
23  T:    →   >can can I just right there-< it's (' kʌmpəni)
24  L1:       (' kʌmpəni)=
25  T:        =(' kʌmpəni)=
26  L1:       =(' kʌmpəni)=
27  T:        =(' kʌmpəni) yeah=
28  L1:       =yep=
29  T:        =yeah not (kʌm'pɑːni) (' kʌmpəni)
30  L1:       (' kʌmpəni)
            (16 lines of discussion omitted)
47  L1:       reasons against giving her a new heart, (1.0) uh (1.5) you
48       →    remember drug (' kʌmpəni) ( ) family allowed drug
49       →    (' kʌmpəni) give them money
```

(Loewen 2002 (5 December C12))

In extract 2 a problem with linguistic form (mispronunciation of *company* with stress on the second syllable) causes a problem in communication for the learners, which necessitates a temporary switch from the discussion (the main business) to a focus on linguistic form in lines 5 to 16. It is evident in line 9 that L1's mispronunciation has created a communication problem for L2. First of all, L1 and L2 jointly manage the repair without the help of the teacher, who is present. L2 initiates repair in line 9, then conducts other-initiated other-repair in line 13, with L1 displaying uptake of the repair in line 14. In line 17 the learners return to the meaning focus. However, although L1 was able to display uptake of the repaired item when the focus was on form (line 14), he reverts to the incorrect pronunciation (lines 18 and 22) when the focus shifts back to meaning and fluency as the debate continues. So although L1 displayed uptake of the correct pronunciation when this became the object of the interaction, he was not able to show that the correct pronunciation had become routinised when the focus of the interaction moved back to discussion. In line 23, T notes that L1 has continued to pronounce this item incorrectly and switches the interactional focus back to form again with other-initiated other-repair, drilling the pronunciation of the item. L1 again displays uptake of the correct pronunciation in lines 24, 26 and 30. Subsequently, when the focus again shifts back to debate of the topic, we find that L1 is now able to display uptake of the corrected item in lines 48–49. L1 does not display continued uptake of a correction of linguistic form when performed by a peer, but does do so when it is performed by the teacher.

The above extract demonstrates the importance of a contextual approach to repair and learning (Seedhouse 2004); a learner may be able to produce a linguistic item correctly and appropriately in one L2 classroom context but not in another. Uptake, then, cannot be demonstrated by drilling or repetition of an item in tightly controlled interaction in a form and accuracy context. Evidence of uptake is more convincing when a learner is able to produce the item independently when the focus is on meaning and fluency, as in lines 48 and 49.

The extract also illustrates the frightening complexity involved in trying to track individual learning items in the very fluid and variable environment of classroom L2 learning. We have focused above on one learner's acquisition of one aspect of a lexical item. Mastering a word 'completely' may require knowledge of its orthographical and phonological form, meanings, grammatical behaviour, associations, collocations, frequency and register (see Elgort and Nation's chapter, this volume). So far as we can tell from the interaction, L1 is able to use the word 'company' correctly and appropriately in a sentence and as part of a discussion – it is only the pronunciation of the word which is creating a problem.

The paradox of tracking 'learning' in classroom interaction is this. If we wish to introduce and track a particular 'learning item' (whether lexical, syntactical or discoursal), then we need to keep very tight control of the interaction in order to ensure that the learners are compelled to produce the item we wish to track. However, it is only when control of the interaction is relaxed and the focus switches away from linguistic form, and learners have freedom to organise the interaction and encode meanings for themselves, that more compelling evidence of learning is produced, as in lines 48 and 49. The problem is, however, that when control of the interaction is relaxed, participants may take it in a number of unexpected directions and the targeted learning item may never occur. Moreover, in the extract above one learner has the floor for a length of time and can be tracked. In many classroom settings around the world this is unusual, and whole-class interaction is common. Finally, we should note that 'learning' is defined here as a change in learning state which moves it closer to a native-speaker standard, in relation to pronunciation in the above extract.

Portraying learning processes

We have detailed above the problems and complexities of tracking and providing clear evidence of 'learning' in relation to specific items in L2 classroom interaction. This was essentially a 'product' orientation to learning, viewing one individual item as a learning outcome. We will now change tack to a 'process' orientation and consider how it is possible to portray the process of learning in interaction in its own terms. Seedhouse (2004) proposed that a CA process analysis of learning in relation to classroom data can be conducted in three stages, by asking the three questions below.

1) What can we say about the learner's learning state or current ability in L2?

The extract showed that, although L1 was able to contribute to the discussion, his mispronunciation of one lexical item created trouble which impeded the discussion. Apart from the pronunciation, he appeared to be able to use the lexical item correctly and appropriately in the discussion. L1 is able to construct a multi-clause sentence correctly (lines 18 and 19), whereas sometimes there is grammatical incompleteness (lines 47–49).

2) What can we say about the learning environment in terms of input to the language -learning process and facilitation of upgrading as a result of the interaction?

We noted that correction of L1's pronunciation was conducted by a peer and then by the teacher. We can see a clear juxtaposition of actual developmental level with that achieved through collaboration with the teacher. Uptake of the peer correction was displayed by L1 in a controlled environment but not in a freer environment. Uptake of the teacher's correction was displayed by L1 in both a controlled and a freer environment. The interactional evidence suggests that L1 has now learnt the correct pronunciation of 'company' by line 48. 'Learning' here is taken to mean a shift from a learning state in which the word was pronounced incorrectly to one in which it was pronounced correctly. The shift is towards a native-speaker norm of pronunciation. However, there is still no guarantee that he will not revert to the incorrect pronunciation in a few months' time or in a testing setting – we have noted the difference in L1's performance between interaction focused on form and interaction focused on meaning, separated in time by a number of seconds.

3) How does the process of instructed L2 learning develop?

Classroom interactants are displaying to each other their understanding of each others' utterances, and of what is being learnt, by means of and by reference to the organisation of turn-taking, sequence and repair. In line 2, L1 displays an analysis or understanding of L3's turn in line 1. We know what the understanding is by reference to the interactional organisations; a turn after a question will normally be construed as an answer because of the interlocking organisations of turn-taking and sequence. In line 2, L1 displays his cognitive state in relation to the question, namely that he doesn't know the answer but does have potentially relevant information: 'they will go to Australia too'. L3's turn in line 3 confirms that L1 showed a correct analysis of L3's previous turn. So we know what L1's understanding is by reference to the turn-taking system, L having been specifically allocated a turn by the question in line 1 and by reference to sequence organisation, which tells us that line 2 is an answer to the question. This is confirmed by L3's turn in line 3. In interactional sequences, then, evidence in relation to socially-distributed cognition is available and piles up, layer upon layer.

Let us now try to conceptualise what factors are involved in an individual's cognitive state in such a stream of interaction at line 2 of extract 2. We noted above in relation to conversation that any utterance is an analysis of the prior turn, it performs a social action in response, and it positions the speaker in a social system. It displays an understanding of the current sequential and social context and also renews it. It documents the speaker's cognitive, emotional and attitudinal states. In line 2, then, L1 displays the ability to perform appropriate social actions in a sequential system. As we said above, in the specific case of the L2 classroom, any utterance by the learner in L2 may perform two additional functions in addition to those already mentioned. First, the learner's utterance may in addition be delivered in the L2 and may thereby document his/her actual developmental level as well. In line 2 of extract 2 L1 is able to produce a linguistically well-formed sentence. Second, interactants in L2 classrooms are always displaying to one another their analyses of the current state of the evolving relationship between pedagogy and interaction. So in line 2 of extract 2, L1 displays his correct analysis that the current relationship between pedagogy and interaction is for him to debate with L2 which patient should receive the heart transplant. In this specific turn, L1 shows evidence of coping well with the complex demands of L2 classroom interaction.

Next we will conceptualise the factors involved in the same individual's learning state in line 24 of extract 2. L1 repeats exactly what the teacher says, copying the corrected pronunciation. It might be supposed that such 'parroting' involves little in the way of cognition. However, any turn in L2 classroom interaction is the nexus of many different levels of organisation. In line 24, L1 displays his analysis that the relationship between pedagogy and interaction has shifted instantly and is very different: it is now for him to repeat exactly what the teacher says. L1 has to recognise that T's turn in line 23 is a correction, specifically of his pronunciation; T does not identify the nature of his action. In lines 23 and 24, the focus has suddenly switched to foreground the two additional functions specific to L2 classrooms, namely documenting learning state and also the relationship between pedagogy and interaction. We noted above in relation to ordinary conversation that the organisations of turn and sequence are mechanisms for displaying and checking understanding, and the organisation of repair is a mechanism for repairing breakdowns in mutual understanding. In L2 classrooms, these organisations become adapted to the institutional goal of L2 learning by integrating these two additional functions specific to L2 classrooms.

So we can see that a part of what is meant by the learning state of a learner involved in L2 classroom interaction is inextricably entwined and engaged with the unique sequential, social and pedagogical environment in which he/she is engaged. It is argued that this part of the individual's learning state can be portrayed emically, in situ, that is, in that unique sequential environment. This is not to suggest that this provides anything like the whole picture, nor that the methods employed by SLA and psychology are not useful in portraying other aspects of the full picture in relation to cognition. The point to be made, however, is that if we wish to fully understand the processes of cognition in relation to instructed L2 acquisition, it is vital to understand how L2 classroom interaction is organised.

Because learning is entwined in the progress of the interaction, it is very difficult to isolate and extract specific phenomena with certainty. For example, in extract 2, we could ask why correction performed by a peer did not result in continued uptake whereas that performed by the teacher did. By contrast with the peer, the teacher carried out an explicit and prolonged correction sequence with native-speaker pronunciation. It is also possible in the above extract that other identity characteristics were relevant. L1 and L2 were of different genders and ethnicities and it is possible that L1 was 'resisting' being corrected by L2. There is some interactional evidence to support this in lines 8 and 16. Alternatively, it could be that it was repetition of the correction by the teacher which proved crucial for learning. However that may be, we can conclude from extract 2 that it is not necessarily sufficient for correction to be performed and for uptake to be immediately displayed – crucial issues are who performs the correction, how they perform it, and in what interactional setting the uptake is displayed.

Furthermore, we saw that sequential environment is vital to the evaluation of learning: a learner may be able to produce a linguistic item appropriately in one sequential context but not in another. We should be very aware of this when attempting to evaluate evidence for learning. Often it is assumed that a speaking test will provide evidence as to whether a learner has learnt a particular linguistic item or not, as if the test provided a direct insight into underlying competence. However, any speaking test has its own interactional organisation which may be compared with other varieties of interaction (Seedhouse and Egbert 2006); learners may produce a spoken item correctly in one interactional environment but not in another. Any talk produced by L2 learners is always entwined with the social, sequential and contextual environment of the talk and cannot be isolated to provide a 'true' or 'objective' insight into a learning state. Production of a spoken item by a learner is socially and sequentially constructed and, crucially, varies according to the interlocutor (Brown 2003).

Classroom interactional competence (CIC)

The discussion now turns to a conceptualisation of classroom interactional competence (CIC). In the same way that we have seen that interactants display and orient to learning through interactions which are co-constructed, they also demonstrate differing abilities to jointly create discourse which is conducive to learning. CIC focuses on the online decisions made by teachers and learners, and considers the extent to which these actions enhance learning and learning opportunity. From the extract of data below, we consider how teachers and learners display CIC and discuss the implications of this for gaining closer understandings of the relationship between L2 learning and interaction.

In this section, we consider how notions of learning through interaction can be extended by looking at the ways in which interactants display varying degrees of classroom interactional competence (CIC), defined here as 'teachers' and learners' ability to use interaction as a tool for mediating and assisting learning' (Walsh 2006: 130). The assumption is that by first understanding and then extending CIC, there will be greater opportunities for learning: enhanced CIC results in more learning-oriented interactions.

The notion of interactional competence was first coined by Kramsch (1986: 370): 'I propose [...] a push for interactional competence to give our students a truly emancipating, rather than compensating foreign language education'. Since then, many researchers have struggled with the concept without really coming to a convincing and workable definition. More recent references emphasise the fact that interactional competence is context-specific and concerned with the ways in which interactants co-construct meanings *together*, as opposed to looking at features of *individual* performance which lie at the heart of communicative competence. In an attempt to identify specific features of interactional competence, Young (2003) points to a number of 'interactional resources' including specific interactional strategies like turn-taking, topic management, signalling boundaries, and so on. Markee (2008) proposes three components of interactional competence, each with its own set of features:

- language as a formal system (including grammar, vocabulary, pronunciation);
- semiotic systems, including turn-taking, repair, sequence organisation;
- gaze and paralinguistic features.

As Markee himself says (2008: 3), developing interactional competence in a second language involves learners 'co-construct[ing] with their interlocutors locally enacted, progressively more accurate, fluent, and complex interactional repertoires in the L2'.

Given the context dependency of interactional competence, we are attempting here to identify some of the features of *classroom* interactional competence (CIC). How are meanings co-constructed in the unfolding interaction? What do participants do to ensure that understandings are reached? How do they deal with repair and breakdown? More importantly, how does CIC influence learning? In what ways are interactants able to create, maintain and sustain 'space for learning'? Space for learning refers to the extent to which teachers and learners provide interactional space which is appropriate for the specific pedagogical goal of the moment. It does not simply mean 'handing over' to learners to maximise opportunities for interaction. Rather, creating space for learning acknowledges the need to adjust linguistic and interactional patterns to the particular goal of the moment. Again, the emphasis is on promoting interactions which are both appropriate to a particular micro-context and to specific pedagogic goals.

In language assessment circles, it is now widely predicted that interactional competence will become the 'fifth skill', along with speaking, reading, listening and writing (the English Profile 2009). Given that interlocutors display varying degrees of interactional competence in their joint construction of meanings, we are suggesting here that teachers and learners also need to acquire a fine-grained understanding of what constitutes classroom interactional competence and how it might be achieved. Not only will such an understanding result in more engaged and dynamic interactions in classrooms, it will also enhance learning. In the data, there are a number of ways in which CIC manifests itself.

First, and from a teacher's perspective, a teacher who demonstrates CIC uses language which is both convergent to the pedagogic goal of the moment and also appropriate to the learners. Essentially, this entails an understanding of the interactional strategies which are appropriate to teaching goals and which are adjusted in relation to the co-construction of meaning and the unfolding agenda of a lesson. This position assumes that pedagogic goals and the language used to achieve them are inextricably intertwined and constantly being readjusted (Seedhouse 2004; Walsh 2003). Any evidence of CIC must therefore demonstrate that interlocutors are using discourse which is both appropriate to specific pedagogic goals and to the agenda of the moment.

Second, CIC facilitates interactional space: learners need space for learning to participate in the discourse, to contribute to class conversations, and to receive feedback on their contributions. Interactional space is maximised through increased wait-time, by resisting the temptation to 'fill silence' (by reducing teacher echo), by promoting extended learner turns, and by allowing planning time. By affording learners space, they are better able to contribute to the process of co-constructing meanings – something which lies at the very heart of learning through interaction.

Third, CIC entails teachers being able to *shape* learner contributions by scaffolding, paraphrasing, re-iterating and so on. Essentially, through shaping the discourse, a teacher is helping learners to say what they mean by using the most appropriate language to do so. The process of 'shaping' contributions occurs by seeking clarification, scaffolding, modelling, or repairing learner input. In a decentralised classroom in which learner-centredness is a priority, these interactional strategies may be the only opportunities for teaching, and occur frequently during the feedback move (cf. Cullen 1998). Elsewhere (see, for example, Jarvis and Robinson 1997), the process of taking a learner's contribution and shaping it into something more meaningful has been termed *appropriation*; a kind of paraphrasing which serves the dual function of checking meaning and moving the discourse forward.

We turn now to a consideration of how features of CIC manifest themselves in classroom data. The extract below is taken from an adult EFL class where the teacher is working with an upper-intermediate group of learners who are preparing to do a listening comprehension about places of interest. There are a number of features in the extract which show evidence of CIC.

Extract 3

The teacher is preparing to do a listening task about places of interest.

```
1   T:      okay, have you have you ever visited any places ↑outside
            London?=
2   L1:     =me I stay in (.) Portsmouth and er:: in Bournemouth
3   T:              [where've you been?
4   L1:             [in the south
5   T:              [down (.) here? (pointing to map)
6   L1:     yeah yeah
7   T: →    ↑why?
8   L1:     er my girlfriend live here and (.) I like this student
9           place and all the people's young and a lot (.) er go out
10          in the (.) evening its very [good
11  T:                                  [right
12  T: →    anybody else? (4) Have you been anywhere Tury?
13  L2:     Yes I have been in er (.) Edinbourg ((mispronounced)),
14          (())=
15  T:      =so here here ((pointing to map))=
16  L2:     =yes er Oxford (.) Brighton (.) many places (())=
17  T:      =and which was your favourite?=
18  L2:     =my favourite is London
19  T: →    (.) ↑why?
20  L2:     because it's a big city you can find what what you [want
21  T:                                                        [mmhh
22  L2:     and do you can go to the theatres (1) it's a very (.)
23          cosmopolitan [city
24  L:                   [yes
25  L2:     I like it very much=
26  T:      =do you all (.) agree=
```

```
27  LL:    =yes (laughter)

28  T:             ((3)) laughter)

29  T:     has anybody else been to another place outside London?

30  L:     no not outside inside

31  T:     (.)mm? Martin? Anywhere?

32  L3:    =no nowhere=

33  T:     =would you like to go (.) [anywhere?

34  L3:                              [yes yes

35  T:                              [where?

36  L3:    well Portsmouth I think it's very (.) great=

37  T:     =((laughter)) cos of the students   [yes (.) yes

38  LL:                                        [yes yes

39  L3:    and there are sea too

40  T:     Pedro?

41  L4:    it's a (.) young (.) place

42  T: →   mm anywhere else? (3) no well I'm going to talk to

43         you and give you some recommendations about where you

44         can go in (.) England (.) yeah
```

(Carr 2006, DVD 12 task-based learning)

We can ascertain from this context (and from the lesson plan accompanying these published materials) that the teacher's main concern is to elicit ideas and personal experiences from the learners. The corresponding talk confirms this in a number of ways. First, there is no repair, despite the large number of errors throughout the extract (see, for example, lines 2, 8, 13, 36, 39): the teacher chooses to ignore them because error correction is not conducive to allowing learners to have space to express themselves. Second, the questions she asks are often followed with expansions such as 'why'? (see, for example, 7, 19) which result in correspondingly longer turns by learners (in 8, and 20). Again, we would claim that both the teacher's questioning strategy and the longer learner turns are evidence of CIC since they facilitate opportunities for both engaged interaction and learning opportunity. Third, we note that there are several attempts to 'open the space' and allow for wider participation of other learners. This occurs, for example, in 12 (*anybody else* plus a 4-second pause), in 26 (*do you all agree?*), in 42 (*anywhere else* plus a 3-second pause). On each of these occasions, the teacher is attempting to include other students in the interaction in a bid to elicit additional contributions. Again, her use of language and pedagogic goals are convergent, ensuring that learning opportunities are maximised.

Other features which show evidence of CIC include:

- the use of extended wait time, pauses of several seconds (in 12 and 42) which allow learners time to think, formulate and give a response. Typically, teachers wait less than one second after asking a question (see, for example, Budd Rowe 1986), leaving learners insufficient time to respond;
- the use of requests for clarification (in 3, 5, 15) which serve to ensure that understandings have been reached. Not only do such requests give important feedback to the students, they also allow the teacher to ensure that the other students are included by clarifying for the whole class;
- minimal response tokens which tell the other speaker that understandings have been reached without interrupting the 'flow' of the interaction (see, for example, 11 (*right*), 21(*mmhh*). Again, the use of such feedback is further evidence of convergence of pedagogic goals and language use;
- evidence of content feedback by the teacher who responds to the message and not the linguistic forms used to articulate a particular message. In extract 3 above, for example, the teacher responds in an almost conversational way to almost all of the learners' turns. She offers no evaluation or repair of learner contributions, as would be the 'norm' in many classroom contexts. Instead, she assumes an almost symmetrical role in the discourse, evidenced by the rapid pace of the interaction (note the overlapping speech in 3–5, 33–5, and latched turns in 14–18 and 25–7).

In the same extract, there are a number of features of CIC which we can highlight from a learner's perspective. First, there is recognition on the part of L1 that the appropriate reaction to a question is a response, the second part of that adjacency pair, as evidenced in lines 2, 4, 6 and 8. Not only does L1 answer the questions posed by the teacher, but he is able to recognise the precise type and amount of response needed, ensuring that his contributions are both relevant and timely. He is also sufficiently competent to appreciate that a question like 'why' in line 7 almost always requires an extended response, which he provides in 8.

His CIC is sufficiently advanced to appreciate that the teacher's focus here is on eliciting personal experiences – while his responses are adequate and appropriate, they are certainly not accurate; yet this is of little or no concern given the pedagogic focus of the moment. This learner has correctly interpreted the teacher's question as a request for further information where accuracy is less important than the provision of that information.

L1 also displays CIC in terms of his ability to manage turns, hold the floor, and hand over his turn at a particular point in the interaction. He responds quickly to the teacher's opening question, as indicated by the latched turn in 2 and turn continuation in 4, indicated by the overlapping speech. As well as being able to take his turn and hold the floor, this learner (L1) also recognises key signals which mark a transition relevance place – the teacher's *right* and accompanying overlap in lines 9 and 10 signal to this learner that it is time to relinquish his turn at talk and hand over to another learner. While it is the teacher who 'orchestrates the interaction' (Breen 1999), nonetheless, L1 has to be able to take cues, observe key signals and manage his own turn-taking in line with what is required by the teacher. He must also recognise that his own contributions are largely determined by the teacher's, and by the specific pedagogic goals of the moment.

In this section, we have seen how one teacher and a group of learners display CIC through their co-constructed interactions. The point we are making here is that CIC is one aspect of learning in formal contexts: teachers and learners, by making appropriate interactional choices through their online decision-making, both facilitate the co-construction of meaning and also display to each other their understandings. CIC manifests itself through the ways in which interactants create space for learning, make appropriate responses 'in the moment', seek and offer clarification, demonstrate understandings, afford opportunities for participation, negotiate meanings, and so on. These interactional strategies help to maintain the flow of the discourse and are central to effective classroom communication. They offer a view of learning through interaction that is different from but complementary to that provided by a conversational analytic perspective, which focuses mainly on turn design, sequential organisation and repair. Taken together, we propose that the two perspectives on classroom interaction advocated here (socially-distributed cognition and classroom interactional competence) offer a comprehensive approach to understanding and assessing learning in a formal, class-based context.

Conclusions

Finally, we reflect on how the methodology of Conversation Analysis (CA) has shaped our findings and our conceptualisation of learning. CA tends to reveal the complexity and heterogeneity of L2 classroom interaction. By contrast, discourse analysis (DA) approaches may tend to homogenise the interaction, showing it as a series of IRF patterns. The same point applies to coding schemes, which isolate individual features of interaction for quantitative treatment.

The CA approach we have adopted in this chapter has led to a process orientation and to a focus on socially-distributed cognition rather than on individual cognitive states. CA's primary interest is in the social act, whereas a linguist's primary interest in normally in language. CA therefore does not treat language as an autonomous system independent of its use; rather, it treats 'grammar and lexical choices as sets of resources which participants deploy, monitor, interpret and manipulate' (Schegloff et al. 2002: 15) in order to perform their social acts. This means that a CA study of learning will tend to move towards a holistic portrayal of learning processes through interaction rather than the acquisition of discrete linguistic items. In extract 2 we showed that it is certainly possible to use CA to track an individual's acquisition of learning items, but that this is a problematic and time-consuming undertaking. We also showed that learning processes may be portrayed in situ, entwined with the evolution of interaction. Our analysis suggests that a CA approach focusing on learning processes and socially-shared cognition may combine fruitfully with more product-oriented approaches focusing on individual cognitive states.

Finally, we considered how a conceptualisation of classroom interactional competence (CIC) may help us to gain a fuller and closer understanding of the ways in which interactants collectively create space for learning. In the data, we saw how both teachers and learners collectively create space and use that space to negotiate and achieve meaning. We suggest that the interactional strategies used by teachers and learners to support each other and assist the process of meaning-making are both central to effective classroom communication, and a clear indication of classroom interactional competence. While there is still a lot of work to do in terms of accurately conceptualising and describing CIC, we firmly believe that such understandings are necessary in order to help both teachers and learners develop levels of interactional competence which will support learning.

9
Adaptation in Online Voice-Based Chat Rooms: Implications for Language Learning in Applied Linguistics

Chris Jenks

> Whatever the degree or nature of contact between neighboring peoples, it is generally sufficient to lead to some kind of linguistic interinfluencing.
>
> Sapir (1921: 205)

Introduction

In this chapter, I will use conversation analysis (CA) to investigate how speakers of English as an additional language (EAL) converse in online voice-based chat rooms. The chat rooms that I investigate are a relatively new communicative environment. Here multiple interactants from all over the world interact in the spoken medium, in very much the same way as text-based chat rooms. The term 'additional' refers to the fact that the interactants investigated here are not in 'second' or 'foreign' language classrooms, but are communicating in non-educational settings where the relevance of English as a second/foreign language (S/FL) varies from interactant to interactant.[1] It is vital to make this distinction at the outset, as any investigation of language learning must identify what is meant by language. Additional language is a more context-sensitive term which acknowledges that for some interactants, formal classroom language learning is only one of many settings in which English is used and learnt. More importantly, the identities and discourse that are often associated with S/FL learning are not ubiquitous (for example, language learner; see Kurhila 2004).[2] So, for example, the communicative

147

goals in online voice-based chat rooms are not necessarily to learn pre-determined 'target' grammatical rules from an expert in a linear fashion, as one would typically experience in language classrooms. Rather, using and learning English in these settings requires communication with interactants from diverse social, linguistic, political and geographic backgrounds. Language learning here entails, in addition to, say, learning *new* words and/or grammatical rules, adjusting and then deploying *existing* linguistic knowledge in order to accommodate and/or incorporate the communicative norms established in any given chat room. Language, as understood in this chapter, is a social-interactional resource for co-constructing meaning (Brouwer and Wagner 2004). Therefore, language learning can be observed as changes situated in social interaction. As reasons, purposes, norms and expectations of communication change according to the context in which language is used, language learning is conceptualised as a multi-directional change (or adjustment) in language that fulfils a socio-communicative goal. With this conceptualisation, language learning can, but need not, be investigated as the acquisition of new grammatical knowledge over time (cf. Markee 2008). Knowledge of how to appropriately deploy existing social-interactional skills in new or different ways is also an important aspect of language learning (Sfard 1998). Language learning will, consequently, be investigated by uncovering how interactants make communicative changes or adjustments, a process I am calling adaptation, according to the contexts in which they find themselves interacting.

Before presenting the data, I will discuss the different ways in which CA has been applied to investigations of language learning, and identify how CA will be used in this chapter.

CA-for-SLA

CA-for-second language acquisition (hereafter, CA-for-SLA) is a term commonly used to characterise conversation analytic investigations of language learning (Markee 2000), though not all conversation analysts adopt this term (for example, Seedhouse 2005). In this chapter, CA-for-SLA will be used as an umbrella term to capture all CA-inspired studies of language learning (see Brouwer 2008).[3]

In a seminal special issue on CA-for-SLA, Markee and Kasper (2004) provide an overview of what CA-inspired studies of language-learning entail. In relation to the cognitive theoretical underpinnings of SLA research (see Gass and Selinker 2001), they argue that conversation analysts have adopted two divergent views. One view, referred to as the strong view of CA-for-SLA, is to abandon the cognitive tradition of SLA research, and adopt a social conceptualisation of language and language learning (for example, Mondada and Pekarek Doehler 2004). The second view, referred to as the weak view of CA-for-SLA, is more ambivalent about the bedrock, cognitive conceptualisations of language and language learning in SLA research (for example, Markee 2004), and sees room for discussion between CA and cognitive traditions. As stated in the previous section, my understanding of language is that it is a multi-functional social-interactional resource. Language exists because it is a social phenomenon (Volosinov 1973), and therefore the social context in which interactants find themselves using and learning language must play a more prominent role in SLA research (Block 2003). That said, in this chapter I adopt a strong view of CA-for-SLA. It is important to note, however, that a strong view of CA-for-SLA does not require rejecting contributions made by cognitive SLA researchers. Rather, a strong view of CA-for-SLA believes that only social conceptualisations of language and language learning are epistemologically and methodologically suitable for CA. (See Pekarek-Doehler, this volume.)

Markee and Kasper (2004) go on to distinguish between data-driven and theory-driven CA-for-SLA studies. A common criticism of CA-inspired studies of language learning is that CA does not possess a learning theory (Gass 1998; Hall 2004; He 2004). Conversation analysts are, therefore, split with regard to how to pursue investigations of language learning. Data-driven CA-for-SLA studies are often characterised as being ethnomethodologically-grounded (Markee 2008). Within this approach, conversation analysts let their data set speak for itself (see Francis and Hester 2004). That is, language learning becomes a topic of analysis only when the interactants are demonstrably orienting to it in some social-interactional way (for example, Brouwer 2003). A data-driven approach to CA-for-SLA '... is neutral and agnostic in relation to learning theories ...' (Seedhouse 2005: 175). Here language learning is an *observable* set of practices and actions deployed in social interaction.

Conversely, theory-driven approaches use exogenous theories to help inform and shape understandings of learning (for communities of practice, see Young and Miller 2004; for sociocultural theory, see Mondada and Pekarek Doehler 2004). Here researchers argue that an ethnomethodological or data-driven approach can only capture language learning as a set of interactional practices, whereas '... language learning probably needs to be conceptualised as a social process' (Brouwer and Wagner 2004: 32). Although Brouwer and Wagner do not make explicit the differences between social practices and social processes, it is clear that the absence of overt references to language learning in CA compels many CA-for-SLA researchers to look elsewhere for conceptualisations of language learning (for example, learning how to be part of a community; Lave and Wenger 1991). With a theory-driven approach, language learning is an observable set of practices and actions deployed in social interaction, and CA is still used to uncover these practices and actions, though the theory, say communities of practice, plays an important role in how the analyst interprets the data. It is perhaps more appropriate to say that this approach is theory-informed, rather than theory-driven.

The approach that I adopt in this chapter is largely ethnomethodological or data-driven in that my initial reason for analysing the present data was to uncover how participants of online chat rooms interact (see Jenks 2009a). In other words, my observations of language learning are a result of an 'unmotivated' attempt to uncover the interactional and sequential organisation of online chat rooms. My analysis was unmotivated in that it was my objective to let the data set speak for itself. As a result of this objective, I have uncovered instances where interactants display learning. Again, a data driven approach to language learning does not require an exogenous theory. Rather, the analyst must show how language learning is situated in and through the talk and actions of the interactants under investigation (see Schegloff 1991).

A final CA-for-SLA distinction can be made between pure CA and linguistic CA (Seedhouse 2005). This distinction relates to how faithful researchers are in interpreting and applying CA. Over the years, CA has uncovered a number of conversational features that have been shown to be fundamental in co-constructing meaning (for example, Sacks et al. 1974). Within applied linguistics, the features of turn-taking and repair have been perhaps the most notable (Schegloff et al. 2002). The appeal of examining turn-taking and repair is that both features are ostensibly compatible with applied linguists' concern for investigating the interactional organisation of classrooms, language learning, and non-native communication, to name a few. However, it cannot be said that applied linguists have interpreted and applied CA's findings systematically and unproblematically.

On the one hand, for example, a pure CA approach examines turn-taking and repair as conversational features that are contextually-embedded in the sequential environment of social interaction (Seedhouse 2007 also calls this ethnomethodological CA). By taking turns and/or repairing talk, interactants reveal how they perform social action, and respond to other's social action (Psathas 1995). Applying CA requires researchers to examine and discuss conversational features as they are sequentially deployed and oriented to by interactants. Therefore, with pure CA, conversational features are examined from an emic, participant perspective (see Markee 2000). Here conversational features are context-bound, and consequently should not be examined outside the sequential context in which they occur (for example, Markee 2004). On the other hand, a linguistic CA approach examines conversational features outside the context in which they occur. Here researchers see conversational features, such as turn-taking and repair, as units of analysis. That is, conversational features are examined within exogenous theoretical frameworks that may or may not be concerned with CA's attention to the social and sequential aspects of interaction (see theory-driven approaches; for example, Young and Miller 2004). As a result, conversational features are treated as units that may be coded and quantified for the purpose of testing exogenous theories. Although linguistic CA has contributed much to our understanding of language and language learning (see Cameron 2001), some conversation analysts would argue that decontexualised examinations of conversational features are 'flawed' as they do not, for example, provide an account of how cognition sequentially manifests and is socially-distributed, two key elements of conversation analytic studies of language learning (Markee 2008: 405).

In this chapter, I will adopt a pure CA approach to investigating adaptation in online voice-based chat rooms. This is because I believe any study that claims to use CA must adhere to its theoretical and methodological principles. Again, this means seeing language as a social-interactional resource, and examining social-interactional issues, such as language learning, from an emic, participant perspective. Table 9.1 below summarises the CA-for-SLA discussion. It is important to note that a strong view does not require one to adopt a data-driven approach

Table 9.1 Characteristics of CA-for-SLA

Role of cognitive SLA theories	*Strong view*: cognitive SLA theories are inappropriate for CA-for-SLA	*Weak view*: cognitive SLA theories may be appropriate for CA-for-SLA
Role of exogenous theories	*Data-driven*: 'let the data speak for itself'; unmotivated looking	*Theory-informed*: adopt exogenous theories of language learning
Role of CA	*Pure CA*: strict application of CA	*Linguistic CA*: loose application of CA

and strictly apply CA, just as a weak view does not necessarily mean the researcher will use exogenous theories and loosely apply CA.

Language learning in chat rooms

Within cognitive-inspired classroom-based SLA research (see Gass 1998), language learning is often conceptualised, evaluated and discussed, as a learner's ability to acquire the knowledge of using language according to institutional and/or linguistic standards (for example, 'native speakers'). For example, for political and socio-historical reasons, Korean EFL students may be required to learn American English, while the teaching of British English may be more common in Singapore. The teaching of standards is to be expected as many classroom language learners will be evaluated accordingly (cf. Canagarajah 2007). As such, classroom language learning is often seen as a linear process (that is, acquiring new knowledge over time), where learners progress along a continuum according to their ability to appropriately use native (or institutional) standards (for example, from true beginner to native-like proficiency). The language that is used within this continuum is often referred to as interlanguage (see Gass and Selinker 2001). Here changes in interlanguage, often evaluated in grammatical terms and through various testing means (Mackey and Gass 2005), are representations of language learning. Classroom language learning and assessment are often fixed to a continuum (native or institutional standards), and as a result, deviations from the target standard are seen as deficiencies in learners' communicative competence. As a result, language learning is often conceptualised as unidirectional.

While the interlanguage continuum may be a reality for many classroom language learners, there is a world outside of classrooms that is not institutionally bound to mastering or mimicking native (or set) standards. For example, though the chat rooms that I investigate here have been created and advertised for English language practice, the onus of determining what language to use, and therefore what language to learn, is with the interactants. At times interactants may topicalise and therefore make relevant their desire to reach set standards, for example when interactants verbalise their wish to sound grammatical or American or educated, while in other situations such standards may be inappropriate (Jenks 2009a). In other words, target standards are not fixed, but rather organic and negotiable. For instance, interactants outside of classrooms may find themselves in situations where they must learn how to be unidiomatic, despite their knowledge of what is 'correct' (for example, Firth and Wagner 2007). In these situations, the utility of demonstrating grammatical competence is replaced by the need to socialise in a way that is conducive to established norms or standards. In online voice-based chat rooms, standards vary from room to room, and are often negotiated on a turn-by-turn basis. In other words, there are no pre-determined, fixed standards of language use and learning. As such, online voice-based chat rooms provide opportunities for multi-directional language learning (Canagarajah 2007), which includes, but is not limited to, the demonstration of sociolinguistic competence (see Leung 2005). For instance, learning how to demonstrate the communicative competence necessary to be an accepted member of a chat room is of paramount importance (Sfard 1998). Though knowing how to use English is a prerequisite for communicating, becoming a member often requires interactants to move beyond the learning and demonstration of appropriate grammar and lexis (for example, shared understanding of popular culture, using humour to promote affiliation, telling jokes, singing songs). In other words, because the task of practising English, veiled or explicit, entails a social-interactional pressure to become part of a community of chat-room participants, interactants must learn how to design their talk and interaction in a way that is acceptable, funny, grammatical, or whatever has been determined appropriate at any given micro-interactional moment (Jenks 2009a). Below I will show how language learning occurs as a result of this fluid and organic process of determining appropriate language use.

The data

The analyses from this chapter come from a large corpus of approximately 45 hours of online voice-based chat-room audio recordings. My observations below are from a single 49-minute recording of a chat room entitled 'Welcome English Beginner'. The chat room comprised seven interactants. Many of the interactants have met for the first time. The three interactants that appear in the following extracts are from Korea and Turkey (two and one, respectively).

My analyses will focus on how, over the course of 15 minutes, one interactant adapts to the situation in which he finds himself communicating. Specifically, the interactant learns how to change his existing knowledge of an interactional practice to accommodate his fellow interactants. The interactional practice that I will be examining is self-identification. Here interactants self-identify who they are, before or after an utterance (for example, 'This is Bob, hello, how are you?' or

'Hello, how are you, this is Bob.'). Self-identifications are potentially important in online voice-based chat rooms as there may be up to ten interactants communicating in the absence of non-verbal cues (see Jenks 2009b). The learning of self-identification is related to the mastery of what Canale (1983) calls sociolinguistic and strategic competence. Accordingly, my analysis of language learning is concerned with interactants' competence to speak the language of chat rooms. In other words, language learning is underpinned, in part, by the knowledge of sociocultural norms, and the ability to put this knowledge into practice (Hymes 1972).

The first of three extracts starts five minutes into the exchange. June has been getting acquainted with an interactant who is no longer in the chat room. The extract begins with James first introducing himself to June, and then proposing a communicative rule to resolve the difficulties some interactants have been experiencing with taking turns and overlapping talk.

(1) 5:02–7:13

```
001 James:  June? (,) hello June?

002 June:   yes (0.4) yes↑ i'm↓ June↑

003         (0.2)

004 James:  hello yeah (.) hello my name's James so okay? yeah

005 June:   yes

006 James:  i- think- that- you- are- host of this group so i

007         think that (0.6) you have to c[ontrol

008 June:                                 [yeah

009 James:  some process you know (.) there are a lot of (rules)

010         and big echoes so we should (.) i think that we- we

011         can (.) i- in my opinion we want to make some kinda

012         rule (0.5) if someone says he↓llo:↑ (.) after that

013         (.) we want to have to say the↓ eye-dee name for

014         example me:: (.) hello my name's

015 June:   yes=

016 James:  =James after then we have to say (it) you know (.) a

017         lot of people say we- we can't understand who is-

018         who is speaking an: so how can we:: answer the some
```

```
019            questions (.) so: and you are both so↓ we are guests
020            okay=
021 June:      =yeah
022 James:     (i said) uh:
023 Sky:       hello
024 James:     (it was) good- g- room or in Skypecast you will make
025            a good- condition or allow me so i hope so
026 June:      ye::s
027            (0.6)
028 James:     yeah
029 June:      yes
030            (0.7)
031 Sky:       <he:↓llo↑<
032 June:      and then sorry (0.5) because the- eh:: five minutes
033            ago (0.8) there's some problem in my computer so::
034            (.) i just wonder (0.6) at the time it's okay so::::
035 Sky:       yes
036 June:      we make(ness) of that. of our:: room. how bout we
037            talking about (0.8) uh: <what is your problem<
038            (0.5) >what is your problem> (0.8) i think you have
039            a problem in your place in your work (.) or when you
040            studying, or anything (0.9) yeah then i just think a
041            kinda gap (1.0) yeah (0.7) if you have a problem
042            just (2.5) just say it (.) may::be↓ there is some
043            people can solve that problem (1.2) eh- uh actually:
044 James:     so y-
045 June:      actually::
046 James:     okay yeah yeah
047            (.)
048 June:      yes hehehe
049            (0.9)
050 James:     okay so
051 Sky:       [(you-)
```

```
052 James:   [yeah so yeah eh-em hello my names James and June
053          said that w- if we have a big problem so (0.4) you
054          can or some other person solve the our problem okay?
055          (0.5) yeah (.) so=
056 Sky:     =you[r name's James?]
057 James:        [in my case    ] yeah (0.9) >yup>
```

In lines 001–005, James and June exchange greetings and names. This exchange serves to not only introduce both interactants, but also provides the interactional space to engage in extended talk (Schegloff 1986). Although greetings and introductions are routine and mundane in many settings, there are different interpretations and expectations of how to engage in these interactional practices in multi-participant online voice-based chat rooms. For example, in lines 006–020, James' extended turn reveals his understanding of how one should address fellow interactants ('in my opinion we want to make some kinda rule (0.5) if someone says he↓llo:↑(.) after that (.) we want to have to say the↓eye-dee name'). Here James is proposing that interactants self-identify before engaging in extending talk. James' communicative rule is noteworthy as it follows several instances of confusion, disruption and overlapping talk in the first five minutes of this chat room session. By proposing a new communicative rule, James is suggesting that he and fellow interactants adjust (or change) their way of interacting with each other.

In lines 016–018, James reveals why this communicative rule is important ('a lot of people say we- we can't understand who is- who is speaking an: so how can we:: answer the some questions'), and in lines 024–025, what will happen as a result of self-identifications ('in Skypecast you will make a good- condition'). In so doing, James verbalises his understanding of how to maximise comprehensible communication in chat rooms. Although June provides acknowledgement tokens throughout James' extended turn (that is lines 15, 21, 26, 29), it is not clear whether June, the host, believes the communicative rule of self-identification should be adopted. In lines 32–43, June engages in his own extended turn, where he proposes a topic of discussion ('if you have a problem just (2.5) just say it (.) may::be↓ there is some people can solve that problem'). After James and June exchange more acknowledgement tokens (lines 46–50), James provides a report of June's proposed topic ('hello my names James and June said that w- if we have a big problem so (0.4) you can or some other person solve the our problem okay?'). What is particularly noteworthy in James's report is the way he designs his turn to follow the communicative rule of self-identification ('hello my names

James ...'). Here James is addressing fellow interactants according to the communicative rule he established minutes ago. In other words, James is putting into practice his knowledge of what he believes is appropriate language use. In line 56, Sky responds to the topic report by confirming James's name, which James provides in line 57.

In the first extract, the interactants of this chat room have experienced some difficulties with regard to communicating with each other. In order to maximise comprehensible communication, James proposed a new communicative rule that he believes his fellow interactants should follow. Though it was not clear whether, and to what extent, this communicative rule has been accepted by the chat room, James later followed his own advice and addressed his fellow interactants by self-identifying. As a result, James not only revealed his understanding of how to communicate in this particular chat room, but he was also shown to demonstrably orient to the communicative rule of self-identification when he later put this knowledge into practice.

A few minutes later, after the interactants have been discussing one of June's proposed topics of discussion, Sky provides an evaluation of living with a mental problem.

(2) 10:09–10:49

```
001 Sky:    you know how it feels to have a mental problem (0.8)
002         it sucks man (0.4) i tell you it sucks (.) yeah (.)
003         mmhm
004         (0.3)
005 James:  yeah so=
006 Sky:    =yeah?
007 James:  i think that (.) hello my name is James so
008         (0.9) hello?
009 Sky:    i know [your
010 James:         [yeah=
011 Sky    =names James we know (0.2) [you
012 James:                           [okay
013 Sky:    said i[t
014 James:        [yeah ye[ah
015 Sky:            [like (.) i do[n't
016 James:                   [yeah
017 Sky:    know how many times (.) maybe fifteen times (0.4)
018         your names James (0.7) we memor(hh)ised yo(hh)ur
```

```
019              n(hh)ame already hahahaha (.) haha you don't have to
020              say it any[mo(hh)re
021  James:             [yeah=
022  Sky:      =hahaha [aha
023  James:            [yeah yeah okay (0.8) okay so i th[ink
024  Sky:                                              [haha
025           ha[haha
026  James:     [that i hope that (goes to) (1.0) i want something
027           that meanings uh: an:: uh: (.) my friend live in U↑K
028           (.) now in this room and uh: (0.4) she stayed in UK
```

In line 005, James acknowledges the previous evaluation ('yeah'), and produces a discourse marker that signals he is attempting to engage in extended talk ('so'). In line 006, James is given the interactional space to do so, as Sky's acknowledgement token returns the conversational floor back to James ('yeah?'). This exchange is important as it reveals Sky's orientation to James' attempt to continue speaking. Though Sky does not explicitly signal that he knows it is James who is attempting to engage in extended talk (for example, 'yeah, go on James'), the acknowledgement token demonstrates that Sky is ready to listen (Nofsinger 1975). In line 007, James continues with a statement ('i think that'), restarts, and then formulates a new utterance. Despite Sky's readiness to listen, James chooses to preface his utterance with a self-identification ('hello my name is James so'). As a result, James aligns himself with his previously declared communicative rule. Here James is again communicating with his fellow interactants according to his understanding of how best to do so. That is to say, by verbalising what he believes is the best way of communicating in this chat room, and then deploying this communicative rule in subsequent instances, James displays his understanding of how to participate with his fellow interactants (see te Molder and Potter 2005).

In lines 009 and 011, Sky responds to James's self-identification by stating that he and others know James's name ('i know your names James we know'). Sky subsequently provides an inflated assessment of James's previous practice of self-identification ('you said it like (.) i don't know how many times (.) maybe fifteen times (0.4) your names James'). In lines 018–020, Sky then declares that the chat room has memorised James' name, and that James's practice of self-identification is no longer needed ('we memor(hh)ised yo(hh)ur n(hh)ame already hahahaha (.) haha you don't have to say it anymo(hh)re'). While it is not entirely clear whether Sky's laughter serves to demonstrate that the practice of self-identification is humorous and/or functions as a way to ridicule James for repeatedly doing so (cf. Jefferson et al. 1987), Sky's assertion that James no longer needs to self-identify serves to repudiate the practice. Sky's utterance is also the first instance where James's understanding (or competence) of how best to interact is questioned. Though the extract ends with James providing several acknowledgements, it is not clear whether he believes he should, or will, change his behaviour. In the second extract, James continues to adopt his previously declared communicative rule. In so doing, James demonstrably orients to his understanding of how best to communicate with his fellow interactants. However, in this instance, Sky verbalises his epistemic stance on the practice of self-identification by revealing that he does not believe James needs to continue with this communicative rule.

Approximately eight minutes later, after the interactants have been discussing national food-eating practices, Sky states that he does not eat pigs, has never seen one in person, and does not eat meat.

(3) 18:51–19:23

```
001  Sky:    i don't eat pigs I've never seen pig in real life i
002          don't eat meat
003  June:   oh
004  James:  yeah yeah pig so (1.0) hel↑lo↓ Sky? (0.6) hello↑
005  Sky:    hello? (0.6) hello=
006  James:  =yeah yeah (.) hello you know my names James yeah
007          so i wonder you know:
008  Sky:    [[hehehe ((inaudible)) ]]
009  James:  [[there's a lotta      ]] yeah [yeah
010  Sky:                                   [hehehe
011  James:  you (think about) over fifteen minute okay? (.) you
012          know my name is so yeah (0.4) i won[der
013  Sky:                                       [yeah
014  James:  you know in:: in this room there are a lot of
015          Koreans so but i dont know where you come from from
```

In lines 001–002, Sky identifies his food-eating practices with regard to pigs and meat. In line 003, June then responds to this statement, and later, in line 004, James attempts to address Sky ('hel↑lo↓ Sky? (0.6) hello↑'). After receiving confirmation from Sky ('hello? (0.6) hello'), James begins to take his turn at talk ('yeah yeah'). It is at this very sequential place where in previous instances James was observed deploying the practice of self-identification. However, in line 006, James adjusts his understanding of how to communicate with Sky by designing his turn in a way that reflects his previous interactional encounter (that is, extract 2). This is evidenced in the way James verbalises his understanding of what Sky knows ('you know my names James'). At the same time, James changes the way he addresses Sky (cf. 'my name is James'). The change from 'my name is James' to 'you know my names James' represents an epistemic shift (cf. te Molder and Potter 2005), one where James has learnt how to adjust his knowledge of address according to the situation in which he finds himself communicating.[4] After some laughter from Sky (lines 008 and 010), James utters what appears to be a reference to Sky's previous repudiation ('you (think about) over fifteen minute okay?'). In lines 011–012, James repeats his previous verbal report of what Sky knows ('you know my name is').

The learning of how to address interactants can be traced over the course of 15 minutes (see Markee 2008). In extract 1, James proposed a new communicative rule that he believed his fellow interactants should follow. By doing so, James verbalised his understanding of how best to interact given the communicative difficulties some interactants were experiencing. Later in the same extract, James followed his proposed rule and addressed his fellow interactants by self-identifying. In extract 2, James continued to deploy the practice of self-identification, though in this instance, Sky repudiated the communicative rule. In extract 3, James abandoned the practice of self-identification and opted to preface his turn with a statement that assumes Sky already knows who is speaking. The three extracts show how James adapts his knowledge of language use according to who he is speaking to (cf. interactional recalibration; see Schegloff 2000). In other words, James adjusted and then deployed his existing knowledge of language use in order to accommodate and/or incorporate the communicative norm established in the chat room (see Sfard 1998).[5] Here language learning occurred as changes situated in social interaction.

Conclusion

In this chapter I have examined language learning as a social-interactional accomplishment. This entailed observing language learning as a process that is situated in the turn-by-turn moments of talk and interaction (Firth and Wagner 2007). Specifically, I have shown how one interactant verbalises his communicative competence by proposing a new rule, and then adapting this rule according to the situation in which he finds himself communicating (that is, recipient design; see Sacks et al. 1974).[6] That is to say, language learning involves adapting one's behaviour in a way that is conducive to established norms or standards. The change in behaviour, or language learning, was situated in the practice of self-identification. An understanding of how to appropriately deploy the practice of self-identification was negotiated in situ. That is, appropriate language use was determined collaboratively and organically by the interactants, for the interactants (Canagarajah 2007).

These observations have implications for applied linguistics. First, because norms and standards vary from chat room to chat room, there are often no pre-determined, fixed standards of language use and learning. While interactants of online voice-based chat rooms may, and in fact do, make relevant their desire to learn a 'native' standard, on many occasions this is overshadowed by the need to use and learn the language of, for example, narrative, humour, popular culture, compliments, and of course address. This type of language use and learning should not be undervalued in any discipline, including SLA. Though the learning of grammar and lexis in a linear fashion may be of paramount importance in language classrooms, in non-educational, institutional settings, like the one investigated in this chapter, language learning can also be incidental, interactional, and multi-directional.

Notes

1. Although English as a lingua franca, multilingual communities, and language use in non-educational settings are all issues which have been shown to expand our disciplinary purview of additional language learning (see, for example, Canagarajah 2007), some interactants may nonetheless see themselves as second or foreign language learners of English (Block 2003).
2. Firth and Wagner (2007) discuss, in detail, the need to do away with deficit interpretations of learning (for example, interlanguage), and highlight the role lingua franca encounters and multilingual community interaction have in studies of additional language learning.
3. By using the term CA-for-SLA, I am not implying that CA should somehow conform to SLA research, or that CA-inspired studies of language learning belong to the disciplinary remit of SLA. While conversation analysts and second language acquisitionists could both convincingly argue that CA has no business in SLA research, these arguments are auxiliary to the aims of this chapter.

4. As a point of interest, it is worth mentioning that James does not use the practice of self-identification with any of the other interactants of the chat room after extract 3.
5. Firth and Wagner (2007) provide similar observations with regard to how an interactant adopts a previously unknown word in subsequent interactional encounters.
6. Some conversation analysts (for example, Lee 2006; Markee 2008) and applied linguists (for example, Kramsch 1986) use the term 'interactional competence' to denote the doing and learning of all things interactional. While there is nothing inherently wrong with this term, those who adopt it do not make explicit the differences, if there are any, between interactional competence and the more classic subcomponents of communicative competence (for example sociolinguistic issues, discourse, and strategic competence). Furthermore, it is unclear whether, and to what degree, interactional competence is a cover term for Hymes's (1972) earlier statements on how talk and interaction are context-bound (see also Hatch 1978).

10
Limitations of Social Interaction in Second Language Acquisition: Learners' Inaudible Voices and Mediation in the Zone of Proximal Development

Amy Snyder Ohta

Introduction

This chapter considers the oral and literacy skills development of language learners via analysis of interviews about the zone of proximal development (ZPD), and how this construct relates to language-learning experiences. This study is grounded in a sociocultural approach to L2 learning, where learning is defined as a process by which the L2 becomes a tool for the mind and for social interaction. Researchers may access learning processes by observing changes in participation, regulation patterns, how learners use mediational tools and access (or not) various supportive resources, or, as in this chapter, through self-report. Data analysis from a sociocultural perspective provides a holistic view of human development that considers cognition, social interaction, interactive settings and learner histories from an integrated perspective (Lantolf and Thorne 2006; van Lier 2004). Here, learning in the ZPD is examined via the perspectives of 17 learners of Asian languages who were interviewed regarding the ZPD and how it applies (or does not apply) to their own language learning. In this chapter, learning in the ZPD is defined as progress in L2 use in other contexts, with the understanding that growing independence retains a stamp of the learning processes through which it developed. This chapter focuses on three limitations of social interaction for language learning that were reported by interviewees, considering how learners overcame these limitations. The limitations discussed by the learners were 1) difficulty in retaining language provided by interlocutors, 2) over-reliance on interlocutor assistance, and 3) inability to handle too-difficult conversational topics.

What is the Zone of Proximal Development?

The ZPD is part of a sociocultural approach to language and development, which views essentially human mental functions of cognition and mind as semiotically mediated by mental tools which are social/cultural/historical in origin (Negueruela 2008). *Mediation* refers to how people use 'culturally constructed artifacts, concepts and activities to regulate (that is, gain voluntary control over and transform) the material world or their own and each other's social and mental activity' (Lantolf and Thorne 2006: 79). Language is the primary mediational tool relevant to thinking, learning, and other cognitive processes. Language does not occur only inside the head, but also functions socially – thinking is mediated through social interaction. From early childhood, adults and peers mediate the child's cognition such that adult cognitive processes retain their social character. Related to learning, help-seeking and help-incorporating processes, whether or not they involve social interaction (Ohta 2006), retain the dialogicality through which they were dynamically formed, and continue to develop, in the social world. The ZPD describes how learning may occur through socially-mediated processes.

Vygotsky (1978: 86) defined the ZPD as:

> [T]he distance between the actual developmental level as determined by independent problem solving and the level of potential development as determined through problem solving under adult guidance or in collaboration with more capable peers.

Vygotsky was talking about children, but today this term is related to both child and adult development, and to academic and practical skills. Interest in the ZPD and its implications for second and foreign language (L2)[1] learning has also grown, with more ZPD-focused L2 research and learning applications.

Newman and Holzman (1993) remind us that the ZPD is not a cause-and-effect 'space' where interaction results in learning (what they call 'tool-for-results'). Rather, the ZPD is a transformative, meaning-making activity where assistance is part of a dynamic interaction. Newman and Holzman (1993: 49) define 'making meaning' as:

> [...] the toolmaker (our species) making tools-and-results using the predetermining tools of the hardware store variety (including nature and language) and the predetermined tools of mind developed by them to create something – a totality – not determined by them. It is the meaning in the emerging activity, not the preconceived imagining followed by its realisation, which is transformative, revolutionary, and essentially human.

Language learning also harnesses such revolutionary and transformative creative processes, involving 'learners constructing meaning-making tools in a[n] L2 and in the process, changing both the circumstances of their language development and who they are as learners' (Negueruela 2008: 190).

The key to the ZPD is mediation of cognitive processes by the other in shared activity. Wertsch (1985: 71) explains that the ZPD is 'jointly determined by the child's[3] level of development and the form of instruction involved; it is a property neither of the child nor of interpsychological functioning alone'. This is critical in understanding how the ZPD works in intellectual development, in creating the *potential* for further development (Chaiklin 2003; Negueruela 2008). Development is not inevitable: 'The fact that the learner is able to solve a task through help from an expert does not mean that he/she has developed; it simply means that the *potentiality* is there' (Negueruela 2008: 199).

The ZPD emerges when the learner's established abilities are stretched through developmentally appropriate challenges and support that allow the learner to outperform the current developmental level. Vygotsky (1987: 213) claims that 'all productive instruction' moves beyond the learner's established mental functions, leading development by forcing the learner 'to rise above himself' because the classroom 'demands more than the child is capable of'. Too much assistance or instruction that lacks challenge and stays within the learner's range of ability does not lead to development. Effective help in the ZPD is contingent upon the need for assistance and is graduated, according to individual needs (Aljaafreh and Lantolf 1994; Lantolf and Aljaafreh 1995). Also important is *withdrawing* assistance to promote learning, that is, independent

Internalisation may begin with activity in the ZPD.[2] These processes are partially observable in social interaction as social facilitation promotes the learner's acting ahead of the current developmental level.

performance. Lantolf and Aljaafreh show the effectiveness of this sort of assistance. Peers also provide appropriate assistance through strategies such as waiting and prompting, avoiding unnecessary help, and promoting independent functioning (Ohta 2001a).
Vygotsky's main point about learning is that learning leads development (Vygotsky 1987). This does not mean that learning causes development. Learning is 'the actual, historical dynamic of *the being ahead of ourselves activity*' (Newman and Holzman 1993: 149, italics mine). The linguistic activity involved in interaction and joint problem-solving is not separate from cognitive processes, but is formative. For Vygotsky, the main point isn't skill development; most important are the new cognitive mechanisms developed through the processes of performing beyond the learner's capability.

The ZPD in SLA

Through interaction in the ZPD, the learner uses the L2 in a way that he or she can reach with assistance, but not yet fully grasp, and human development is interwoven into this process. The studies by Lantolf, Aljaafreh and Ohta cited above are L2 studies, and many other L2 studies involve the ZPD (such as, Brooks 1992; Donato 1994; Guk and Kellogg 2007; Huong 2007; Lantolf 1994; the articles in Lantolf and Poehner 2008; McCafferty 2002; Nassaji and Cumming 2000; Ohta 1995, 2000a, 2000b, 2001a, 2001b, 2002, 2006; Ryberg and Christiansen 2008; Swain and Lapkin 1998; Watanabe and Swain 2007). To better conceptualise the ZPD's role in classroom L2 development, I have revised Vygotsky's (1978) definition of the ZPD:

> For the L2 learner, the ZPD is the distance between the actual developmental level as determined by individual linguistic production, and the level of potential development as determined through language produced collaboratively with a teacher or peer. (Ohta 2001a: 9)

Learning is evident as functional system components shift and learners become more independent and utilise less support. Adults have a highly developed capacity to incorporate various mediational tools into their cognitive processing. Ohta (2006: 176) has proposed that through human development, the processes in the ZPD are internalised such that the ZPD can be considered 'a tool used by cognitively mature adults as they go through life seeking new skills and new knowledge'. As children develop literacy skills their ability to gain assistance through literacy-based activity increases. Adults apply these tools also to manage tasks that are beyond the present developmental level. Dialogic processes encompass both social processes and processes through which learners use other cultural artifacts such as reference materials. Poehner and Lantolf (2005: 238) emphasise that development is not about 'the individual acting alone, but the interpersonal functional system formed by people and cultural artifacts acting jointly'. This involves mediation via previously learned language (Swain and Lapkin 1998), private speech (Berk and Diaz 1992; Ohta 2001a), inner speech (de Guerrero 2005), writing (DiCamilla and Lantolf 1995), and reading (Ohta 2006). Learners mediate their cognition by manipulating established cognitive tools when learning a second language. Here, all of these cognitive tools are understood to facilitate learning in the ZPD as they work together with the learner to form a functional system for a particular L2 task. Any activity that brings learners at the edge of their developed abilities together with developmentally appropriate assistance is part of the ZPD.

The study

Research questions

The research questions addressed by this study relate to how the ZPD applies to language-learning experiences. The interview protocol first elicited information about study methods, how these changed as learners progressed, then asked questions about how learners manage(d) difficult areas of language learning and how this changed with growing proficiency. Finally, learners were asked about the ZPD and how it related (or not) to their language learning. The goal was to better understand how each learner functioned when a gap was encountered between what the learner could do with the language and what the learner wanted to accomplish, how that gap was filled (or not) through interaction with help-sources, and how this impacted language learning. Learners explained whether and how language learning occurred as they reported their experiences with interaction and study of the L2.

Participants

Seventeen learners of Asian languages were interviewed. Table 10.1 lists study participants by pseudonym, Asian languages studied, language-learning background, and year interviewed.

Table 10.1 Participants, languages, language-learning background and year interviewed

Participant Pseudonym	Language(s)	Language-Learning Background	Year
Brandon	Japanese, Korean	4th+ (Japanese), 2nd year (Korean), 2 years studying in Japan	2009
Sandra	Chinese	3rd/year studying, year working in China (2 years in China)	2009
Tina	Chinese, Korean	Grad/summer studying in Korea	2009
Larry	Chinese	3rd/2.5 years working in China	2009
Max	Chinese	4th/summer studying in Taiwan	2009
Beth	Japanese	4th/year studying in Japan	2009
Lydia	Chinese	4th+/year studying in China, including 2 years of research in China	2009
Lance	Korean, Classical Chinese	Grad/6 years in Korea	2009
Wendy	Tagalog	1st	2009
Sam	Japanese	1st	2009
Heather	Chinese, Hebrew[4]	3rd (Chinese)/year studying in China, 2nd (Hebrew)	2009
Scotty	Korean	2nd/summer studying in Korea	2009
Niles	Japanese, Korean	Unknown[5] – Highly proficient in Japanese	2006
Mark	Japanese	3rd	2006
Evelyn	Chinese	4th(Japanese)/2 years in Japan, Grad (Chinese)/internship in Taiwan	2006
Victor	Chinese	Highly proficient in Chinese	2006
Sanjay	Sanskrit	Grad	2006

Key: 'Languages': Languages discussed in the interview. Most studied other languages also. Course level: Current enrolment or recent completion of that year of college-level instruction. Year: 2009 data were collected for this study. 2006 data are also discussed in Ohta (2006).

Interview procedure

Interviews ranged from ten minutes to an hour in length. Interview questions are listed in the appendix. Questions 1–9 were used in both interviews, with questions 10 and 11 added for the 2009 interviews. These questions were a flexible guide, adapted to the circumstances of each interview. Interviews were audio-recorded using Audacity 1.2.5 software.

Analysis

Interviews were transcribed for a qualitative analysis based on themes discussed by the participants. These were listed on an MS Excel table, with transcript excerpts posted by theme for analysis across participants and within the context of each individual's interview.

Results

Previous research has shown how learners benefit from assistance in classroom settings – they later use the language gleaned from assistance-related episodes (Ohta 2000a, 2001; Swain and Lapkin 1998). In the present study, all learners detailed helpful episodes, explaining their developmental utility and a variety of mediational tools and learning strategies[6] harnessed to promote learning or manage difficulties, as well as classmates', teachers' and target natives' involvement in collaborative problem-solving. Findings demonstrated how the participants worked through problems encountered in the ZPD, learning through interaction with help-sources. A subset of learners discussed some limitations of social interaction for language learning and, in some cases, how they worked through these difficulties. Related to the ZPD, learners reported three problem areas: 1) difficulty in retaining language provided by interlocutors, 2) over-reliance on interlocutor assistance, and 3) inability to handle too-difficult conversational topics. The first two of these relate to the social interactive context of receiving conversational assistance. The third relates to a limitation of the ZPD: that interactive assistance cannot overcome a proficiency gap that is too large. Here, each problem area is introduced, along with how learners harnessed mediational tools to overcome difficulties.

Difficulty in retaining language provided by interlocutors

Learners talked about the usefulness of interlocutor assistance with completing utterances. In fact, they reported actively eliciting this assistance via circumlocution, or 'trailing off' so that the native-speaking interlocutor might finish the utterance. This illustrates how the ZPD functions in ordinary talk, as the learner incorporates the interlocutor into his or her functional system, resulting in co-construction or other assistance that permits participation beyond the learner's current abilities. Beth, for example, describes 'trailing off':

> If I got unsure of the whole honorifics thing I'd get to the end and start leaving verbs off because that's where most of the decisions[7] are. So I found I could be a little bit vaguer about what I was doing if I used verbs less frequently. (Beth 2009)

Collaboration with native speakers seems an ideal form of assistance. Encounters where the learner incorporates interlocutor language into his or her utterances may begin the process of internalisation.[8] Max relates a similar experience:

... I knew this concept or this term or this structure before but it just wasn't coming to me and then when I would try and would get prompted with the correct version then I'd say 'yes, yes, that's what I meant' and that would reinforce what I was struggling for. (Max 2009)

Interlocutor prompting provides Max with an appropriate nudge of assistance in the ZPD. Max's effort pushed him to the edge of his current developmental level; the helper's prompt allowed him to access what he needed to function ahead of himself, promoting his active use of the language in the future.

However, results also underscore that we cannot assume that assistance in the ZPD means that a word or structure is learned, nor that learning in this context is a speedy, linear process. Learner perceptions of learning processes confirm that the path from social interactive assistance to language learning is not straightforward. Even when they elicited social interactive assistance, learners did not necessarily do so after applying effort (like Max did), nor did they necessarily evaluate it as helpful in learning the language. Some reported difficulty retaining language provided in interactive contexts; conversational collaboration may have the downside of producing comfortable interactions that lack a developmental challenge. Larry talks about using circumlocution to converse with people in China. Note that the narrative is in the historical present tense as Larry discusses his journeys:

If can't say it in Chinese ... I just use a bunch of adjectives and they say 'Oh yeah it's that' and I say 'Yeah it's that' or I go 'I've never heard that word before but I'm sure that's the word for it'. ... What happened ... in class and in China was I'd kind of say half a sentence and then trail off because I wasn't quite sure how I could make it all fit together and then the other person would finish it for me: 'Oh you mean XYZ'. (Larry 2009)

Larry reports using this strategy both when living in China and in language classes. However, he also reported that he neither *retained* nor developed the ability to *use* language provided in these contexts. These particular bits of language did not become mental or social interactive tools for Larry. Evelyn (2006 Corpus) discussed the same problem: when talking about interlocutors providing needed vocabulary, Evelyn remarks, 'they say okay and five minutes later [poof] ((hand gesture showing it's gone))'.

Over-reliance on interlocutor assistance

As Larry talked about using circumlocution, he showed excitement at the effectiveness of this strategy and how rewarding it was to participate in interesting conversations. However, he explicitly states that these episodes did not help to build his production skills:

> People's willingness to do that was – on the one hand that doesn't facilitate developing your vocabulary because I always knew I could fall back on that. ... [It's] functional communication but on the other hand it's not really helping my production ability at all <not if you develop the strategy of relying on it>[9] which I totally did.

While assistance in the ZPD would seem an ideal incubator for language learning, it is potentially, but not necessarily, helpful. Larry demurs that what he experienced 'doesn't facilitate developing your vocabulary'. He settled into a pattern of relying on interlocutors to finish his utterances, relieving him of the responsibility for doing so. He implies that he didn't try to do what was difficult. In sociocultural terms, this can be described as dependence on *other regulation*. Interlocutor assistance was part of the functional system he relied upon, and he did not push himself to learn the new vocabulary presented or to complete his own sentences. Instead of working to become *self regulated*, to become an independent L2 speaker, he relied on what others would willingly supply. His lack of effort was in dynamic relationship with interlocutor over-suppliance of assistance, which was not withdrawn to promote independent functioning.

Reliance on other regulation might not be a problem if learners could retain what was collaboratively constructed, developing the ability to use these new linguistic tools. However, learners report that what is quickly provided is incorporated into a conversation that is moving rapidly, resulting in problems with retention. Mere comprehension of the vocabulary and structures provided, without additional effort applied, does not ensure that the learner can recall them later, much less produce them.

Inability to handle too-difficult conversational topics

When a learner's goal was to participate in interactions that far exceeded his or her current ability, interactive help fell short. In other words, to work *beyond* his or her own ZPD, collaborative construction was not sufficient. This issue was raised by Brandon, who wanted to do *more* than he was currently able to do in the L2 for an assignment in his second-year Korean class:

> [For the assignment,] we could ask them what's your job or something like that but I wanted to get more into politics and ask like what they think of the Obama administration and how it effects the Korean economy and stuff like that. And how the Obama administration talks about responsibility and how that affects the Japanese responsibility in history and stuff like that. (Brandon 2009)

Brandon's limited Korean made his language study less interesting and he reported that this was frustrating when he compared his Korean with what he could accomplish in Japanese, an L2 in which he is highly proficient. Korean L2 collaborative interaction could not provide enough support to leap this hurdle.

Moving beyond the limitations of social interaction: Mediation in the ZPD

The learners who reported limitations of social interaction also reported how they managed these situations, to transform them into learning opportunities. Learner interactions were transformed by their active engagement with semiotic tools and focused efforts to do something about the limitations of social interaction they encountered. The learners incorporated various mediational devices into their learning activity, including their own 'voice', literacy tools and other languages.

Inaudible voices in the ZPD

Much L2 research related to the ZPD considers verbal and physical (gestural, eye gaze, and so on.) behaviour of participants as recorded and transcribed. Such research analyses collaborative processes evident in the audible voices and visible behaviour of participants, relating these processes to L2 learning. However, another mediational resource is the learner's own inaudible voice that shapes help-seeking episodes.

Eun et al. (2008) discuss the notion of a 'third voice' in considering dialogicality in tutor-tutee dialogue. They state (ibid: 135):

> The current conceptualization of the ZPD defines the verbal inter-action between the more capable and less capable participants within the ZPD as the main mechanism of development.

Applying Bakhtin's (1981: 136) notion of dialogicality, they explain that dialogue consists of not only speech, but also interactional and cultural histories, including participants' goals and agendas:

> [D]ialogic interactions are based on the first voice of the more capable participant and the second voice of the less capable participant. In addition, there is an *inaudible third voice* that mediates the perceptions and interpretations of the first voice within the zone. This third voice is based on a larger linguistic context, in which it engages in dialogic interactions with the first voice. (Italics mine)

Eun et al. conceptualise this third voice as something like high-stakes testing that constrains *the tutor* in tutor-tutee interactions. In conversation, however, a more proficient speaker's agenda may simply be to get through or enjoy a particular conversation, or s/he may be interested in helping the learner with the L2. These differing agendas form inaudible voices that variously mediate interpretations of the learner's talk and how the interlocutor should respond. The learner also has an inaudible voice that shapes his or her effort and interaction with any source-of-assistance. The learner's inaudible voice is closely related to motivational thinking (Ushioda 2001) and learner goals, and relates to how the learner participates and perceives the importance (or not) of new language. This voice is evident in the learner's engagement and activity – what the learner *does* with the language provided through assistance and, as a result, how well the learner retains such language. Results suggest that mediation of the learner's inaudible voice may either perpetuate the limitations of social interaction, or transform social interaction into a place where language learning occurs more readily.

Let us consider the involvement of learners' inaudible voices in mediating interactional and learning processes as they encounter the three limitations of social interaction discussed above: 1) difficulty in retaining language provided by interlocutors, 2) over-reliance on interlocutor

assistance, and 3) inability to handle too-difficult conversational topics. Analysis examines learner choices about how they mediate their
learning processes and challenge themselves to harness (or not) various
mediational tools to promote learning. Results show how learners apply
effort to adjust to or to shape how interlocutors mediate their learning
processes (embracing withdrawal of support and selecting language-
exchange partners), how they incorporate literacy tools (mediation
through writing, reading, and language analysis), and how a different foreign language is harnessed to mediate L2 learning. In each case,
effort enables learners to transform problematic social interactions into
learning opportunities.

Difficulty in retaining language provided by interlocutors

Evelyn: Mediation through writing, reading, and language analysis.   Larry
did not retain language provided by Chinese interlocutors and Evelyn
illustrated with a gesture how a word offered by an interlocutor in
social interaction disappears. Evelyn wanted to retain new words from
social interaction. This desire alone did not result in retention. Rather,
she harnessed learning strategies, actively engaging with the language
beyond social interaction. She reported that immediately following an
interaction,

> ... I'd write down the pronunciation and then I'd go look it up and
> ask 'is it this?' and maybe they'd say yes or no ... and on the computer
> I had a database of words I actually thought I'd use again. (Evelyn
> 2006)

Evelyn followed up conversation with writing pronunciation in a notebook, using a dictionary to find the Chinese characters, writing those
down, and returning to the interlocutor to ask about the expression and
characters. Finally she decided whether or not to include the language
in her database. Evelyn harnessed mediational tools – writing, reading,
the L1 (bilingual dictionaries), further L2 interaction, and technology.
She likely also used other mediational tools that she does not report –
L1 and L2 inner speech used to retain the word long enough to write
it down (repeating the word to herself), for oral/mental rehearsal, as
well as for linguistic analysis. Evelyn engaged in these processes at work
where she had her notebook and computer database. Assistance in the
ZPD through the interlocutor's provision of new language was the first
step in a multi-sensory process Evelyn followed that helped her to learn
Chinese.[10]

Over-reliance on interlocutor assistance

Larry: Embracing withdrawal of support. Larry was satisfied with conversations with Chinese people and became dependent on their oversuppliance of support. Unlike developmentally-tuned support in the ZPD which creates an intellectually challenging interactive environment that promotes development, the support Larry experienced created comfortable interactions without intellectual challenge that Larry claims did not help him to learn Chinese. While the same sort of interactions may have proved helpful earlier in his learning, when higher-frequency vocabulary and structures were encountered, this was not currently true. When Larry returned home for graduate school, the inaudible voices shaping Larry's interactions began to change. At first, what changed was the inaudible voice of his new interlocutor – his Chinese teacher. Interlocutors in China followed the norms of ordinary talk: co-construction is common, and helping a learner to develop is not part of the agenda. But in graduate school, Larry's teacher's interactions were shaped by a different inaudible voice – her goal of fostering independent language skills. Larry describes how his teacher does *not* finish his sentences, and the positive impact this has had on his development:

> [When] I can't formulate the sentence and trail off the teacher just calls on someone else – she's like I'm not going to deal with you. But that's also been good because now I'm formulating sentences before I try talking and have to try to say all of it. At this point the teacher is withdrawing support and that is really helping me to think what am I really going to say, how am I going to end this. (Larry 2009)

In China, co-construction relieved Larry of the burden of sentence formation and lexical retrieval. His Chinese teacher has withdrawn that support. This experience was transformative for Larry, re-shaping his own inaudible voice. His experiences in Chinese class revealed that he was not as fluent as he had hoped. He began to view social interaction as a place where he works to formulate his own sentences. Larry now expends effort to do what is difficult for him. His inaudible voice is evident in the mediational resources he incorporates into his interactions as he uses inner speech for 'formulating sentences before I try talking', applying effort to 'try to say all of it'. He reaches beyond what he can do with ease to attempt what he may or may not be able to do. As a result, Larry can receive L2 support that is more finely tuned to his developmental needs. Larry reports that his efforts are paying off in improving his Chinese.

Tina: Selecting language exchange partners.   Tina was aware of the problem of too much assistance. She was not satisfied with the status quo
presented by ordinary conversation with Koreans who would finish her
sentences:

> I find that I learn a lot better if someone can just *start* to finish the
> sentence. And then I can *finish* finishing the sentence. If they can
> provide me with enough help that it feels helpful ... but not so much
> help that I feels like there's just no point ... I've found that if ... some-
> one can kind of say 'Well it sounds like you're thinking of maybe this
> verb or maybe this verb'. If they give me a choice I'll remember what
> I'm looking for, or I'll remember one of them and won't know the
> other, and then I'll try to learn that one as well. (Tina 2009)

Tina realised the tendency for interlocutors to provide too much assistance. She even found herself guilty of this: 'I find with a lot of language
partners I've had there's a kind of a sort of tension. You don't want
them to feel stupid so you just finish it for them' (Tina 2009). Through
her college course, Tina is matched with different language-exchange
partners. She explained how she meets with different partners, then
chooses those willing to provide smaller nudges of assistance that are
helpful in promoting her learning. These smaller nudges allow Tina to
outperform her current developmental level. Her inaudible voice shapes
her interactions via choice of interlocutors able to provide developmentally appropriate support in the ZPD; they provide an appropriate level
of collaboration, a mediational tool that allows Tina to do what she can
for herself, push herself to do more, get help when needed, and progress
in learning Korean.

Inability to handle too-difficult conversational topics

Brandon: Using other languages as mediational tools.   Brandon, a learner
of Korean who is highly proficient in L2 Japanese, provided the most
striking example of working to overcome the limitations of social interaction. Brandon wanted to do interviews on politics, not mundane daily
life. These desires shaped Brandon's interactions – instead of settling
for working just a bit beyond his linguistic ability (and within what
would be his ZPD in terms of his social interactive skills in Korean), he
harnessed mediational tools available via his proficiency in Japanese,
a language with morphosyntactic similarities to Korean. Japanese and
Korean are similar enough that word-for-word translation can be done
easily. Using Japanese allowed Brandon to do a project on politics,

something he could not have managed without using it as a mediational tool:

> So I did the questions in Japanese first and then I translated them into Korean ... Then some of [my interviewees] would type up the answers beforehand [in Korean] so I could look it over before the interview. So what I'm doing now is translating that [into Japanese] and in the process learning a whole bunch of new words. So I'm translating what they gave to me first and then I try to listen to what they say and transcribe that, and then I show it to them and they correct it and give it back. (Brandon 2009)

Brandon's inaudible voice – his interest in talking politics and willingness to put effort into preparation in order to be able to do so – allowed him to outperform his own Korean. He harnessed various mediational tools to accomplish this: writing (in Japanese and Korean), reading (written responses), translation (both J–K and K–J),[11] dictionary work (using J–K/K–J dictionaries), writing (transcription), technology (email, video, and YouTube) and interpersonal assistance (eliciting transcript corrections). Brandon applied much of this effort prior to the interviews by corresponding with interviewees via email and reading/translating their replies. He learned enough to interview in Korean and follow the interviews, which he video-recorded and transcribed. He had his interviewees correct the transcripts, then translated them into Japanese, working to fully understand each entire interview. Brandon created many ZPDs for himself as he interacted with various help-sources, incorporating what he learned along the way to keep outperforming his present developmental level. And, he reported that knowing and using Japanese in this way has helped him to learn Korean much faster than his English-speaking peers who don't know Japanese. While translation (along with use of the L1) has been rejected by some L2 pedagogues, others note that using a language that a learner is highly proficient in can promote language learning (Anton and DiCamilla 1998; Cook 2001b; Laufer and Girsai 2008; Stern 1992).

Conclusion

The foundations of linguistic life are social interactive, providing a rich context for language learning. However, the spoken word is ephemeral, quickly fading. People do learn language through social interaction – they repeatedly encounter common vocabulary and structures that they can incorporate into their linguistic activity. However, as learners become more proficient, conversation may seem less helpful as the vocabulary and structures encountered are less common. They may experience interactions which are successful in terms of communication goals, but which don't push language development forward as assessed by whether or not they were able to remember and use new forms in the future. Conversation includes a range of procedures designed to address trouble-sources (Sacks et al. 1974), but is not designed to create developmentally appropriate *challenges*. To be developmentally optimal, interaction must present a challenge that is mediated by just enough, but not too much, assistance, and by appropriate withdrawal of assistance to promote self-regulation. Another limitation of social interaction is that ZPDs only emerge when the task is just beyond what a learner could do without assistance. When challenges are way beyond the learner's developmental level, collaborative processes are not sufficient. These are the limitations of social interaction discussed by participants in the present research.

These can only be considered to be limitations because of what isn't visible in interactions the inaudible voices of the learners. If we observed Tina's or Evelyn's or Larry's interactions, we might feel they exemplified the usefulness of collaboration and co-construction between native and non-native speakers, not realising the problems these learners faced with developing a useful command of language introduced in conversation. The effectiveness of social interaction for language learning cannot, therefore, be measured only by observing interactive processes. These processes seldom reveal what was learned – what becomes a tool for the learner to use for comprehension or production in future L2 activities. Incorporation of assistance does not guarantee development. It makes sense to consider the ZPD as a zone of *potential*, not *proximal*, development (Negueruela 2008).

Some learners are not content with having to rely on strategies that result in interlocutor support – they apply effort to learn new language. The interview results show how inaudible voices are integrated into learners' social interactive behaviour, visible in how they harness mediational tools before, during and after social interaction to guide their own learning processes and outcomes. Larry, Evelyn, Tina and Brandon demonstrate that learning need not be constrained by the limitations of social interaction. We see how Larry's own voice changed through pedagogical experience, how Tina shaped her interactions through choice of interlocutor, how Evelyn focused on workplace interactions as a place to learn Chinese through multi-sensory and multi-modal interaction with the language, while Brandon harnessed L2 Japanese, technology, and literacy skills to ratchet up his functionality in Korean. These reports exemplify how dialogicality moves beyond the audible voices of participants, incorporating learner goals and histories as well as mediational tools.

However, it is not the case that these learners overcame the limitations of social interaction *because* they applied particular strategies. What superficially may appear to be cause-and-effect (or to use Newman and Holzman's (1993) term, *tool-for-results*) processes, showing that learners used certain strategies and thus had certain outcomes, are actually dynamic processes that are permeated by the learners' inaudible voices within a broader context. To better understand language learning we need a dynamic *tool-and-results* (Newman and Holzman 1993) understanding that considers learning in the context of learner histories, motivational thinking, and learning goals that work together to form the inaudible voices that silently participate in each individual's learning activity. While collecting learner histories was beyond the scope of this study, such histories might be useful to provide a better understanding of the dynamic systems at work and of why some learners apply effort to overcome the limitations of social interaction while others do not. Even so, the limited data considered here still evidences how deeply learning processes are mediated by each person's language-learning goals, and how these inaudible voices transform social interactive opportunities into places where developmentally appropriate challenges are joined with developmentally appropriate assistance in multiple modalities in the ZPD.

Appendix: Interview questions

1) What methods do you use to study [language name].
2) Have these changed as you have become a more proficient speaker? If so, how?
3) Have these changed as you have become a more proficient reader? If so, how?
4) What is the role of native speakers or others who are more proficient in your language of specialisation than you are? Do you make use of their expertise? If so, how? How has that changed over time?
5) How do you handle linguistic situations (speaking, listening, reading or writing) that are beyond your individual ability now? How is that similar to or different from how you handled such situations when you were less proficient?

6) Are you familiar with the term 'Zone of Proximal Development (ZPD)'? If not, may I explain?

7) How does the concept of the ZPD fit with your experiences learning and studying your language of specialisation? How does it diverge?

8) How do you feel your ability to work within your ZPD has changed as your language proficiency has improved? What are the 'gaps' you encounter today when working with your language of specialisation? How do they differ from those encountered earlier in your language-learning career?

9) Internalisation in the ZPD is considered something that moves from the 'between people' space to being an individual resource. Do you see similarities or differences with the process of learning language from textual sources?

10) Part of the idea of the ZPD is growing independence as assistance is incorporated at first, and then gradually is no longer needed. Does this idea jibe with your language-learning experiences? Are there any ways you are 'dependent' on particular resources more than you would like to be at this point in your learning? If so, please explain.

11) What is the role of other linguistic helps in your learning and how has this changed as your proficiency has grown? How has this changed over time?

Notes

1. The abbreviation 'L2' is used to refer to any foreign language, whether it is a learner's second or third, or any subsequent, language.

2. For further discussion of the ZPD in the context of Vygotsky's writings, see Chaiklin (2003), Guk and Kellogg (2007), and Poehner and Lantolf (2005).

3. Scholars discussing Vygotsky's work were often interested, as was Vygotsky, in child development. Here, these ideas are applied to the language learning of adults.

4. All participant interviews focused on Asian language study, except for this interviewee, an L2 speaker of Chinese whose most recent learning experiences relate to studying modern Hebrew.

5. For the 2006 Corpus, I did not solicit participant details regarding time spent abroad.

6. Learning strategies involve incorporation of a wide range of mediational tools. Nation's (2001) taxonomy of vocabulary-learning strategies is a good example of this. Takac (2008, pp. 54–6) provides a list of features of language-learning strategies.

7. The 'decisions' Beth refers to are both lexical (which verb to choose) and morpho-syntactic (whether or not to use passive or causative morphology, or include an auxiliary verb, for example).

8. I do not claim that internalisation is immediate, but that collaborative construction is part of internalisation processes as language-to-be-learned emerges in social interaction.
9. Language between < > marks was uttered by the interviewer.
10. Kojic-Sabo and Lightbown's (1999) study of 90 language learners also found that learner effort, including time spent studying and incorporating a variety of learning strategies, is important in vocabulary development and promoting higher proficiency.
11. I recently taught an undergraduate course in Japanese SLA and a number of students did in-depth interview case studies on the topic of the impact of knowing other foreign languages on learning Japanese. Subjects who knew Korean all reported relying heavily on K–J and J–K translation at elementary and intermediate stages of learning Japanese. Learners who knew other foreign languages such as Chinese or French did not report using translation to facilitate learning Japanese.

11

English as an Additional Language: Learning and Participating in Mainstream Classrooms

Constant Leung

Introduction

English as an Additional/Second Language (EAL) within the National Curriculum in England raises a number of complex conceptual issues regarding the notion of additional/second language learning within a broader context of communication in school.[1] The National Curriculum sets out the statutory content specifications for subjects such as English, mathematics, science and others for primary and secondary schools. From a historical perspective linguistic diversity has been a recognised feature of British school life since the 1960s, when appreciable numbers of New Commonwealth citizens arrived in the UK. According to recent official figures, 14.4% of primary pupils and 10.8% of secondary pupils are classified as having 'a first language other than English' (DCSF 2008). The EAL figures have seen an increase of 1% p.a. since 2005. It is generally estimated that on average 40% of school pupils in urban areas are EAL at present. Given Britain's continuing dependency on migrant labour, linguistic diversity is likely to continue to intensify. For that reason, issues related to EAL are likely to figure more prominently in future school curriculum discussions. Although this highly situated discussion is focused on the school context on England, many of the issues raised would be relevant to education systems across Europe, North America, and other world locations where linguistic minority students participate in regular school programmes through an additional/second language.

School curriculum responses to linguistic diversity have undergone some radical changes in the past 50 years. In the 1960s and 1970s the main response in the UK was to provide specialist English language teaching outside the regular school curriculum. Since the 1980s, mainstreaming of language minority pupils has been the officially endorsed curriculum policy and practice; a major assumption of the particular form of mainstreaming that has been implemented in England is that EAL learners can develop their English language knowledge and skills through participation in ordinary curriculum teaching/learning activities, and specialist English language tuition is not seen as necessary.[2] This chapter attempts to provide (1) a descriptive and analytical account of the current policy positions in relation to additional language learning inspired by a rendered version of the work of Krashen and Cummins, and (2) some analytical and evaluative comments on the current policy dispensations with reference to a piece of naturally occurring classroom data drawn from a school-based ethnographic study.

In the opening section I will look at the notion of language learning as presented in the current official curriculum document. This will be followed by a description of the current policy positions highlighting their theoretical and ideological underpinnings. Next I will present some classroom data to interrogate the pedagogic assumptions in the current policy positions. Then the discussion moves on to an analytical account of the pedagogic affordances and limitations of these policy positions with reference to some empirical data. The chapter will close with a suggestion that an alternative epistemology should be adopted to address the pedagogical issues associated with additional language learning in mainstream curriculum contexts.

In this discussion I use the term 'policy' to refer to formal statements, as well as quasi-policy and other discursive expressions found in official guidance and professional discussions. In relation to the analysis of the EAL curriculum the notion of learning is seen through a social constructivist lens – learning is understood as situated in social interaction (including classroom interaction), and as part of a transactional process of meaning-making and meaning-taking (for example, Wells 1995). Furthermore, an integrated content–language view of learning is adopted. That is, language learning and curriculum content learning are not regarded as two separate processes; they are seen as co-occurring in the self-same moment. EAL pupils in mainstream curriculum classes are expected to engage in subject content learning and English language learning at the same time. EAL isn't a subject in its own right in the National Curriculum, and it isn't given content specification (unlike subjects such as mathematics). So what goes on in the subject learning activities is, for the EAL learner, in effect part of their EAL learning (and using) experience. The content–language integrated perspective adopted in this chapter, drawing on Systemic Functional Linguistics (for example, Halliday and Matthiessen 2000), holds that there is no conceptual separation between language and socially engendered meaning; they are mutually constituting (see Leung 1996, 1997, 2005; Mohan 1986, 1990; Mohan and Slater 2004). Language is seen as a resource for meaning-making; subject content meaning is expressed through language (as a major semiotic resource). In a classroom context, language is a means for talking about and learning about school subjects and the world more generally. Thus the language used by teachers and pupils in interaction can be seen as a window into moments of learning, and learning can be seen as a window into moments of language use and acquisition.

EAL in the mainstream

The mainstreaming of EAL pupils, and EAL as an educational provision, gathered momentum in England in the late 1970s. This move was spurred on by a progressive disenchantment with the perceived lack of effectiveness of an English language-focused approach (for example, the provision of English language courses which displaced the ordinary age-appropriate curriculum) and, perhaps more importantly, the growing ideological acceptance of the principles of equal opportunity (see, for example, Bullock Report 1975; Swann Report 1985). In the emerging professional consensus it was generally held that minority pupils should participate fully and directly in the mainstream curriculum irrespective of their English language proficiency, and that any separate curriculum provision for these pupils would be (and should be) regarded as a form of indirect racial discrimination (for example, Commission For Racial Equality 1986). Access to and participation in the whole curriculum was now *the* criterial consideration. (See Leung 2001 for a detailed discussion.)

The pedagogical assumptions accompanying mainstreaming include the following: the learning of English is best achieved through maximum naturalistic engagement with curriculum activities in the English language (see the characteristics associated with Language$_6$ in Cook's chapter); the development of an additional language does not require dedicated language provision and pedagogical responses; and pupils' first-language knowledge can be used to assist the development of additional languages. In addition, an affectively supportive and non-racist school environment is a prime motor for successful learning (including English language learning).

These assumptions about language learning have drawn on the work of Krashen and Cummins. Krashen's (for example, 1982, 1985; Dulay et al. 1982) concept of comprehensible input argues that to acquire new language knowledge and skills, learners must understand what they hear and read in their target language; in other words, comprehension will lead to acquisition. His work has been explicitly acknowledged in recent curriculum guidance documents, for example 'Pupils learning English as an additional language' (DfES 2006).[3] His well-known conceptual distinction between language acquisition and language learning are interpreted as follows:

- The **acquired** system is a subconscious process very similar to that which children undergo when they acquire their first language. It requires meaningful interaction in the target language where the focus is on natural communication.
- The **learned** system is the result of formal instruction and is a conscious process which results in explicit knowledge about the language, for example grammar rules. (DfES 2006: 12, original emphasis)

In this rendering, the similarities between first language development and additional language development are made prominent. The role of comprehensible input in additional language 'acquisition' is elided to that of first language development. For example, 'For a young child acquiring L1, understanding [comprehensible input] could be enhanced by pointing to an object; for an older pupil acquiring L2, it could be the use of diagrams or other visuals to illustrate text' (DfES 2006: 12). Nonconscious language acquisition processes are held to be more important than conscious language learning (as in first language development), and EAL learners need 'regular exposure to words and structures at an early stage' through 'meaningful practice of a particular structure in the context of normal classwork' (DfES 2006: 12). In this Krashenian account there is some recognition of the differences between first and additional language development, but they are largely regarded as matters related to time and language lag factors. EAL learners will go through the same experiences as first language learners, but at a later time/age.

Cummins's ideas can clearly be seen in the advice on using students' first language (see discussion on NCC advice above). This reflects Cummins's long-held position on the potential benefits of bilingual education (for example, Cummins 1984, 1993, 2000 Chapter 4;

Cummins and Swain 1986). Cummins, like Krashen, also stresses the importance of understanding meaning in communicative context. While Krashen treats language as an undifferentiated body of linguistic resource for communication, Cummins distinguishes between two types of language proficiency in school and curriculum contexts: Basic Interpersonal Communication Skills (BICS) and Cognitive Academic Language Proficiency (CALP) (for example, Cummins 1984, 1992,[4] 2000, 2008). These are configured in the current policy formation in the following way:

> [Cummins] describes the acquisition of Basic Interpersonal Communicative Skills (BICS) as occurring within **two years** of exposure to English. Cognitive Academic Language Proficiency (CALP) to the level of their English-as-a-mother-tongue (EMT) peers, however, may take a **minimum of five years** and usually longer. Cummins's research has shown that because the pupils appear so fluent in everyday social language, teachers are unaware of the need for explicit teaching of academic language. The need for all teachers to be teachers of language in the context of their subject cannot be overstressed and nor can the advantages of such an approach for their EMT [English as mother tongue] peers. (DfES 2006: 14, original emphasis)

This representation of Cummins's work here also elides additional language development to that of first language development: all students, EAL and EMT alike, would benefit from the same pedagogic considerations.[5]

The mainstreaming of linguistic minority pupils has meant, *inter alia*, that all pupils regardless of their language backgrounds should participate in the same classroom activities and processes, and all teachers (not just language specialists) are advised to adopt practices that would enable EAL learners to participate in curriculum activities. Additional language learning is seen as part of curriculum communication, which conceptually obviates the need to treat EAL as a distinct discipline. These assumptions have been reflected in the key policy pronouncements since the mid-1980s. The National Curriculum Council Circular No.11 is a good example of the kind of injunctions issued to teachers:

> Language teaching is the professional responsibility of all teachers ... The National Curriculum is for **all** pupils ... Bilingualism is not,

in itself, a sufficient reason for disapplication from the National Curriculum.[6] (NCC 1991: 1, original emphasis)

Teachers were advised to adopt classroom activities that would minimise language demand and maximise participation:

- Work can be carried out in different language and peer groups, such as: monolingual groups to encourage the use of preferred languages ...
- Matrices, true/false exercises, data presentations and other display work can help to ensure that achievement is not entirely dependent on proficiency in English ... (op.cit.:2)

This particular interpretation of mainstreaming of linguistic minority pupils was given its fullest professional articulation in the officially-endorsed Partnership Teaching model (Bourne and McPake 1991), which sets out the principles and practice for whole-school staff development. General support for this approach has also received support from a number of teacher educators (for example Meek 1996, and Travers and Higgs 2004).

While endorsing the equal opportunities and non-racist principles of this approach, a number of researchers have questioned the pedagogic soundness and professional viability of this particular policy interpretation of mainstreaming (for example, Creese 2002, 2005; Franson 1999; Leung 2001, 2002; Leung and Creese 2008; Leung and Cable 1997). The key conceptual and pedagogic issues raised in these discussions include the validity of the assumption that mainstream curriculum activities constitute sufficient support for the language and other learning needs of different types of EAL learners;[7] the insistence on incidental and diffuse English language learning through curriculum (subject) activities; and the absence of EAL as a distinct school curriculum area and a main subject discipline in initial teacher education. In a fundamental sense the traditional identity of an additional language learner, which the conventional additional/second language education literature would discuss in terms of teaching and learning issues such as target-language needs, curriculum content, teaching methods, pupil characteristics such as age, aptitude, motivation and so on (for example, Hinkel 2005, Part IV; also see Toohey 2000, Chapter 1 for a related discussion), have been obliterated in this particular conceptualisation of mainstreaming.

Unlike much of the scholarly discussions in additional/second language education, where there is a working assumption that there are moments in classroom activities which are recognisably focused on language teaching and learning, in this conceptualisation of the mainstream there isn't such a moment. And yet paradoxically, in the logic of the 'communication equals learning' principle, all classroom activities are about language teaching and learning. As a reflection of this perspective, a good deal of the official quality indicators of current EAL policy and practice have been couched in terms of opportunities to take part in mainstream activities and pedagogic strategies that would promote such pupil participation.[8]

Conferred pupil identities

A review of the current policy statements suggests that the conventional idea of the language learner – someone who would benefit from language teaching – has been replaced by the notion of a multifaceted English language user-learner. Four main facets can be identified; each of them can be seen as an aspect of 'conferred EAL pupil identities'. By this is meant, following Bourdieu (1991: Chapter 10), the creation of a category of individuals by policy discourse so that the people in question are invested with certain qualities and not others. The conferring of an identity in policy terms, in this sense, is an attempt to impose and delimit what is legitimate to see and to discuss as EAL provision. This is an important conceptual point because a good deal of the policy discourse turns on how the EAL pupil is seen and projected, as the following discussion will show. Four pupil identities can be found in the relevant curriculum literature:

(1) The EAL pupil as a user of the opportunities generated through direct participation in the learning of English and curriculum subjects:

> ...pupils learn English most effectively in a mainstream situation where bilingual pupils are supported in acquiring English across the whole curriculum alongside English-speaking pupils. (DfES 2003: 29)

(2) The EAL pupil as an individual of equal moral worth to be supported:

> ...they [linguistic minority pupils] must have opportunities to glisten – to surprise and delight us with their insights and phrasing, to state as Chlève [a Francophone pupil from Congo] does

that 'one day I will get a new life in a new world'. (Travers and Higgs 2004: 32)

(3) The EAL pupil as an 'ignored' and 'diffident' individual in the classroom:

[Referring to an official report on the success of a special project on EAL:]

[The project has] built up my confidence...before I used to sit back and not ask for help. Now school is an opportunity. (DfES 2007: 6)

(4) The EAL pupil as a less competent user of English in need of help:

[Teacher giving advice to pupils:]

...if you didn't use that word [in science] you might have to use 20 words to express yourself and you're wasting time, and the examiners might still not be sure that you've got it right...you need to be quite precise...quite short...straight to the point. (DfES 2007, video segment)

The first of these identities asserts the pedagogic merits of mainstream provision for the EAL learner. The second endows the EAL learner with the capacity to make use of mainstream provision. Together they emphasise the need to provide pupils with opportunities to develop their full potential. The third spells out the negative consequences when the EAL learner does not participate actively because the mainstream environment isn't sufficiently supportive. The last acknowledges the need for the EAL learner to achieve an expected level of proficient language use. It would be fair to say that although all four of these identities populate the current policy documents, the first two of these have been the most frequently and prominently invoked in the past 30 years. For that reason the first two are particularly significant in this discussion (this point will be revisited later in relation to the empirical data). An important question here is: How can we make sense of these identities?

These curriculum pupil identities can be seen as ideological constructions, very much akin to chronotopic constructions,[9] designed to locate groups or categories of pupils in a particular position vis-à-vis an official policy configuration in terms of public expectations, individual rights and entitlements, and social obligations; at the same time they project selective pupil attributes and curriculum trajectories within particular policy parameters.

An analysis of these EAL pupil identities would provide us with a grasp of the underlying values and assumptions, which can help account for the kind of additional language teaching/learning provision afforded by the current provision.[10] I will now elaborate on the four EAL pupil identities mentioned earlier.

(1) *The EAL pupil as a user of the opportunities generated through direct participation in the learning of English and curriculum subjects.* This is essentially a modernist conceptualisation within a liberal individualist framework which sees that individuals are detached from any particular community in any pre-ascribed way. Sampson (1989: 915) argues that since the onset of the modern era (circa sixteenth century):

> Individuals were constituted as entities apart from any particular community; they had priority over it and so could freely choose the forms of association to which they would subject themselves. In turn, the community became an *instrumentality* for individuals, a necessity required so that individuals could pursue their personally chosen purposes in life…. (Original italics)

The depiction of the EAL learner as an individual who has the capacity to exploit the opportunities afforded by an English-speaking school community to further their own interests in relation to English language learning is clearly in line with this modernist view. It also allows policy discourse to eschew the more conventional concerns with curriculum content and specialist pedagogy. Here the obligation of the individual EAL pupil, irrespective of age, socioeconomic and language background, is to make use of the opportunities afforded (for example, to engage in mainstream activities) and the obligation of the education system is to reduce obstacles to participation (for example, the assumption that all teachers are language teachers; the use of pupils' home/first languages to facilitate learning in English; and the use of visuals and other means to enhance participation). The epochal order that underpins this EAL pupil identity is that of the untrammelled language learner overcoming obstacles and making advances through engagement with a projected curriculum environment that represents a common level playing field for all pupils. Seen in this light the mainstream curriculum is not primarily about what is to be learned, but is more concerned with offering opportunities for the learner to engage in learning.

(2) *The EAL pupil as an individual of equal moral worth to be supported.* This EAL pupil identity is in some sense an adjunct to identity (1) above. The emphasis here is on the importance of allowing the individual to

enjoy the affective benefits of a common level playing field imbued with humanistic values. For instance, in an autobiographic statement Vo (2004: 6–7), a former learner of EAL who is now a teacher, recalls her happy days in primary school when she was an 'A' student:

> I loved my primary school and strongly believe that my progress was made quicker because of the way I was treated. From day one there was total inclusion. It was…obvious in terms of appearance that I was different from other children. But the school allowed me to attend regular lessons. I was made to be part of my class's assembly play and Christmas play like everyone else. I was punished when naughty and praised when good. There were no concessions…Since I felt that I was on equal par with everyone else it gave me confidence to behave like everyone else, and ultimately I tried to speak and learn like everyone else.

In this account Vo goes on to contrast this happy and successful experience with that of her secondary school, where she found the environment 'threatening' and where '… like everyone else who was a millimeter outside the "norm band", [she] was picked on for being different' (op cit.: 7). From the point of view of language learning, the task of the curriculum is to remove all potential social and affective hindrance for the individual. This is an endorsement for the 'don't treat people differently' approach.

In a description of the progress made by a French-speaking pupil from Congo after 18 months in school, Travers and Higgs (2004: 29) observe that

> Chlève has made remarkable progress. He is an articulate, able student, keen to learn. He had also been supported and challenged in the steps he's made. He has been provided with opportunities to work collaboratively, have access to artefacts, visual resources, to read and analyse models of fluent writing…Above all, perhaps, he's been noticed, his strengths recognised…A relationship has developed between Chlève and his teachers and other pupils, enabling learning and language development to happen…We as teachers need to ensure that we get to know our pupils and value and include their experiences of communities, cultures, language learning.

Where further learning is required it is framed in this agentive way: 'He has had a go at writing in the past tense…he is still learning the English tense system and he will need to be supported in developing a more varied and extensive vocabulary' (loc.cit.). Notice that the contribution of the teacher is characterised as providing 'support'. Indeed in this description of success there is no mention of language-teaching approaches or curriculum content. The celebratory narrative is about the individual pupil who actively makes use of the opportunities afforded by the teacher and other pupils.

(3) *The EAL pupil as an 'ignored' and 'diffident' individual in the classroom.* This EAL pupil identity is often presented in the context of an injunction to teachers to pay more attention to the positive values of the current policy (identities 1 and 2 above).

> While a proportion of [bilingual] pupils are fully fluent in English and another language, many more will require support to develop their skills as confident speakers and writers of English.[11] (DfES 2003: 28)
>
> ... [EAL] pupils may be reluctant to speak, read or write in some subjects... depending on how familiar they are with the lesson content or how comfortable they feel in the class or group. (QCA 2000: 8)

In Vo's (2004: 8) own words, when things fell apart for her in her secondary school '... I stopped wanting to express myself. I thought people would never understand and would only laugh at the differences in me. I wanted to blend into the background....' Where the curriculum is not supportive of the individual affectively and socially, little learning is achieved.

(4) *The EAL pupil as a less competent user of English in need of help.* In a sense the EAL pupil as someone who is in need of help with their English is implicit in the policy recognition of EAL as a pupil-oriented issue. As a language learning and teaching issue, however, EAL has tended to be addressed as a *learning language through curriculum participation and communication* issue through identities (1) and (2). The assimilation of EAL pedagogy into English as a mother tongue, through everyday curriculum communication, has been the official policy position since the inception of the National Curriculum, and more recently affirmed explicitly in a statement on using common criteria to assess both English mother-tongue and EAL pupils (DfES 2005). The kind of EAL 'help' envisaged under the current dispensation is routed through the lens of an elided 'first and additional languages as one' position, as illustrated by the teaching of literacy within the curriculum subject of English in recent years.[12]

Participation in classroom interaction

The discussion of conferred pupil identities as ideological constructions suggests that they are designed to underpin particular policy options, and to direct attention to selective aspects of curriculum provision and pedagogy. The mainstreaming policy puts a high premium on active participation in curriculum activities and respect for pupils as persons of equal moral worth. These are clearly important considerations in any educational process. The question is how far they can account for what goes on in the classroom in general, and in curriculum content and language learning in particular. This is primarily an empirical question. To explore this further we now turn to some empirical data. Extract 1 (below) is a segment of a mathematics lesson, lasting approximately two and a half minutes.[13] The data were collected by means of a radio-microphone carried by the focal pupil. The ordinary non-contrived everyday-ness of this particular pupil-teacher interaction makes it particularly relevant for our discussion here. The focal pupil is Sairah (pseudonym), a Year 9 (14-year-old) secondary school pupil from a Kurdish Iraqi background. Sairah was not a beginner-level learner of EAL. At the time of the data collection she had been living in England for five years. Her English language was assessed as between Levels 3 and 4 English (National Curriculum subject). It is generally held that Year 9 pupils should be at Level 5 (Level 8 is the highest). The transcript begins at a point when the pupils were completing their exercise individually; the teacher was moving around the classroom to help individual pupils. There was general chatting in the classroom.

Extract 1

Mean, Median and Mode

```
S  =  Sairah
S1 =  another pupil
[  ]  noise/comments related to utterance

001   S:   miss?
002        miss you know for the median when I you know
003        compare them together I've got 7 and 7 in the middle
004   T:   7 and 7 in the so you've got two numbers in the
005        middle
006   S    yeah [and they are the same
007   T         [because you've got an even number of numbers isn't
```

```
008        it?=
009   S    =yeah=
010   T    =so that's 1 2 3 4 5 6 7=
011   S    =yeah there are 20 (.) 26
012   T    right so what you do is you add them up (.) the 7 and the 7
013        and divide them by 2
014   S    oh okay
015   T    right? you get if it is 7 then you'll get 7 isn't it?=
016   S    =yeah?=
017   T    =because 7 and 7 is 14 di[vided by (unclear)]
018   S                             [yeah (.) yeah      ]
019   S    7
020   T    if it was different numbers if it was 7 and 8 then you
021        would have to=
022   S    =7.5
023        ((Background classroom talk, teacher moving away?))
024        ((Teacher returns, after approx. 6 seconds))
025   T    what if you had if you had median (.) I'm sorry mode what
026        then
027   S    mode?
028        ((Classroom background noise))
029   T    if you have two 7s and two 8s (2) then what would your
030        mode be?
031   S    7.5=
032   T    =no if all the rest of the numbers were appearing only
033        [once=
034   S1   [miss?
035   S    =yeah=
036   T    =and 7 and 8 was appearing twice
037   S    hmmmn
038   T    then you can have two modes (.) 7 and 8 because it is the
039        most frequent number
040   S    would you have 7.5?
041   T    =no that, that (unclear) if it [was the mean  ]
042   S                                    [so if that was] yeah
```

```
043   T   =right? if it is a mode then you can have two modes

044   S   (unclear)

045   T   so what numbers (.) right you've got 8 more her    isn't it?=

046   S   =yeah=

047   T   =and if I gave you a set of numbers and I said no pencil

048       [T responding to another pupil] if I gave you a set of

049       numbers there 1 2 3 3 4 8 9 8 8 7 6 5 7 7 (.) so what's the

050       mode there? (.)    you've got 1 2 3 8s and 1 2 3 7s isn't

051       it?=

052   S   =yeah=

053   T   =so the mode will be 8 (7)=

054   S   =8 and 7?

055   T   =8 and 7=

056   S   =okay=

057   T   =so you have two modes (.) okay?=

058   S   =okay yeah
```

We will adopt Scollon's (1996) discourse framework of production and reception roles, which is itself an extension of Goffman's (1981) work on 'production format' roles. This framework comprises two parallel sets of discourse roles:

Productive		Receptive
animator	*mechanical*	receptor
author	*rhetorical*	interpreter
principal	*responsible*	judge

(Scollon 1996: 4)

The three productive roles are usually played by the same person in an act of social communication: the participant speaker uses their own voice (animator) to express their meaning (author) and normally they will take responsibility for what they say (principal). In parallel, when a person hears something (receptor) they normally try to make sense of what they hear (interpreter), and would make a decision as to what to do with what they hear (judge) in their response. In most everyday situations these productive and receptive roles tend to be played out voluntarily on a moment-by-moment basis.[14] The relevance of this discourse framework lies in its capacity to determine the degree/extent of *understanding* on the part of the participants in classroom interaction and communication. Why is understanding important here? It is important because understanding is very much part of the meaning-making process.[15] Consistent with the 'learning through curriculum participation and communication' view adopted by the mainstreaming policy discourse is the social constructivist idea that learning is situated in interaction and is part of a transactional process of meaning-making. Wells (1995: 238; see also Wells 2002; Alanen et al. 2008) puts it in this way:

> ... as soon as the situated and transactional nature of the learning and teaching encounter is recognised, it becomes clear that learning is as much a social as an individual endeavour and that meanings that are constructed occur, not within, but between individuals ... furthermore, these meanings, far from being neutral and value-free, are shaped by the social activities from which they arise and toward which they are directed. In simpler terms, what we learn depends crucially on the company we keep, on which activities we engage in together, and on how we do and talk about these activities.

Achieving and sharing understanding of what is being talked about is clearly part of the meaning-making process. The interpreter-author and judge-principal roles in the Scollon framework can help make this process analytically more visible because the utterances associated with these roles reflect the extent to which participants have made sense of each other's meaning/s.

To turn to the data at hand, both Sairah and the teacher were engaged in a sustained way in a mathematics task on mean, median and mode. Both were 'on task' throughout this sequence of exchanges. I will focus primarily on Sairah's utterances. Sairah's initiation and posing of a question in the form of a task-completion frame in lines 001–003 signalled that she wanted to confirm her understanding of the procedural steps involved in working out a mathematical median (animator, author and principal). Her use of the term 'compare' (line 003) might have indicated a slight misunderstanding (or lack of knowledge) of the procedure (as suggested by the teacher's utterance in line 010). And this might have led to the teacher's extended effort to work out the answer with Sairah. In line 004 the teacher started what appeared to be an explanation of how one would deal with two numbers of the same value in the middle position of a distribution of numbers, and this effort stretched over several subsequent turns (lines 007, 008, 010, 012, 013, 015 and

017). Sairah seemed to follow the teacher's mathematical working in these turns; for instance, in line 011 she jumped in with an answer during the teacher's counting up of the numbers in the distribution, and in line 022 she gave the correct answer for the averaging of the two median numbers. So far then, Sairah's participation in this interaction displayed all six productive and receptive roles, and she showed understanding of her teacher's expressed mathematical meanings.

However, things appeared to become considerably less clear for Sairah from line 025 onwards. The teacher's switch to the concept of 'mode' seemed to touch on a concept unfamiliar to Sairah. Her echoing of the term 'mode' in the teacher's question with a question tone signalled unfamiliarity (line 027, reception with uncertain interpretation), and this is confirmed in line 031 when she gave an incorrect answer to the answer on mode (incorrect interpretation and authoring an incorrect answer): 7.5 is incorrect because it represents the mean of 7 and 8, whereas a mode is the most frequently occurring value in a distribution of numbers. In this particular case there were two such values, 7 and 8. The teacher at this point attempted, once again, to work out the reasoning for the calculation of mode with Sairah in lines 032, 033, 038, 039. But Sairah did not appear to have understood this exposition, and repeated her previous answer '7.5' in line 040.

Despite her apparent struggle with the concept of mode, Sairah continued to display all six productive and receptive roles in her interaction with the teacher. This suggests that Sairah was interested in continuing with this piece of mathematics work. At that point the teacher explicitly corrected Sairah by saying 'it was the mean' (line 041) and went on to restate the steps involved in finding the mode in lines 047–051. Sairah's response 'yeah' in line 052 can be interpreted either as a signal of understanding or as a localised follow-on response to the teacher's tag question 'isn't it'. From a mathematics content point of view, however, this response does not indicate that Sairah had made use of her teacher's explanation. After the teacher reconfirmed the answer in line 053, Sairah repeated '8 and 7' as a question (line 054, incorrect interpretation of the information supplied), signalling continuing difficulties in grasping the concept of mode. Insofar as Sairah was making an effort to provide some sort of answer, this seems to indicate her interest in continuing with the interaction with the teacher (by playing the receptor, judge, animator, author and principal roles); the role of interpreter was much less easy to ascertain in this moment of interaction. The teacher re-confirmed the answer in lines 055 and 057 again, and Sairah's 'okay' in lines 056 and 058 served to complete this particular interaction. Both of these turns seem to be acknowledging responses (receptor role). The lack of explicit display by Sairah that she had been able to follow the teacher's reasoning does not, of course, preclude the possibility that she might have some sense of the meaning of mode at some level. There was, however, little in the data to suggest that Sairah actually made use of her teacher's exposition to produce an explicitly task-oriented response (no interpreting, judging and authoring, let alone taking responsibility as principal) in these final exchanges. There is in fact very little sign of understanding on Sairah's part from line 025 onwards. The 'what' (content meaning) in the interaction was not grasped. Therefore, in all probability Sairah was adopting a reactive coping strategy; she simply accepted the teacher's proffered answer at the close of this interaction.

Beyond social participation

In terms of the curriculum pupil identities discussed earlier, it is quite clear that Sairah was a user of the opportunities generated through direct participation. She cannot easily be seen as an ignored and diffident pupil. She took the initiative in approaching the teacher and participated in the exchanges in ways that would suggest engagement. Her attempts to check understanding, even when she appeared to have difficulties in grasping the meaning at hand (for example, line 51), suggest that she knew her right to engage the teacher as a pupil. In that sense she was comfortably aligned in this interactional frame with the teacher. The teacher responded to Sairah attentively, and even took it upon herself to extend Sairah's initial question, and she raised the issue of mode. The data would suggest that in this episode she treated Sairah as an individual of equal worth. She did not back off when Sairah appeared to be struggling with the concept of mode. She repeated and reformulated the content information in slightly different ways, and in so doing she was also providing helpful models of language use. She persisted with her effort (line 029 onwards) and gave an explicit judgement when (line 041) Sairah supplied an incorrect answer. In this sense Sairah was offered no 'concessions' as an EAL pupil; there was no backing off on the part of the teacher.

In fact, there is little in the data to suggest that Sairah was treated as a less competent user of English. Superficially then, the data in this episode would suggest that Sairah was a fluent speaker of English in the everyday sense. Her difficulties in following the teacher's exposition on mode point to a complex issue in terms of understanding subject content through English in a classroom context. It is well recognised in the established EAL literature that there is a difference between fluency in the use of everyday social communication and ability to use English for academic purposes; indeed Cummins's BICS and CALP tap into this difference (also see Scarcella 2003; Schleppegrell and Colombi 2002, among others). But for curriculum subject teachers who have not been trained in EAL, this is not an easy distinction. This problem, in all probability, has been made worst by the fact that in England teachers in general have been actively encouraged to see EAL development as part of classroom communication, and to regard active pupil participation in tasks as a positive sign of language development. So, as long as there is communication on subject content and there are signs of pupil engagement, then the EAL part of the teacher's job can be said to have been accomplished. In this case the teacher is a maths specialist, and from the data it is quite clear that she was very much concerned with the mathematics content. Her exchanges with Sairah do not betray any signs of specific attention to potential language difficulties.[16]

There is, then, a reasonable case for saying that while participation in classroom activities can provide opportunities for meaning-making and meaning-taking, and understanding and learning can be achieved along the way, successful outcomes are, however, not automatically assured.

Learning in social participation: Action and mind

In the earlier discussion on curriculum pupil identities it was suggested that they serve to underpin policy options and to foreground selective aspects of curriculum and pedagogical provision. These identities, once established, are durable within the lifetime of a particular policy regime and in time they can become criterial indicators of 'quality' of educational provision. For instance, one can readily see traces of the four curriculum pupil identities in this OFSTED (2001: 11) guidance for secondary school inspectors:

When observing a lesson, note whether some or all of the following features are present – all are important for developing bilingual learners:

- enhanced opportunities for speaking and listening;
- effective models of spoken and written language;
- a welcome environment in which bilingual pupils feel confident to contribute ... ;

and again in a more recent version:

> All EAL learners have a right to access the National Curriculum ... Pupils learn more quickly when socialising and interacting with their peers who speak English fluently and can provide good language and learning role models. (OFSTED 2008: 17)[17]

Seen in this light, the officially preferred curriculum pupil identities have displaced other views and perspectives. Let's suppose that a school inspector, armed with the above OFSTED guidance, observed the same interaction between Sairah and her mathematics teacher. On the criteria set out by the official guidance it would be very likely that this interaction would contribute to a favourable judgement of the quality of teaching and learning in this lesson. But how 'good' was this interaction in terms of learning? The answer depends on how far one would want to go beyond the confines of the officially preferred pupil identities.

Two issues stand out immediately. First, does participation mean achieving understanding and learning? There is a reasonable case to say that, despite active engagement with the task, Sairah and her teacher did not accomplish a shared understanding of mode in any explicit way. As shown by the analysis of this part of the interaction, Sairah showed little sign of active use of the information given to her. Yet in participation terms she was an active user of the opportunities generated through direct participation. By any account, she played her part as an active participant, and the teacher responded to her in a pedagogically sanctioned way. In a sense both Sairah and the teacher did and said all the 'right' things to play themselves as teacher and pupil. Ivanič (2006: 13), for instance, suggests that participants in communication can construct themselves and one another by 'address – the way we are talked to by others' and 'by affiliation – the way we talk like others'. Sairah talked like a pupil: she asked curriculum-related questions, and she showed appreciation by acknowledging the information given to her. The teacher talked to Sairah like a teacher by giving her relevant information on subject-based concepts and by extending Sairah's initial question to cover a related concept. This raises the very interesting question of how far active participation in classroom activities is by itself a useful indictor of a desirable educational quality. It would seem possible that one can talk and behave like a projected 'good' pupil in a seemingly supportive environment, without achieving understanding and learning.

Second, is the conferred identity of 'the EAL pupil as an individual of equal moral worth (don't treat people differently)' potentially inimical to 'the EAL pupil as a less competent user of English in need of help'? In an educational environment where teachers are encouraged to include EAL learners in all classroom activities, and where they are informed that curriculum-related communication is good for EAL development, it is not difficult to see that this kind of advice can be used as a licence for teachers to 'treat everyone the same', leading to a kind of 'homogenised' view of pedagogy. But if pupils are not to be differentiated in terms of participation in curriculum activities, how would one go about approaching the EAL pupil as 'a less competent user of English in need of help'? To be sure, individual teachers, drawing on their experience and common sense, do make efforts to provide differentiated support for their pupils. The point here, though, is that there is inherent tension in policy articulation.

Take as an example Sairah's apparent difficulties with mode. Her problems might have begun with the way the question on mode was phrased and presented by the teacher (line 025). This initiated a new topic in an informal question which included a slip of the tongue and self-correction. This might have added to Sairah's initial uncertainty as to what was being asked of her. The teacher went on immediately to ask an if-then question on mode without responding to Sairah's answer, which might have been intended as a clarification request (line 027). Given the level of classroom noise at that moment it was possible that the teacher did not hear Sairah's question. It is a moot point here whether the teacher should have continued with the mathematics procedures and whether she should have defined the concept of mode at this moment. The important issue here is that the apparent lack of understanding on the part of Sairah did not appear to have been registered by the teacher. This failure to communicate meaning effectively could be seen as an instance of a pupil failing to learn a piece of mathematics. Although it is beyond the scope of the present discussion, it would be interesting to consider which of the English language expressions used might have contributed to the communication failure. For instance, one might ask how far negatively framed conditional expressions such as 'not if...' (line 032) might have added to the pupil's language and communication difficulties.

In a context where there is little systematic EAL professional training, particularly for curriculum subject teachers, it is far from obvious what helping EAL pupils' English might entail. Of course, some areas of language may be more amenable to teacher action than others. For instance, most teachers, irrespective of their subject specialisms, would find it relatively easy to conceptualise what 'teaching vocabulary' might mean. It would be far more difficult to grasp the complexities of talk, because talk in interactional contexts (when language is in flight) is difficult to monitor and control. Perhaps it would be important to emphasise that this discussion is not designed to blame teachers for dereliction of duty. Rather, the point is that helping pupils to develop their English language is not an easy task, not something that can be achieved without considerable professional and infrastructural support, articulated within a theoretical framework that grapples with the meaning of learning in context.

As pointed out a little earlier, both Sairah and her teacher played their part well in enacting the parts of pupil and teacher – they engaged in curriculum-based communication in an active way. And in terms of the 'learning through curriculum participation and communication' view, this should be seen as a happy episode of teaching which will lead to learning of both subject content and EAL. The analysis above, however, suggests that engagement itself may not automatically lead to understanding, let alone learning. Engaging in mathematics tasks through an additional language introduces further layers of communicative complications. The issue here is that if social participation cannot be seen as a facilitator of both curriculum content and EAL learning, then we would need a different epistemic understanding of social participation and meaning sharing.

Instead of seeing classroom participation as paving the way towards learning, it may well be necessary to see participation in social activities as a moment in which both engagement and cognition are constituted and revealed at the same time. Social activities, particularly those related to curriculum learning, in the classroom are not completely random happenings; many classroom activities are either planned or routinised. As such they can be regarded as part of a social practice. Schatzki (1996), working in a Wittgensteinian tradition, proposes a notion of social practice that is directly relevant to this discussion.

> A practice may be identified as a set of considerations, manners, uses, observances, customs, standards, ... principles and rules ... specifying useful procedures or denoting obligations or duties which relate to human actions and utterances. (Schatzki 1996: 96)

The course of a person's action, however, is not prescribed by established practice in a preordained way. An individual's action in any given situation depends on the understanding they have of their own goal (however defined) and 'the motive ("sentiment") out of which a particular action conducive to wished-for condition is "chosen"' (Schatzki 1996: 96). Social practices are therefore background considerations which individuals can choose to observe or ignore in pursuance of their goals. A significant aspect of this view of social practice, for the present purposes, is the non-separation of action or interaction (participation) and mind (cognition).[18]

> ...behavior and expressions on the one hand and understanding and language on the other are bound together within social practices...'mind' is how things stand and are going for someone. These matters are expressed in bodily activities and formulated in 'mental state' language. Mind is thus constituted within and carried by practices, where these locutions are used and people acquire the abilities and readiness to perform and to understand a range of bodily doings and sayings. (Schatzski 1996: 24, emphasis added; see also Wittgenstein 1953, 2001: 135–6c)

On this view, the episode of interaction between Sairah and the teacher discussed earlier would suggest that in the extended exchanges 'things' were not going well for Sairah as far as understanding (and learning) of the concept of mode was concerned. From line 025 onwards Sairah's apparent difficulty in grasping the mathematical idea of mode was evinced by her utterances. Her repeated return to the idea of mean when the teacher had gone on to mode must be seen as an instance of, at best, unclear and uncertain understanding of the teacher's utterances.

By adopting this more holistic integrated action and mind perspective on curriculum participation, it is possible to go beyond interaction and participation as indices for learning in a somewhat formalist and unproblematised way, and to pay attention to moment-to-moment meaning- making and sharing (or the lack of it). Seen in this light, much of what happened after line 025 would signal the dangers of treating participation synonymously with understanding and learning. Sairah did not seem be able to follow the teacher's questions and explanations. An integrated view of action and mind would better alert us to the points at which failure to achieve understanding and learning has occurred, and we would be in a better place to explore the sources of the difficulties in the interactional moment. Such an integrated view would endow the analysis of classroom interaction and classroom discourse with greater diagnostic and explanatory precision in relation to the notion of learning adopted in the mainstreaming policy (see Seedhouse and Walsh, this volume). All of this would enable us to open the way to investigate the language and content learning issues in the mainstream classroom in non-superficial ways.

Notes

1. The devolved nature of political administration in the UK means that the public education system in England is quite different from that in Scotland, Wales and Northern Ireland. The discussion on EAL in this chapter relates largely to developments in England. EAL is the preferred official term used by the curriculum authorities in England. In other education systems terms such as English as a second language or English language/English language learners are preferred.
2. It is interesting to note that for the past 20 years school curriculum policies in England have tended to increase content specifications, except for EAL. (For a discussion on historical developments see Edwards and Redfern 1992; Leung and Franson 2001; Rampton et al. 1997; Leung 2007, 2009.)
3. Although researchers have noted the influence of Krashen and Cummins in the official EAL curriculum formation for some time (for example, Leung 1996), explicit official acknowledgements of their work have only appeared relatively recently.
4. The 1992 version is drawn from the 1984 text.
5. References to first language development are found in the work of both Krashen and Cummins because researching additional language development necessarily involves learners' background language experience. Whether these researchers would rhetorically and theoretically blur the distinction between first and additional language development in this way is a moot point. Given that the work built up by these researchers is directly connected to additional/second language education, this blurring of first and additional language development is more likely to be a particular case of policy-oriented rendering.
6. The term 'bilingual' is often used in official documents to refer to EAL learners; 'Bilingualism' here denotes EAL learning.
7. Some EAL learners in mainstream schools are beginners with background schooling in another language, while others are from long-settled ethnolinguistic minority communities who may be fluent speakers of local varieties of English for everyday purposes, but they may need to further develop their capacity to use English for academic purposes. See Harris (1997) for a discussion.
8. See Note 2.
9. Bakhtin (1981: 84) uses this term to refer to '... the connectedness of temporal and spatial relationships that are artistically expressed in literature'. The protagonists in narratives are often endowed with particular characteristics: 'The chronotope as a formally constitutive category determines to a significant degree the image of man in literature as well.' (Bakhtin 1981: 106).
10. The various national strategies (for example, DfEE, 2001), designed to raise academic achievements for the whole school population, in the past ten years or so have tended to be prescriptive in terms of curriculum specification.

11. The label 'bilingual pupils' is often used in a general and sometimes confusing way in the official curriculum documents. It includes bilingual or multilingual pupils from minority communities who are UK-born and have high levels of competence in English, and pupils from a variety of community backgrounds (including those from outside the UK) who are learners of English.

12. The introduction of the National Literacy Strategy (DfEE, 1998), with its explicit specifications for the teaching of structural features of English at word, sentence and text levels, has created some opportunistic backwash into official EAL guidance. In more recent official EAL guidance publications, elements of the prescriptions for the teaching of structural features (with an English-as-a-mother-tongue orientation) have been incorporated into EAL discussion (for example, DfES 2007). However, there is little discussion on how these structural features are meant to be taught within a differentiated pedagogical perspective that would address the diverse needs of EAL pupils at different ages with different language learning needs.

13. This piece of data is an extract of a much larger corpus collected for the ESRC-funded project entitled 'Urban classroom culture and interaction', RES-148-25-0042.

14. Furthermore, they do not have to be played by the same person, either as speaker or hearer. For instance, a secretary may take a message (receptor) and pass it on without needing to interpret it, let alone judge the value or merit of the message content. Similarly a bilingual interpreter may provide a rendition of what they hear (animator and author, in the language of production) without taking responsibility for the content of the message. So much depends on what a person can and/or would want to claim in a particular interaction in a moment-by-moment basis.

15. Also see Stubbs (1983: Chapter 9) for an earlier discussion on 'acknowledge', 'accept' and 'endorse'.

16. Perhaps it should be pointed out that with English-as-a-first-language pupils, their participation in learning activities is not automatically regarded as a sign of content (and language) learning. Researchers such as Mary Kalantzis and Bill Cope, for instance, raise issues such as the need to make use of appropriate technologies and the need to switch into appropriate language registers and genres in their discussions on learning (see http://newlearningonline.com/multiliteracies/).

17. Much of this resonates with Krashen's (for example, 1985) and Krashen and Terrell's (1983) arguments, and perhaps with the wider communicative language teaching literature. But these possible influences have not been acknowledged in official documents.

18. Schatski (1996: 23) argues that although the idea that 'mind is social' is fairly commonplace, it is important to see how the relationship between 'mind' and 'social' is construed in Wittgenstein's work: '... most contemporary theories treat mind as either an abstract apparatus or an underlying cognitive one that is functionally or causally responsible for bodily functions... In Wittgenstein, by contrast, mind is a collection of ways things stand and are going that are *expressed* by bodily doings and saying.' (Original italics.)

12
Participation and Instructed Language Learning

Joachim Appel

Introduction

The following chapter explores the relationship between participation and learning. It does so for a particular type of learning situation, a young learners' class taught in a teacher/whole-class alignment. The chapter addresses the following research question: How does participation contribute to the instructed learning of a foreign language?

Instructed language learning is one particular, context-specific type of language learning. It has two aspects, an interactive one and a cognitive one. Since verbal data on classroom interaction are studied here, an evaluation of learning will necessarily have to rest on student and teacher utterances in interaction, including verbal but also non-verbal features of language (such as prosody and paralinguistic features). These features can be shown to display comprehension of participation frameworks, comprehension of targeted forms, and uptake of these forms.

Instructed language learning means that students learn subject-specific forms of participation. Mastery of these forms can be inferred from the degree of coordination between teacher and student actions. This coordination is made possible through mutual understanding of the interactive meaning of these actions. In the data such understanding can be seen, for instance, in the teacher's reactions to student contributions. Reactions include confirmation, insistence on the intended framework, or realignment. Examples of these can be found in the data.

The cognitive element in instructed language learning is represented by the notion of academic task structure (Erickson 1982). The academic task structure of a lesson is an agenda that has been planned by the teacher. It comprises a focus on certain features of language and a series of steps and tasks learners are intended to go through. Both steps and tasks have been designed on the base of the logic of the subject matter. With regard to academic task structure learning can be evaluated through instances of student use of the form(s) targeted. These range from an imitation of a model to more independent use. Comprehension of forms focused on in the academic task structure can be evaluated through student contributions.

In order to address the question of how participation contributes to instructed language learning, a concept of participation is developed that can be used for analysing classroom discourse (part one of this chapter). This concept will refer to five aspects: a macro and micro level of interaction, speaker and listener roles, and the multiparty nature of classroom discourse. In part two of this chapter the notion of academic task structure is developed with the help of classroom data. The focus of the academic task structure in these data is the regular plural of nouns in English. Part three shows how academic task structure is realised through participation frameworks installed and learned by students and the teacher. Part four looks at evidence for student uptake of the form focused on in the academic task structure.

Participation

Participation refers to the question: Does someone have access to interaction, and in what capacity? As a speaker? As a hearer? As someone who is merely listening in? As someone who controls the content of what she says, or as someone who merely gives her voice to ideas and words decided on by others?

Participation has been discussed in different fields of research, most prominently in the analysis of verbal interaction (Goffman 1981) and in linguistic anthropology (Duranti 1997; Goodwin and Harness Goodwin 2004). In linguistic anthropology participation is defined as 'actions demonstrating forms of engagement performed by parties within evolving structures of talk' (Goodwin and Harness Goodwin 2004: 222). Taking this definition as a starting point, a number of aspects characterising participation can be identified. First, participation operates within 'evolving structures of talk', that is, within a wider context and longer stretches of interaction. These structures are dynamic. Second, participation includes a 'demonstration' of actions that make observable what sort of involvement is intended by participants. Third, participation includes different and changing forms of involvement. Fourth, participation may involve more than two parties.

Goodwin and Harness Goodwin's definition refers to conversation, and especially to the telling of stories in conversation. The following part of this chapter tries to apply the above aspects of participation to language teaching interaction. Drawing on research literature and on classroom data, participation can be shown to operate on four levels:

Macro level

Participation operates on a macro level of classroom interaction, that is, over longer stretches ('phases', 'episodes') of interaction within a lesson. Typically these stretches of interaction have relatively stable participation frameworks. Some of them have been identified in early research on participation. Philips (1983) gives a typology of alignments she found in the classrooms studied by her: the teacher and the entire class, the teacher and a small group, the teacher and an individual student, and students working individually.

Macrostructures are, for instance, rituals and routines. Extract 1 is an example of such a routine. At the beginning of a lesson the teacher hands out nametags (cf. Appel 2007 for a more detailed analysis). Each time she gives a nametag to a student she asks the question 'How are you?' The child then answers and is given a nametag.

Extract 1

```
001 T:   And Bastian? Bastian how are you?
002 S1:  I'm fine thank you.
         standing, sits down when he has obtained his nametag
003 T:   Kilian? Who is Kilian? That's you?
         is given nametag, remains seated
004      Christine? Christine, how are you?
005 S2:  I'm fine.
         stands up to collect nametag, answers while standing
006 L:   And Sandra? Silvi? Silvi how are you?
         both collect their nametags
```

The way the children are expected to participate is highly routinised and clearly set out. They get their nametag, answer 'fine' or 'fine thank you', and sit down. Their understanding of the pattern of participation is supported by physical action. They can learn how to participate by observing others. A detailed analysis of a macrostructure is given in the next part of this chapter: see especially extract 4 and extract 6.

Micro level

Participation also operates on a micro level of interaction. Participation frameworks are communicated in an indirect and implicit way. They are demonstrated to participants through so-called contextualisation cues. These contain information as to how a particular utterance is to be understood (Auer 1992; Gumperz 1992a, b). Contextualisation cues are typically non-referential and non-lexical. Code switching (Auer 1995), and especially prosody and paralinguistic features (Auer 1992), can function as contextualisation cues. From the point of view of the teacher such cues (voice, tone, pitch, tempo) are resources for classroom management (Dorr-Bremme 1990).

Consider (004) – (006) in extract 1. In (004) and (006) there is contrastive stress on 'you'. This serves as a contextualisation cue containing information as to how (004) and (006) are to be understood in interactive terms. It indexes the series-character of the interaction. (004), for instance, points backward and forward in the history of interaction. Before Christine is asked in (004), Bastian has been asked in (001). It is likely that after (004) someone else will be asked, in our case Silvi in (006). In this way contrastive stress as a contextualisation cue contributes to the predictability of the series of exchanges.

Speaker and hearer roles

Participation refers to the various speaker and listener roles suggested by Goffman's (1981) notion of 'footing'. The concept of footing had originally been developed to address the inadequacy of a model of communication positing only the speaker and the hearer as participants. Such a model was felt to be inadequate, because it did not account for the various and changing alignments participants take towards each other in interaction. In order to capture these alignments a division of the speaker and the hearer into different roles was suggested by Goffman (1981). On the part of the speaker such roles include that of an animator simply lending his or her voice to words composed by an author, and decided on by a principal who takes responsibility for what is said. Hearer roles include that of a ratified participant (who can be addressed or unaddressed) or a bystander, who can listen intentionally as an eavesdropper or unintentionally as an overhearer (Goffman 1981;

see also Levinson 1988 and Irvine 1996 for a critical account). Extract 2 illustrates how learners act in the participant role of an 'animator'.

Extract 2

```
001 T:    it's a window. Can you say it?
002 S1:   (1.7) it's a window.
003 T:    can you all say it?
004 Ss:   it's a window.
          reciting
```

In the exchange the students lend their voices to words decided on by the teacher as a principal. S1 repeats the phrase 'it's a window'. The teacher then asks the whole class to 'animate' the phrase.

Multiparty discourse

It is one of the merits of CA-led research into footing (Duranti 1997; Goodwin and Harness Goodwin 2004) to have shown that even a small number of participants can create participation structures of considerable complexity. An even greater complexity can be found in whole-class frameworks where teachers address – often simultaneously – the group as a whole, subgroups, and individual students (Lörscher 1986). Participation in the language classroom is multiparty discourse and classroom interaction is a nexus of interrelated speech exchange systems (Markee 2004). These include non-official participation (Toohey 2001; van Dam 2003).

Extract 3 illustrates the multiparty character of participation in the classroom. A dialogue between the teacher and an individual student, that is, a dyadic participation structure, functions in a so-called 'conduit' relationship (He 2003). The teacher overtly addresses an individual student. However, what is said is intended as a model for the whole group.

Extract 3

```
115 T:    Christine? (0.7) ↓How old< are you:. [(5.6)
116 Ss:                    [( ) (Ich mal-)
                           Let me (answer)
117 Sx:   (whispering to her)
```

```
118 T:    ↓How old are you:
119 Sx:   ((whispering))(acht)    Wie alt bist du,
                          eight    How old are you?
120 S:    ↑Eight,
121 T:    =Okay.(1.0) Janine? (1.0) G'morni:ng.
```

On one level we have a teacher-student exchange with Christine as an addressed participant. On a second level, interaction takes place in the unofficial domain in the classroom. Here other students participate in the interaction, supporting Christine, prompting her, and translating for her.

Participation, learning, and academic task structure

Participation has been linked to a wide range of issues related to learning, for example, socialisation (Rogoff 2003), L1 acquisition (for example, Bruner 1983), and school learning (Au 1980; Erickson 1982; Philips 1972, 1983; Sfard 1998; Sfard and Kieran 2001). Goffman's original framework especially has been used for the analysis of language teaching interaction (Abdesslem 1993; Appel 2007; He 2003; Kasper 2004; Mori 2004; van Dam 2002, 2003).

Studies taking a sociocognitive perspective have considered learning and participation as more or less identical. With reference to Lave and Wenger (1991) learning is seen as a 'social accomplishment' and as a development towards fuller participation in the learning situation (cf. Atkinson et al. 2007; Young and Miller 2004).

No doubt learning and participation are closely connected. There is substantial evidence to show that participation can support learning (Atkinson et al. 2007; Hall 1998; Kasper 2004; Mackey et al. 2007; Mori 2004; Poole 1992; van Lier 2000). However, there is also evidence that participation may actually constrain learning. Early research into participation showed how participation structures in a school classroom might restrict the learning opportunities of children who are used to different forms of participation from their family background (cf. Au 1980; Philips 1972, 1983). Participation can constrain learning in various other ways. Teachers may treat pupils differentially and establish subgroups in their class (Hall 1998). Students may be denied access to learning opportunities due to unfavourable participant roles in their peer group (Toohey 2000, 2001). Coordinating participation in pair work might put a strain on learning (Sfard and Kieran 2001). Differing orientations of learners in group work can make task accomplishment difficult (Mori 2004). With regard to language teaching, the IRF-structure customary in classroom discourse may deprive learners of opportunities to practise forms of participation – like initiating topics – that are vital in communication outside the classroom (Lörscher 1986; Schwab 2007). Finally, social considerations (for example, face work) might take precedence over learning (Markee 2004; van Dam 2002).

It therefore seems reasonable to assume that participation cannot simply be equated with learning. The position taken in this chapter is that participation affects learning, for example by providing space and opportunities for cognitive processes (He 2004; Kasper 2004; Mori 2004). In order to understand instructed language learning, both participatory and cognitive aspects of learning have to be considered.

Erickson (1982) has introduced the terms 'academic task structure' and 'social participation structure' to refer to these two aspects of classroom discourse. This distinction has also been used for the analysis of language teaching (Johnson 1995). Academic task structure is defined as 'a patterned set of constraints provided by the logic of sequence in the subject-matter content of the lesson' (Erickson 1982: 154). Social participation structure is defined as 'a patterned set of constraints on the allocation of interactional rights and obligations of various members of the interacting group' (Erickson 1982: 154). Similar distinctions between the goal, theme, subject or 'pedagogical focus' of interaction (Seedhouse 2004) on the one hand, and structures of participation related to this goal on the other, have been used in a variety of studies on language teaching and on teaching other subjects (Johnson 1995; Lemke 1990; Seedhouse 2004; Sfard and Kieran 2001; van Dam 2002; Wells 1993). In the following discussion the term 'participation', which covers a wider range of phenomena, will be used instead of 'social participation structure'.

The academic task structure of a transaction in the classroom represents the cognitive side of learning. It consists of intended learning states (cf. Walsh and Seedhouse this volume), and therefore is an important element in the task-as-workplan (cf. Seedhouse 2004). Academic task structures are characterised by a thematic focus, and the presentation of this focus as a series of tasks in an instructional sequence. This sequence is incremental, with each new step introducing an additional task element for the learner. This can be seen in extract 4 (capital

letters have been inserted in order to identify the logical structure of
the sequence):

Extract 4

A
201 T: >Look here,< (1.0)
202   ↑This (1.4) is – a – ↓p^hear. (1.4)
203 S: P^hhear.
204 T: ↓Pear.

B
205   And here (1.3) are – three – pears.
206 Ss: (softly) three

C
207 T: Hm. . I like pears
208   Ronja
209   Do you like pears?
210 S1: (2.1)
211 T: Magst Du ´pears`? Yes?
        Do you like
212 T: Anna-Sophie, do you like pears?
213 S: Yes.
214   (action)

The macrostructure behind the entire teaching episode studied here
consists of three steps: A-B-C. The same sequence is 'repeated' in extract
6, this time with a different noun. The academic task structure in extract
4 has been designed to proceed in the following sequence. In step A, the
teacher introduces a lexical item by taking a flashcard showing a piece
of fruit (pear, banana, plum, and so on), and holding it up. In step B the
teacher introduces the plural form together with the numeral 'three'
by taking three flashcards showing three pears, bananas, plums, and
so on, and holding them up. In step C the teacher asks students – using
the plural form in her question – whether they like a particular type of
fruit. Students are only required to answer with 'yes' or 'no'.

One fundamental characteristic of the academic task structure displayed
in extract 4 is that – with the exception of (211) – the L2 is the exclusive

medium of instruction. The reason behind this choice is a collectively held belief or ideology in language teaching that learners' L1 should be banished from the L2 classroom. Since the days of the direct method and audiolingualism this belief has been widely accepted in teacher training. It has also been propagated in the teaching context studied here.

In our data the L2 plays a dual role as both the object of instruction (that is, the plural as the focus of the academic task structure) and its medium (that is, use of the L2 to display form and meaning of the plural). At the same time the L2 is only very partly available to the learners. Instruction therefore has to rely on a number of non-verbal strategies to supply necessary information about the input. Steps A and B demonstrate the meaning of the plural by contrasting a single object (step A) with three objects (step B). In (207) the teacher acts out the meaning of the term 'to like'. The 'hm' is performed with paralinguistic features signalling something like 'yummie'. The meaning of the linguistic focus of the academic task structure is presented without recourse to a metalanguage, whether L1 or L2, but implicitly through contextualisation cues relying on paralinguistic features. Such features are not only used in order to display the thematic focus of the academic task structure. They also serve as contextualisation cues that establish coherence between different steps of the academic task structure. In (202) and (205) the teacher uses a rhythmic structure as a contextualisation cue for the coherence between steps A and B. The line (202) is, as the pauses indicate, spoken in a rhythmic pattern, that is, with a 'beat' on every word. This pattern is reproduced identically in (205). By sticking to the same contextualisation cue the teacher links up the logical steps of the academic task structure, that is, the introduction of a lexical item (step A, 202) and the introduction of a numeral plus the plural form (step B, 205). The identical rhythmic pattern connects these steps.

Due to the predominant use of the L2, a lot of information contained in the academic task structure has to be inferred from contextualisation cues. For students this leads to comprehension difficulties. In extract 4 the phrase (209) ('Do you like pears?') has quite clearly not been understood, as the long pause in (210) and the teacher's 'partial' translation in (211) ('Magst Du ´pears`? [*Do you like*] Yes.') show.

Learning to participate – developing participation

In order to get access to learning opportunities, that is, in order to become active in the classroom, students not only have to understand the subject logic behind the academic task structure, but also the participation formats intended by the teacher. Learners have to learn how to participate.

This is especially true for young learners. Young learners are still in the process of learning how to 'do school', that is, learning the mostly implicit 'ground rules' of interaction in the classroom (Edwards and Mercer 1987; Saville-Troike and Kleifgen 1986; Toohey 2000). This is even more difficult if a foreign language is the medium of instruction (Kanagy 1999). In addition young learners have to learn subject-specific ways of participating (Geekie and Raban 1994; Nystrand et al. 2003). The following extract shows how learners are still grappling with a form of participation (a 'footing') specific to the language classroom.

Extract 5

```
400 T:   What's this?
         The teacher holds up a flashcard with a picture of a watermelon.
401 Ss:  What's this?
         choral reply
402 T:   Watermelon. Put it on the table.
```

The participation framework intended by the teacher is that of an elicitation (Allwright 1988). The children are expected to respond as authors (Goffman 1981) with the correct English expression for the object on the flashcard. However, they interpret the utterance in a different framework. They assume the teacher has given them the expression 'What's this?' as a model for a collective answer (Lerner 1993), to which they are to respond in the role of animators. One part of the class answers within this framework, the other part is not quite sure as to which participation framework they should choose. The teacher (consciously or unconsciously) sticks to her original framework and answers her own question. The example shows that students may attribute an utterance to a participation framework that differs from the one intended by the teacher. It also shows how children have to cope with participation frameworks specific to the language classroom.

Differences of interpretation with regard to participant roles occur at several points in the teaching interaction and give some insight into how learners learn how to participate. Extract 6 follows immediately after extract 4. It displays the same three-step academic task structure (A-B-C) as in extract 4. The lexical item 'plum' is introduced (step A), its plural form is given (step B), and students are asked a question containing the plural form (step C).

Extract 6

A

```
215  Teacher:    ↑This,  (1.8)
                 'dramatic' pause
216  S1:         °Plum°
217  S2:         =Plum
218  S3:         [Plum
219  S4:         [ Plum
220  S5:         [    Plum
221  T:          [    Plum,
222              that's ↑right.(2.1)
                 affirming
```

B

```
223              And here - ↑a:re (1.3)
                 shows three plums
224  Ss:         Sree
225  T:          =Three:: (0.4) [plums. (1.7)
226  Ss:                        [ ( )ms
```

C

```
227  T:          I like plums. (1.7)Do you like plums? - Helena?
228  S:          Yes,
229  T:          ↑Mhm,  (0.8)
                 Her intonation signals interest in the content of
                 Helena's utterance.
230              Gelnas. >Do you like> plums?
231  S:          Yes,
232  T:          °↓Good° - this is ↑a::
233  S1:         Banana
```

Although the academic task structure is the same as in extract 4, its realisation through participation differs on all four levels described in the first part of this chapter. Starting on a micro level, let us consider the prosodic contextualisation cues used by the teacher, and the students' reaction to them. Especially for young learners, prosodic cues are vital for understanding participation structures intended by the teacher (Dorr-Bremme 1990; Kanagy 1999; Peters and Boggs 1986; Saville-Troike and Kleifgen 1986). In (215) the teacher leaves a dramatic pause after 'this'. In (216–20) the children immediately come up with the correct lexical item 'plum'. Their replies are spontaneous and uncoordinated. They have taken the long pause after 'this', plus the rising intonation on it, as a contextualisation cue signalling a transition relevance place. There is, however, some evidence that this was not intended by the teacher. In the first exchange of this type in extract 4 (202, 205), no participation in the role of a speaker had been envisaged for students. Combining the teacher's utterance in (215) with student responses in (216–20) does not yield a syntactically complete sentence. (216–20) is therefore an interruption of what the teacher is saying.

How does the teacher react? In (221) she joins in, drawing together the various overlapping replies into one choral utterance highlighting 'plum'. In (222) she acknowledges the children's answers, expressing praise or positive surprise. By reinforcing the students' reply she shows that she is taking a positive attitude towards this unexpected state of affairs. Such a move had already been foreshadowed by her reaction in (204). Here she did not insist on conventional, 'orderly' patterns of classroom interaction. Rather, she accepted the children's reaction as it came.

At first sight what happens in extract 6 is similar to what happens in extract 5. Students have interpreted contextualisation cues in a way not intended by the teacher. In extract 6 and the ensuing interaction, however, the teacher adjusts her participation framework to student participation. This happens on a macro level, that is, over a longer stretch of interaction and in several stages. In (223) the teacher again leaves a gap, because she is fetching the 'pieces' (flashcards) of fruit. The intonation on 'are' in (223) signals 'Where can I find it?', that is, the teacher is looking for the object while asking the question. Lines (223) and (225) therefore accompany the action of looking for the flashcard. They are not exclusively addressed to the children, but have an element of an aside to them. Again the children are able to supply 'three' in (224), although pronounced with an s-sound. The teacher leaves yet another gap after 'three', this time trying to get a reaction. There is no reaction after 'three' and the teacher supplies the correct form herself. Some students join in (cf. the final part of this chapter for a more detailed discussion). The same thing happens in the following extract:

Extract 7

```
230 T:  Gelnas. >Do you like> plums?
231 S:  Yes,
```

```
232 T:    °↓Good° - this is ↑a::
233 S1:   banana
234 S2:   [=banana
235 S3:   [   banana
236 T:    [       bana:na, - >that's right.<
237       And here are ↑three::
238 Ss             =bana
239 T                      =[bananas
240 Ss                     =[bananas,
241 (S)                        bananas
```

In (232) the teacher produces a 'designedly incomplete utterance' (Koshik 2002) and gets a similar pattern of reply in (233–5) to (216–20) in extract 6. Again the teacher 'synchronises' the answers in (236). In (237) the teacher produces yet another designedly incomplete utterance, through which she manages to cue in the class and get a fairly synchronous choral reply. In extract 8 the teacher produces even clearer signals as to what participation she expects.

Extract 8

B

```
245 L:    This is        ↑a::
246 S                         =cherry
247 T:                            cherry
          display speech style, emotional
248 SS:   cherry
          teacher takes flashcards from basket
249 T:    And here are ↑three:: (1.3)
250       Sylvie? (1.1)
251 S:    Cherries
252 T:    Cherries, -
253       These are three cherries. (1.9)
```

In (249) the teacher leaves a gap after 'three' that is spoken with rising intonation. In contrast to earlier B-parts she designates one student,

Sylvie (250), who then supplies the right form. Teacher initiative and student response are by now well coordinated. Looking at a macro level of participation we can see a development. Although the three steps of the academic task structure A, B, and C remain constant over their five occurrences in the data, the teacher has changed her participation framework from one of presentation with no intended speaking rights for the class in extract 4 (202, 205) to one of designedly incomplete utterances in extract 6 (223, 225, 232) and in extract 8 (245, 249), and finally – also in extract 8 – to one of addressing individual students (250). In other words, the teacher has changed the intended participant role from that of an addressed participant, that is, of a listener, in extract 4 (202, 205) to that of an 'author' in extract 8. Both teacher and class have contributed to this change. On the level of multi-party discourse the interaction has moved from uncoordinated replies in extract 6 (216–20) to more structured and better co-ordinated participation in extract 8 (249–52), where only one student speaks at a time.

The teacher not only adjusts the participation structure in order to coordinate her interaction with the children. She also uses participation as a resource for varying the complexity of the learning task. Extract 9 shows how this happens:

Extract 9

B

(...)

```
237 T:    And here are ↑three::
238 SS:                    =bana
239 T:                     =[bananas
240 Ss:                    =[bananas,
241 (S)                              bananas
```

C

```
242 T:    Who likes bananas? (2.0)
          Saphira likes bananas.
243 Ss    hm
244 T:    O::r Lots of people like bananas.
```

In (242) the teacher initiates the C-step of the sequence with a question that differs from those used in (209) and (227). She no longer uses the yes-no question 'do you like?' but asks 'Who likes ...?' Instead of addressing an individual student she now turns to the whole class. The learning task itself has been made simpler, because a non-verbal reaction is an acceptable solution. Threats to students' face are minimised. No one is picked out and put on stage for an individual teacher-student exchange. It is sufficient for students to raise their hands, if they like a certain type of fruit. Because of the non-verbal character of their response students can participate simultaneously. By setting up a new participation format the teacher has provided space for a different kind of student engagement.

Evidence for learning

How do students respond to the learning opportunities afforded through participation? In our data the focus of the academic task structure is on the plural -s. What evidence is there of students having learnt this form? The following instances of learners using the plural form can be found.

Extract 10
```
223      And here -  ↑a:re (1.3)
         shows three plums
224 Ss:  Sree
225 T:   =Three:: (0.4) [plums. (1.7)
226 Ss:             [ ( )ms
```

In (226) students imitate the form presented by the teacher, speaking more or less simultaneously with her. The same happens in extract 11:

Extract 11
```
237 T:   And here are ↑three::
238 SS:              =bana
239 T:               =[bananas
240 Ss:              =[bananas,
241 (S)                       bananas
```

In (239–40) students come in with their solution more promptly and confidently than in extract 10. Again they speak simultaneously with

the teacher. In extract 12 the teacher designates an individual student
in (250), who then produces the correct form in (251).

Extract 12

```
249 T:   And here are ↑three::  (1.3)
250      Sylvie?  (1.1)
251 S:   Cherries
252 T:   Cherries, -
253      These are three cherries.  (1.9)
```

Whether this student is representative of the state of knowledge of the
entire class can, of course, not be decided. The final try for the plural in
extract 13 suggests not.

Extract 13

```
260 T:   it´s a watermelon
261      and these are three::?
262 Ss:  watermelon
263 T:   watermelon[zz]
```

Here students do not supply the plural form. The teacher corrects their
answer, highlighting the voiced plural -s.

Looking at the above extracts, we see there is little uptake of the form
presented by the teacher. This is not surprising, because this is the very
first encounter students have had with the form. In addition the teacher
had, at that point of the lesson, not planned to provide a systematic
opportunity for using the form. Such opportunities, however, arise in
the course of the episode, because the teacher changes her participation framework. Originally she does so because students already know
some lexical items. However, she quickly extends her new framework
of designedly incomplete utterances to the presentation of the plural
form in extract 6 (225) ('Three:: (0.4) [plums'). This shows how teachers' assumptions about states of knowledge in the class can influence
whether a particular participation framework is chosen or modified
(Nassaji and Wells 2000).

One reason for the rather minimal uptake of the new form is that
students seem to make their own selection of the language they use productively. Apart from extract 4 (203) where 'pear' is selected, because

the aspiration of the initial consonant sounds poetically attractive (Appel 2007), the main criterion for selecting an item is whether it is known. This can be seen in extract 6 (224), where 'sree' is known as a numeral. When an item is taken up, this often happens in a process of 'shadowing', where students speak simultaneously with the teacher, as in extracts 14 and 15. In extract 14 (226) students echo the plural form modelled by the teacher.

Extract 14

```
225 T:    =Three:: (0.4) [plums. (1.7)
226 Ss:                  [ ( )ms
```

In extract 15 (240) they produce the plural simultaneously with the teacher:

Extract 15

```
239 T,    =[bananao
240 SS    =[bananas,
241 (S)     bananas
```

It should be noted that the episodes analysed so far lie at the beginning of the lesson. In later phases student show more uptake.

The instances of uptake of the plural -s documented in extracts 10 to 15, and also the student contributions in extracts 4 and 6, show how knowledge is distributed among different participants in the multi-party discourse of a teacher/whole-class framework. Participation in a whole-group setting therefore differs from that in instructional dialogues between the teacher and an individual student which provide the data for many sociocognitive studies (for example, Atkinson 2007). Classroom discourse with young children often means creating a 'proposition across utterances and speakers' (Ochs et al. 1979; Poole 1992). Learning processes in instructed settings are social in the sense that vital parts of them are distributed among different participants who attend to the theme of the lesson within different participation frameworks, for example as addressed individuals or as an intended audience. Multiparty discourse is a potential resource for learning, because knowledge can be aggregated and used for enabling individual students to complete a task (Kanagy 1999). On various occasions in our data different participants collectively contribute to the solution of a learning task. In extract 6 they supply the lexical item 'plum' (216–20), the numeral 'three' (224), and, though in a very subdued way, the plural form (226). In extract 4 Ann-Sophie has heard the partial translation given by the teacher for Ronja in (211). She is then able to answer the question without the help of a translation. The data discussed here therefore suggests that instructed language learning can be seen as an instance of social cognition. Cognition in the classroom observed here is social in the sense that the knowledge of several individuals, including the teacher, and other resources (flash-cards), are brought to bear on the solution of a task. In the data this task is inferring the meaning and form of the plural without recourse to the L1. Our analysis has shown how this is collectively achieved.

Conclusion

This chapter has discussed instructed language learning from two per-spectives, that of the academic task structure and that of participation frameworks behind a particular stretch of language teaching interac-tion. Academic task structure represents the cognitive side of classroom learning. It consists of a thematic or 'pedagogical' focus (Seedhouse 2004). This focus is broken down into a sequence of steps according the logic of the subject matter. These steps are intended to lead the learner to mastery of the focus. Academic task structure is realised through participation. Its mastery often depends on the mastery of forms of par-ticipation related to it. The learners' task therefore encompasses both the steps of the academic task structure and the participation formats related to these steps.

Participation and academic task structure are interrelated at all four levels on which classroom participation operates. The first two levels are connected to learning how to participate. On a macro level the sequence of steps in the academic task structure is kept constant (cf. extracts 4 and 6). On a micro level, however, these steps show a fair degree of variation, because participation is negotiated between stu-dents and the teacher. By going through this process students learn how to participate in the classroom. Their learning is documented by more and more stable and well-coordinated patterns of interaction between them and the teacher. Learning to participate starts at this micro level of participation. Here learners have to interpret contextualisation cues that indicate the interactive meaning of utterances in the classroom, for instance that of teacher interventions.

The next two levels of participation are connected to the focus and logical sequencing of the academic task structure. Participant roles can be a resource for adapting the complexity of the academic task structure. By varying these roles, the character of a learning task can be varied. A student's participant role can be changed from that of a speaker, who actively uses the language, to that of a listener. Likewise it can be changed from that an animator, who simply has to repeat words provided by someone else, to that of a principal, who decides on the content of his or her own contribution. In this way participation can provide a variety of learning opportunities. These opportunities are taken up by learners in different ways. Learners may – at least initially – select linguistic forms already known to them for active use. Or they may simply 'animate' a model provided by the teacher. Finally, multiparty discourse is connected to states of knowledge distributed among a group. These different states of knowledge are collectively used as a resource. In this sense, classroom learning is social cognition.

Last but not least, a word on teaching and the teacher. Seedhouse and Walsh (this volume) have introduced the concept of classroom interactional competence. This chapter has exemplified one aspect of this type of competence. The teacher has shown a remarkable sensitivity towards the potential of different participation formats for student learning. She was prepared to respond to student initiatives, and thus set up participation frameworks conducive to learning. She learned how to do this 'on her feet', that is, in the ongoing teaching situation. The discourse studied here is therefore as much about teacher learning as it is about student learning.

13
Building a Comprehensive Second Language Acquisition Theory

Florence Myles

Introduction

The aim of this chapter is to discuss theory building in second language acquisition research, and in particular how and whether the different schools of research currently active within the field can or indeed need to talk to one another, if we are to build a comprehensive SLA theory. My aim is to draw an overarching conceptual map of the field as I understand it; this will necessarily involve a certain amount of oversimplification, as well as my own theoretical biases.

I will start by describing my own research agenda and its empirical basis, as it has played a crucial part in determining my conceptualisation of the field. I will then outline what I see as the major research questions that need addressing, before exploring the different views of language and of learning which have typically been used to investigate them. I will conclude with the way in which I see them mostly complementing one another, offering answers to different pieces of the SLA jigsaw, rather than necessarily conflicting with one another.

Background

My own research agenda is to document and explain the **development** of French L2 over time, and to relate this analysis to theoretical understandings about the acquisition of second languages in general. Together with my research collaborators,[1] we are interested in the development of all aspects of the linguistic system, that is morphology, lexis, syntax, semantics, discourse, pragmatics, and interfaces between these sub-domains of language (David 2008a, b; David et al. 2009; Myles, 2003, 2004, 2005; Myles et al. 1998; Myles et al. 1999; Rule and Marsden

2006). We are also interested in the pedagogical implications of this research (Mitchell 2003b, 2006).

This work is based on a large database of classroom oral learner French of over three million words (FLLOC – *French Learner Language Oral Corpora*, www.flloc.soton.ac.uk; see, for example, Rule 2004 for a description), containing seven corpora of various sizes. They represent a mixture of longitudinal and cross-sectional data, with most of the learners having English as their L1 (with one Dutch L1 corpus), ranging from complete beginners to advanced learners (final year at university), performing one-to-one and group oral tasks ranging from semi-spontaneous to focused elicitation tasks. We are now also investigating the role of age in early foreign language learning, comparing beginner learners of French aged five, seven and eleven in terms of linguistic development, learning strategies, and attitudes towards foreign language learning.

The context of my research is important to understand, as it has significant implications for the way in which I view language and learning. My aim is to document and understand the development of the L2 system in these learners. I am therefore interested in what learners actually produce in order to fulfil given communicative goals, and how these productions change over time, as well as in the mechanisms underlying this development. My main focus is on the route of development, rather than on what might facilitate and speed up this development. This agenda is not, of course, theory-neutral, given its developmental focus.

Research agendas in SLA

SLA researchers over the last 40 years or so have been addressing very varied research questions, ranging from the highly theoretical, for example the nature of the formal properties of human language and their implications for SLA (Hawkins 2001, 2004; Lardiere 2009; Schwartz and Sprouse 2000; Snape et al. 2009; White 2003) to the very applied, for example what should we teach learners in the foreign language classroom (Cook 2001a; Ellis 2001, 2008b; Lightbown 2000; Pienemann 1984; VanPatten 1996, 2002), with nearly as many research agendas in between as there are researchers. My belief is that all approaches have a contribution to make to a better understanding of the processes involved in second language learning and use, but that it is imperative to be clear about the precise domain of application of each theoretical paradigm. There has been a tendency in the field to assume that one theoretical approach has all the answers, which is of course nonsensical; to give just one example, a theory of, say, interaction will have little to say about the formal properties underlying the learner system, and a syntactic theory will not inform us about the co-construction of identity in L2 interactions.

In order to understand how second languages are learnt, we need to give answers to the following core questions:

1. What is the linguistic system underlying learners' performance, and how do they construct this system, at various stages of development and in each of the following:

   a. Phonology
   b. Morphology
   c. Lexis
   d. Syntax
   e. Semantics
   f. Discourse
   g. Pragmatics
   h. At the interface between these subsystems

2. What is the role of (1) the L1, (2) the L2, and (3) universal formal properties of human languages in shaping and/or facilitating this development?
3. How do learners develop their ability to access and use their L2 system in real time, that is, their processing capability?
4. What are the roles of individual differences and learning styles in shaping and/or facilitating L2 development?
5. How does input/interaction/output facilitate, shape, and/or accelerate the development of either 1 or 3 above (formal system and/or processing)?
6. How does the environment/social context facilitate, shape, and/or accelerate the development of either 1 or 3 above (formal system and/or processing)?

Some of these questions are clearly concerned with the formal properties of human languages (1 and 2), others with internal cognitive characteristics and mechanisms (3 and 4), and still others with socio-cognitive and sociocultural factors (5 and 6).

The use of language routinely involves all three (the formal, the cognitive and the social), making it imperative that we understand each one, as well as how they interact in the acquisition and use of second languages. And it is my belief that different theoretical and analytical tools are required for the investigation of each of these different facets, before we can construct a comprehensive SLA theory encompassing all three types of knowledge/competencies (formal, cognitive, interactive). I do not believe, however, as some theorists would argue, that different views of language or of learning necessarily underpin these different questions: both language and learning in my mind are fundamentally a mixture of the formal, cognitive and social, and although we need different tools to study each one, I do not see them as relying on mutually exclusive conceptions of language or of learning. I will now briefly develop each question in turn.

The objective of questions 1 and 2 is to *document and understand formal linguistic development*. Our knowledge of developmental patterns remains very patchy, especially in languages other than English and in areas other than morphosyntax, and a sound empirical basis for documenting these patterns is crucial. These descriptions will have recourse to formal paradigms not only to describe and analyse learner productions, but also to investigate the interaction and cohabitation of multiple language systems in the same mind (Cook 2003; Cook et al. 2006). There is little doubt that the formal properties of both L1 and L2 play an important role in shaping and/or facilitating development, if only in making it easier to learn closely related languages rather than typologically distant ones, but the exact way in which this interplay works is still not fully understood (see Odlin 1989, 2003). It is also clear that many of the formal properties in evidence in learner languages are not directly traceable to either the L1 or the L2. A range of theoretical frameworks have been used to investigate L2 formal properties, ranging from, for example, Universal Grammar – UG (Hawkins 2001; Snape et al. 2009; White 2003) – to associationist frameworks (N. Ellis 2008; Elllis and Schmidt 1998; MacWhinney 2001). These frameworks have very different views of language, with UG claiming that all human languages have the same basic structure which is a separate, innate module in the mind, whereas associationist or emergentist frameworks claim that languages 'emerge' from communication, through pattern recognition and use. The predictions they make about how languages are acquired are therefore very different, and these can be tested empirically.

As my third question, *How do learners develop their ability to access and use this system in real time (that is, their processing capability)*, indicates, I see the construction of the linguistic system and the development of the ability to use this system in real time as two different kinds of development, relying on different types of internal mechanism.

This dissociation seems obvious when we are confronted with learners who have highly complex linguistic systems but who are very non-fluent, or learners who are very fluent but whose system remains underdeveloped. This process of automatisation of linguistic knowledge is of course not seen by all as independent from its construction, for example in the emergentist/associationist frameworks mentioned above, but I take the view here that although they usually develop in parallel, they draw on different learning mechanisms (see for example Pienemann 2005; Towell 2003, 2007; Towell and Dewaele 2005; Towell and Hawkins 1994).

The fourth question centres on *the role of individual differences and learning styles in shaping and/or facilitating L2 development*. We know that some learners are considerably better than others at learning languages. This is clearly evidenced, for example, by beginner learners in the same language classroom who receive the same input and opportunities for interaction and yet end up with widely different levels of proficiency. Better understanding the role of intrinsic variables such as aptitude and learning style, as well as potentially more extrinsic variables such as motivation and learning context, are important in helping us understand why some learners make more and faster progress than others (for a review, see Dörnyei and Skehan 2003).

The fifth question is about *the role of input and of interaction* in L2 development, and in particular, what kind of input and interaction might facilitate, shape and/or speed up development (Gass 1997; Gass 2003; Mackey 2007; Mackey et al. 2003). Additionally, is any facilitative effect related to the type of input and/or interaction equally prevalent for the acquisition of all sub-domains of language, or is it more evident in the development of lexis, as in the 'negotiation for meaning' studies (Gass and Varonis 1994); or in the acquisition of syntax, as in the study of interrogative development (Mackey 1999)? Furthermore, what role does input/interaction/output play in the acquisition and the development of processing skills?

And my final question is about *the role of the social context*. By social context, I do not mean only in terms of, for example, the social status of the languages in question, but also in terms of the communicative needs entailed by the social context (Firth and Wagner 2007; Jenkins 2007), and in terms of the co-construction of identities, as for example in the work on communities of practice (Norton 2000; Pavlenko and Blackledge 2004). The focus here is neither on learning nor on language, but rather on the wider social context and the role that language plays in it.

This list of questions is not exhaustive of course, but I think it captures the three main research agendas which have prevailed in the field over the last 40 years or so, and which continue to shape the field today:

- question 1 (formal properties of learner language) and question 2 (role of the L1, of the L2 and of universals of languages in L2 development) are concerned with the formal properties of human languages; they focus on language, with different views of language underpinning them; they have little to say about learning;
- question 3 (processing capability) and question 4 (individual differences) relate to internal cognitive characteristics and mechanisms; their focus is on learning, with language having the same status as other conceptual tools;
- question 5 (the role of input and interaction) and question 6 (the role of the social environment) are about sociocognitive and social factors; the focus is the wider social context, with both language and learning being rather peripheral.

The use of language routinely involves all three dimensions, the cognitive, the social and the formal, making it imperative that we understand each one and how they interact in the acquisition and use of second languages. The investigation of each of these aspects, however, has traditionally relied not only on different theoretical and methodological tools, but also on very different and sometimes conflicting views of language and of language learning. The next section will outline these different perspectives.

Differing views of language and of learning

The questions I have put forward as being central to the construction of an SLA theory tend to be associated with different views of language and of learning. Moreover, the importance given to each of these questions will tend to depend on individual researchers' positions on the nature/nurture continuum. Researchers who emphasise the belief that language is primarily socially constructed will prioritise the analysis of the social forces at play in language acquisition and use, while researchers interested in understanding the nature of the formal properties of the language system will focus on the development of the formal system within individuals. Some researchers, of course, do not dissociate between the two and disagree with this dichotomy, but my own view is that, given our current state of knowledge, it is helpful to map the field in this way in order to investigate these different domains, and that both nature and nurture play an important role in language development. At one end of the nature-nurture continuum (Figure 13.1), we have the view that language is socially constructed, and does not exist outside of its social context (Block 2003; Firth and Wagner 1997, 2007; Lantolf 2000; Lantolf and Thorne 2006). At the other end, we have the view that the core of language is an internal formal system, separate from but interfacing with the conceptual, semantic and pragmatic systems (Dekydtspotter et al. 1998; Hawkins 2004; Jackendoff 2002; Schwartz and Sprouse 1996; White 2003). Somewhere in between, we have the view that language is a social construct interacting with internal formal and cognitive mechanisms, and that we have to understand both these internal and external processes.

My own view is that language acquisition is socially driven, but that there is an internal mental structure in which it has to fit (Mitchell and Myles 2004). The principal reasons underlying this belief are, on the one hand, the well-documented developmental sequences similar in all learners irrespective of first language, which to my mind are strong evidence of the formal constraints underpinning and shaping language acquisition, given the multitude of very different learning experiences encountered by learners. On the other hand, I think that the driving force behind language acquisition is primarily social, as evidenced for example by some immigrant communities who do not acquire the language of the country they live in, in spite of plentiful input; or, at the

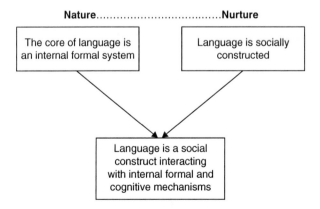

Figure 13.1 Language acquisition within the nature/nurture continuum

other extreme, by communities which switch effortlessly between an impressive number of languages required by the social context. Quite obviously, one's view of language impacts on one's understanding of learning. But I do not think that the nature and nurture ends of the continuum outlined above are necessarily incompatible; they are merely focusing on different aspects of language or of the learning process. And one can investigate, for example, the formal properties of learner language, without denying the important role that learner differences or the social environment can make to speed of acquisition or eventual attainment. Similarly, one can be primarily interested in the development of the processing system without denying that the nature of the linguistic system which learners construct is subject to certain constraints. And researchers can be interested in what learners actually do with their L2 when engaging in various social encounters, and how they co-construct meaning as well as a changing identity, without denying that these social processes interact with cognitive processes.

Before I elaborate any further, I want to very briefly summarise what we currently know about second language acquisition. If we are going to reconceptualise the field and set new agendas, we must not ignore the research findings which have shaped the field to date.

SLA research findings

In their investigation of the research questions listed above, SLA researchers have established a number of well-documented facts which seem to be characteristic of second language acquisition, which can be summarised (somewhat simplistically) as follows (for a comprehensive review, see R. Ellis 2008):

a) Second language learners follow developmental stages in their acquisition of a second (or third) language. These stages are largely independent of the first language of the learner, and of the mode of exposure (naturalistic vs instructed); moreover, these are often similar to the stages followed by children acquiring an L1 (for example the acquisition of interrogation and negation in English L2, of word order in German, and so on.).

b) The linguistic system underlying learner production is rule-governed, but these rules are often unlike the rules underlying either the L1 or the L2: for example, L2 learners go through an early stage where verbs are typically uninflected, even those learners whose L1 and L2 both obligatorily inflect verbs (Housen 2002;

Lakshmanan and Selinker 2001; Myles 2005). Additionally, learners acquire subtle grammatical properties of the L2 which do not seem acquirable from the input alone, and which they have not been taught explicitly (Dekydtspotter 2001; Dekydtspotter and Sprouse 2001; Hawkins 2004).

c) Some properties from the L1 are likely to transfer, others not; moreover, within pairs of languages, properties often transfer one way but not the other. For example, object pronouns are placed after the verb in English (*Peter paints it*) but before the verb in French (*Peter la peint*). French learners of English do not transfer French placement and never produce *Peter it paints*, whereas English learners of French go through a stage of wrongly producing postposed object pronouns in French L2: *Peter peint la* (for a review, see Mitchell and Myles 2004: 79–81).

d) The rate and outcome of the second language-learning process is highly variable, with some learners arguably becoming indistinguishable from native speakers while others fossilise at an early developmental stage; there is some variability in the route of development, both across learners and within learners, but it is relatively limited by comparison.

In attempting to draw a conceptual map of SLA theorising, it is helpful to relate these findings to the three types of approaches briefly mentioned above, namely formal approaches, cognitive approaches and sociocultural approaches. It is important to note, however, that these findings relate primarily to developmental processes rather than L2 use, a more recent field of enquiry. For each approach,[2] I will discuss its domain of application and how it has attempted to account for some of the facts outlined above.

Domain of formal linguistic approaches

The formal linguistic approach (with Universal Grammar being the most influential and productive so far within this range of approaches) has been concerned exclusively with describing and explaining the formal system underlying learner productions. Furthermore, the focus of attention has been primarily on morphosyntax, neglecting other aspects of the linguistic system. This is slowly changing, however, with current interest focusing on interfaces between morphosyntax and, for example, semantics or pragmatics (Dekydtspotter et al. 1999; Juffs 2000), and with phonology gaining momentum (Archibald 2004, 2005, 2009). The view of language characterising this approach is usually modular, with the formal properties of language being part of a distinct structure in the mind, and different aspects of language in turn being modular too (syntax, phonology and so on). The conceptualisation of learning underlying formal linguistic approaches is at best underdeveloped: for example, UG claims that, in the context of first language acquisition, all children need is language around them for acquisition to take place.

This approach has attempted to explain aspects of most of the research findings summarised above (indeed it has been at the origin of some of these findings), as follows:

a) developmental stages
    This approach might argue that, in similar ways to children acquiring their L1, second language learners' hypotheses about the L2 are constrained by the restricted possibilities afforded them by Universal Grammar. For example, the lack of inflected verbs in early stages would be due to learners not having yet acquired the functional projection hosting tense features (the Inflection Phrase),

b) interlanguage rules are often unlike both the L1 and the target language
    The example mentioned above is a case in point: the uninflected verb stage witnessed in second language learners does not reflect either the native grammar or the target grammar when both those languages inflect verbs.

c) selective transfer of L1 properties
    By comparing the formal properties of languages cross-linguistically, this approach enables us to make predictions about transfer. In the example outlined previously whereby French learners of English do not transfer pronoun placement whereas English learners of French do, this would be due to the fact that this property in French is linked to the strength of the inflection phrase which forces verbs (and their clitic pronouns) to rise to a higher position in the syntactic tree, whereas it remains in situ in English as the inflection phrase is weak and does not trigger movement (Herschensohn 2004; White 1996).

d) Variable rate and outcome of SLA process
    This approach does not enlighten us as regards variability in the rate of learning, nor in variable outcomes with learners with the same L1/L2 combination. It has, however, provided us with some testable hypotheses about why some grammatical properties might never become native-like in second language learners. For example,

it has been suggested that grammatical gender is not available as a formal feature to second language learners whose L1 does not have this feature, past the critical period[3] (Franceshina 2001; Hawkins and Franceschina 2004).

The domain of enquiry of formal linguistic approaches is the description and explanation of the formal nature of human languages, including second languages. Therefore, they cannot be made to account for processing mechanisms nor social factors which are outside this domain. Understanding of these is the domain of other theoretical approaches.

Domain of cognitive approaches

Processing approaches have been interested not so much in the formal properties of language, but on how learners gradually expand their linguistic knowledge and learn to access it increasingly efficiently in online production (Ellis 2002b; Harrington 2002; Juffs 2004; McLaughlin and Heredia 1996; Myles 1995; Pienemann 2003, 2008). Like formal linguists, their primary focus has been on the individual and what goes on in the mind of the learner, regardless of context. This is also true to a large extent of the work on individual differences, although the way in which constructs such as anxiety or motivation might be socially and culturally shaped has played some part in this subfield (Dörnyei and Skehan 2002; Dörnyei and Skehan 2003; Robinson 2002; Sawyer and Ranta 2001; Skehan 1989). The view of language underpinning these approaches is usually underdeveloped, and the focus is very much on the learning process. Learning is seen as a cognitive mechanism taking place within the individual, rather than as a social process. The contribution of this line of research to our understanding of SLA has been primarily in putting forward explanations for the large amount of variability in the rate and outcome of the acquisition process (d), but also of developmental stages (a).

Some of the explanations put forward by cognitive approaches can be selectively illustrated as follows:

a) developmental stages
    Processability Theory (Pienemann 1998, 2005, 2008, see also Chapter 5 this volume) has argued that the acquisition of processing in the second language is incremental and hierarchical, thus explaining in a principled way developmental stages, with word-level processing preceding phrase-level processing which in turn precedes sentence-level processing.

b) interlanguage rules are often unlike both the L1 and the target language
   As outlined above, the processing limitations at each stage of development in Pienemann's model will give rise to learner productions which are unlike both native and target languages. In the case of the uninflected verb stage, this will be because learners have not yet gone beyond the phrase-level processing stage.

c) selective transfer of L1 properties
   Similarly, transfer might occur one way but not the other when the processing demands for a particular structure are greater in one language than another, and therefore beyond the current processing capabilities of the learner in the L2 in one direction but not the other.

d) Variable rate and outcome of SLA process
   This is the area in which research on individual differences has had most impact. Work on, for example, aptitude, intelligence, anxiety, motivation, and so on, has found correlations between certain individual characteristics and both rate of learning and eventual success in a second language (Dornyei and Skehan 2002, 2003; Robinson 2002).

The domain of cognitive approaches is the learning mechanisms involved in the SLA process and what impacts upon them. Their underlying assumption is usually that learning a language relies on similar mechanisms to other types of learning, and their methodologies usually come from psychology.

Both formal linguistic theories and cognitive theories have met with some success in explaining some of the findings of SLA research, each bringing particular insights into specific aspects of the process. Both focus on language and/or learning within the mind of the individual learner.

Domain of sociocognitive approaches

Social theorists, conversation analysts and interactionists, by contrast with the two previous types of approaches, focus not on the individual but on the co-construction of knowledge and identity, and the role that social factors play in this process (Firth and Wagner 2007; Lantolf 2000; Lantolf and Thorne 2006; Lantolf and Appel 1994). This work ranges from macro-analyses such as the role of social factors and contexts in the (co-)construction of identity (Jenkins 2007; Norton 2000;

Toohey 2000), to micro-analyses of interactions aiming to investigate, for example, the role of scaffolding and microgenesis (Gánem Gutiérrez 2008; Lantolf and Thorne 2006; Mitchell 2004), or the way in which conversations are negotiated and co-constructed (Pekarek Doehler 2006a; Pekarek Doehler and Ziegler 2007; Seedhouse 2004). This work does not see language as existing outside of its social context and thus often disagrees fundamentally with a cognitive view of language or of learning. Consequently, their focus has not been on understanding which formal properties are being acquired and why, but rather on giving us a glimpse of the actual process of acquisition taking place in real time. Much of this research, however, is less interested in development than in L2 use, and has therefore little to say about changes in the L2 system over the course of acquisition in the longer term.

Because of this shift in focus, sociocognitive models have little to say about (a) developmental stages, (b) interlanguage rules, or (c) selective transfer of L1 properties. By investigating in great detail the kind of language use learners engage in, this approach has the potential to enable us to understand much better how the social context shapes the kinds of interactions learners engage in. This of course might shed some light on the types of interactions and social contexts which are most facilitative for L2 learning, therefore contributing to our understanding of (d), the variable rate and outcome of the SLA process, but this is not the primary goal of many of these approaches. In fact, sociocognitive theories claim that the field has been asking the wrong kind of questions, and that the focus should shift to understanding the social factors at play in the co-construction of language and identity, rather than concentrating on the learning of the formal properties of languages over time, as has been the tendency to date.

SLA theory: The Holy Grail?

To conclude, I would claim that because second language acquisition is a multifaceted phenomenon and, like language itself, it is at the same time linguistic, cognitive and social, different theoretical and methodological paradigms are required to investigate different aspects of the SLA process. Over the past four decades or so, we have moved from a series of binary questions such as 'Is L2 acquisition like L1 acquisition?', 'Is Universal Grammar still accessible to L2 learners?', 'Do L1 properties transfer to the L2?', and 'Is L2 learning like the learning of other skills?', to more subtle and complex questions such as 'What exactly is the role of the L1?', 'Which properties transfer and which do not? Why?', 'What exactly is variable in L2 learning?', 'How do L2 learners make use of their emergent L2 in real communication situations?', and 'How do L2 learners co-construct meaning and renegotiate their identity?'

As in most fields of research, as facts emerge from a growing body of empirical research, the questions raised become more complex and sophisticated. After a necessary period of time when the primary focus is to establish the facts, that is, to document what is actually happening, the time becomes ripe for theorising and investigating possible explanations. This in turn provides empirically testable questions, and as the nature of the facts, and thus the nature of our understanding, becomes increasingly complex over time, the hypotheses being tested become more subtle and powerful.

Each of the different facets of the SLA process is asking different research questions which require different theoretical and methodological tools. They all contribute to a better understanding of SLA within their particular domain. And as the focus of attention shifts to different aspects of the process, different questions are being asked. To illustrate with a concrete example illustrating my multifaceted view of both language and learning as essentially formal, cognitive and social, I will briefly outline the theoretical and methodological design underpinning a research project[4] I am just embarking on. The aim of the project is to investigate the popular belief that young children are better at learning foreign languages than older learners, in spite of at best ambiguous empirical evidence underpinning this belief (Muñoz 2008a, b).

The project will provide similar French language teaching to three groups of twenty beginner English learners aged five, seven and eleven years respectively, and will (a) compare linguistic development in these three age-groups, (b) compare rates of development at different ages after the same amount of classroom exposure, and (c) compare the classroom learning strategies used by children at different ages as well as their attitudes to language learning. These very different agendas require varied theoretical and methodological tools, ranging from the formal to the cognitive and the social. For example, our formal agenda includes testing the Critical Period Hypothesis by investigating whether young children have access to, for example, the formal grammatical gender feature inexistent in their L1, which, it has been argued, is not available to older learners. From a cognitive perspective, we will investigate the role of, for example, different levels of cognitive maturity and of literacy, as well as of learning strategies. And we will draw on sociolinguistic and sociocultural methodologies to shape our investigation of classroom interaction and of attitudes to foreign language learning.

We could not achieve our objective of understanding the role of age in early language learning without taking due account of formal, cognitive and social factors which impact on learning processes. As will have become clear, my own view is that in our current state of knowledge we need to pursue all these varied agendas. Whether and how they eventually come together to produce a comprehensive theory of SLA is some way off as yet. In the meantime it is important to be clear about the domain of application of the various paradigms, and what aspects of the SLA process they can and cannot explain. It is just as unreasonable to ask a theory focusing on the formal properties of language to inform us about processing, as it is to ask a sociocultural theory to inform us about the acquisition of, say, morphology. But we do need to understand all these different aspects of SLA, and we do need to start asking questions about how they interact with one another.

Notes

1. Rosamond Mitchell; Annabelle David; Sarah Rule; Emma Marsden.
2. Please note that in my discussion of the different paradigms, I am merely illustrating from selected theories, rather than presenting a comprehensive picture of all the theories in each paradigm.
3. 'The Critical Period Hypothesis', Lenneberg, E., 1967. *Biological Foundations of Language*. New York: Wiley, suggests that the period during which children can acquire language using innate language-specific mechanisms is limited in time (this time limit is sometimes thought to be around age seven, sometimes around puberty). After this, general learning mechanisms have to be relied upon in order to learn language.
4. Research grant ESRC Ref No: RES-062-23-1545

14
A Framework for Conceptualising Learning in Applied Linguistics
Paul Seedhouse

Introduction

This chapter suggests that researchers in the field of second language learning often start with different basic assumptions about the nature of 'language' and 'learning' (as well as 'second', as Cook points out). This situation has generated a number of disputes in the field: 'The danger is that SLA researchers often do not realise that they are working from different maps and exhaust their energy quarrelling over differences in basic assumptions or patiently defending them against their critics' (Cook's chapter). This chapter therefore seeks to establish the common ground contained in the diversity of views, and to establish a broad framework for conceptualising language learning which can provide a basis for relating studies using different approaches to each other. As we have seen in this volume, language learning is a complex, multifaceted phenomenon. The argument of this chapter is that different approaches are required to study different facets of the phenomenon, and that we need to understand how these different approaches can best work together in the future. One significant achievement of this collection is that it has assembled a group of scholars who are operating in rather different paradigms and enabled them to make explicit their conceptualisations of 'learning', thereby increasing mutual understanding. One frequent complaint in the field of SLA over recent years is that researchers have been attending events with like-minded people, and so a rift between cognitively-oriented and socially-oriented SLA has developed.

Why do conceptions of learning vary so much?

Pulling together themes which have emerged in the collection, I will first summarise why conceptions of learning vary in research into learning and teaching a language. A major factor is multiplexity, or the quality of having many interrelated features. Second language learning is an extremely complex process, involving the interaction of many different components and issues. It is a complex system in the sense in which 'complex' is understood in complex systems research, that is, its order emerges from the interaction of its components. Multiplexity is evident on a number of levels in this collection, as follows:

a) A language has many components, including morphology, syntax, lexis, phonology, semantics, pragmatics and discourse. Learning one component may involve different issues from learning another component. For example, Pienemann (this collection) suggests that L2 grammar development follows universal stages that are constrained by the processability hierarchy. However, no such hierarchy of processability has been claimed in relation to L2 lexical or discoursal development.

b) Each individual component of language may have a number of subcomponents in relation to learning. For example, in relation to lexis, 'learning a word is a process by which different aspects of form (spoken and written), meaning (referential, conceptual, associative/paradigmatic, connotation, interpersonal, sociocultural) and use (morphological, syntactic and collocational features and patterns of use, as well as constraints on use, such as register and frequency) are acquired' (Elgort and Nation's chapter).

c) There are multiple definitions and conceptions of what language is (see Cook's chapter).

d) Second language learning may be investigated on very different scales. One may focus, on the micro level, on whether an individual has learnt a specific phonological point (Seedhouse and Walsh's chapter). Alternatively, one may investigate the overall size and depth of a learner's vocabulary (Elgort and Nation's chapter) or a learner's stage of grammatical development (Pienemann's chapter). Here, there is a much broader perspective on an individual's overall ability in the L2. Studies at these two extremes of scale (and at points in between) may require very different approaches.

e) Learning is both a process (an activity in which learners participate in relation to some kind of exposure to L2) and a product (a

change in cognitive state). However, these two complementary
aspects have often been researched using different methodologies
and epistemologies.

How to compare studies of learning

Because there is such heterogeneity in conceptualising learning in
applied linguistics, it would be helpful if future studies into 'learning'
could adopt a simple protocol briefly detailing the conceptualisation of
learning which is involved. This would specify:

a) the meaning of 'language' involved (preferably using Cook's scheme);
b) the component(s) of language or language use learnt (vocabulary,
    syntax, patterns of participation, and so on);
c) the definition or conceptualisation of learning employed;
d) the criteria employed for the evaluation of learning;
e) the research methodology and epistemology employed;
f) the aims of the research, or research questions;
g) the circumstances of learning;
h) whether learning is being understood as a process, a product, or
    both.

This simple measure would greatly facilitate comparisons across studies,
and enable meta-studies. I will now illustrate some of the issues which
relate to two parts of this protocol, and then give examples of how it
would be used.

The meaning of 'language' involved

Research into second language learning needs to state explicitly the
meaning of 'language' that it is employing. Cook (this collection) suggests the following framework (Table 14.1).

Studies in second language learning should state explicitly which of
these distinct conceptions of 'language' they are investigating. Cook's

Table 14.1 Six meanings of 'language'

$Lang_1$	a human representation system
$Lang_2$	an abstract external entity
$Lang_3$	a set of actual or potential sentences
$Lang_4$	the possession of a community
$Lang_5$	the knowledge in the mind of an individual
$Lang_6$	a form of action

framework for classifying meanings of 'language' also helps us to understand why conceptions of 'language learning' can differ so greatly in the literature: 'views of language learning based on a particular meaning of "language" are often incompatible with views of language learning based on another'. It is not sufficient for studies to state which meaning of 'language' they are using; as Cook points out, 'each implies a particular form of description and analysis'.

The component(s) of language or language use learnt

Elgort and Nation's chapter demonstrates that, when we drill down to the learning of individual components of language, such as vocabulary, the issues involved in learning remain just as complex. I summarise points made in the chapter to show their similarity to points made in relation to language as a whole. Vocabulary learning is inherently ill-defined, multidimensional and variable, and thus resistant to neat classification. Multiple conceptualisations of second language vocabulary acquisition (SLVA) are therefore inevitable and necessary to mirror the complexity of the field. Knowing a word involves knowing many different aspects of the word. Word knowledge can be conceptualised along different dimensions, including formal and conceptual representations. Knowledge can be represented using different parameters: deep/surface, receptive and productive. The complexity of the SLVA domain is reflected in multiple ways of describing and measuring L2 vocabulary knowledge. In this context, it is common to distinguish between the breadth, depth and fluency dimensions. There is a growing agreement among vocabulary researchers that a multiple measure approach is the way forward in assessing the quality of lexical knowledge. The multidimensional nature of L2 vocabulary knowledge is also reflected in multiple conceptualisations of what it means to learn a word in L2. Elgort and Nation's own conceptualisation of what it means to learn a word is represented by three kinds of process. It is fascinating to note that the study of a single component of language (lexis) replicates on a smaller scale many of the issues which have emerged in this volume in the study of the language system as a whole. This phenomenon is known in Complexity Theory as a fractal.

I now illustrate how the protocol outlined above might work in practice by applying it to two chapters in this collection:

Pienemann's Chapter

a) *The meaning of 'language' involved (using Cook's scheme)*: the focus of PT (Processability Theory) is language processing (Lang$_3$), and to a lesser extent the knowledge of language (Lang$_5$).

b) *The component(s) of language or language use learnt*: the development of grammar in L2 learners.

c) *The definition of learning employed*: 'In our cognitive perspective language learning is seen as consisting of two aspects: the development of language processing procedures that permit new linguistic forms to be processed and the discovery of new linguistic forms.'

d) *The criteria employed for the evaluation of learning*: 'Evidence of L2 grammatical learning can be gathered from learners' oral language production using a detailed distributional analysis that identifies the point at which a structure emerges in the L2. In practice, this analytical approach can be simplified and sped up using Rapid Profile.'

e) *The research methodology and epistemology employed*: the Processability Theory (PT) view on SLA focuses on cognitive processes in language acquisition, in particular on a hierarchy of processability which accounts for L2 development in any L2. Evidence of L2 grammatical learning is gathered from learners' oral language production using a detailed distributional analysis that identifies the point at which a structure emerges in the L2. The PT view on language learning has been utilised in a large number of empirical studies of SLA, most of which are based on large corpora of natural or elicited interlanguage discourse. The operationalisation of this conception of learning follows logically from its objective to account for the way in which the target-language grammar unfolds as the learner's language develops. The focus is on emerging interlanguage forms. More specifically, PT utilises the so-called 'emergence criterion' which has been found to be more reliable in corpus studies than accuracy-based acquisition criteria. The epistemology of PT is summarised in the Key Claim and Constructs section of Pienemann's chapter. In PT, an episode of individual language learning must be seen in relation to the architecture of human language processing. An individual's L2 production is taken as evidence for their position on an interlanguage continuum.

f) *The circumstances of learning*: these are not of prime relevance to PT, as it is intended as a universal framework that has the capacity to predict developmental trajectories for any second language. The teachability of language is constrained by processability, and the Teachability Hypothesis boils down to the claim that developmental stages cannot be skipped through formal intervention.

g) *Whether learning is being understood as a process, a product, or both*: in general, PT takes a product orientation to learning, seeing it as a change in cognitive state. PT does not focus on the process of learning in the sense of observable activity in the L2 classroom. However, Pienemann's study clearly does focus on the cognitive psycholinguistic processes or mechanisms which drive learning. His work also portrays grammar learning as a process in the sense of incremental movement along developmental trajectories, and in the sense that learner productions are generated by the language processor.

Pekarek Doehler's Chapter

a) *The meaning of 'language' involved (using Cook's scheme)*: primarily $Lang_6$, a form of social action, and also $Lang_3$, a set of actual or potential sentences. Pekarek Doehler sees language and social action as mutually constitutive or reflexively related: 'language form is analysable in the first place as a contextualised solution to an interactional problem'.

b) *The component(s) of language or language use learnt*: the empirical analysis focuses on the lexico-grammatical item 'adorer'. However, the argument is that evidence for learning this specific item is embedded and embodied in the multimodal detail of social action, and cannot therefore be isolated and extracted in any meaningful way.

c) *The definition of learning employed*: 'learning is seen as a socio-cognitive process that is embedded in the context of locally accomplished social practices. Learning a language is not the mere internalisation of linguistic knowledge that can then be simply put to use, rather it consists of the continuous adaptation of linguistic and other semiotic resources in response to locally emergent communicative needs. It involves the routinisation of patterns of language-use-for-action through repeated participation in social activities.'

d) *The criteria employed for the evaluation of learning*: interactional development is documented in terms of how turn-taking and sequential organisation change over time within recurrent interactional practices (for example, opening a story). Alternatively, the analysis can focus on single instances of interaction and document the interactional configuration of linguistic patterns. In this case, evidence for learning is provided by observing that linguistic constructions, that have been worked on interactionally earlier, are now re-used within a new communicative (micro-)context.

e) *The research methodology and epistemology employed*: Conversation Analysis, which is based on the principles of ethnomethodology.

Two scales of the time axis are currently investigated. The first relates to change across larger time-spans as addressed by longitudinal (or cross-sectional) studies that are designed to capture some dimensions of the outcome (*product*) of learning – that is: a state of competence at a time X, X+1, and so on. The second is concerned with how participants, within short time-spans, work their competencies in real time through the moment-by-moment unfolding of talk. These studies are designed to capture some dimensions of the *process* of learning, and typically focus on the learning of specific linguistic items or patterns.

f) *The circumstances of learning*: here, group work in a French L2 lower-intermediate class in Switzerland, where French is one of four official languages. Analysis focuses on naturally-occurring social interaction.

g) *Whether learning is being understood as a process, a product, or both*: 'Learning is seen as a sociocognitive process that is embedded in the context of locally accomplished social practices and their sequential deployment.' However, the chapter also tracks the learning of a specific item (lexico-grammatical) by a specific individual over time and evaluates the evidence of learning, that is, shows a product orientation as well.

The protocol enables more complete comparison of studies of learning by requiring authors to be explicit about the different elements of their conceptualisations of learning. Use of the protocol should also make clearer how the different elements relate to each other, and whether or not they form a coherent whole.

Definitions of learning

Here I list the conceptualisations of learning employed in the different chapters of this collection. The different definitions can be related to the different research methodologies employed, to the different components of language studied, and to the aims of the research.

Elgort and Nation adopted a cognitive psycholinguistic view of L2 vocabulary learning and teaching, which is primarily interested in changes that occur in the individual cognitive state and factors that affect these changes.

Seedhouse and Walsh: in this chapter, learning is defined as a change in socially-displayed cognitive state.

Ohta: this study is grounded in a sociocultural approach to L2 learning, where learning is defined as a process by which the L2 becomes a tool for the mind and for social interaction.

Jenks: language, as understood in this chapter, is a social-interactional resource for co-constructing meaning. Therefore, language learning can be observed as changes situated in social interaction.

Pekarek Doehler: learning is seen as a sociocognitive process that is embedded in the context of locally accomplished social practices and their sequential deployment. Learning a language centrally involves the continuous adaptation of linguistic and other semiotic resources in response to communicative needs that emerge locally, through the course of communicative practices.

Larsen-Freeman: learning is not the taking in of linguistic forms by learners, but the constant adaptation of their linguistic resources in the service of meaning-making in response to the affordances that emerge in the communicative situation, which is in turn affected by learners' adaptivity.

Leung: language is seen as a resource for meaning-making; the language used by teachers and pupils in interaction can be seen as a window into moments of learning, and learning can be seen as a window into moments of language use and acquisition.

Appel: instructed language learning is one particular, context-specific type of language learning. It has two aspects, an interactive one and a cognitive one.

Pienemann: in our cognitive perspective language learning is seen as consisting of two aspects:

a) the development of language-processing procedures that permit new linguistic forms to be processed; and
b) the discovery of new linguistic forms.

All of the above definitions conceptualise learning as involving change. Many of the definitions refer to learning involving both a cognitive and a social element. Ellis's chapter develops a definition of learning (pp. 44–46) which is intended to be sociocognitive in nature, and hence to bridge the social and cognitive divide. By adding elements from the above definitions to Ellis's, the definition below is proposed as one which amalgamates the insights of this volume:

Second language learning involves both a sociocognitive process and a change in cognitive state. It involves adapting linguistic and other semiotic resources to communicative needs. It represents an adjustment in a complex adaptive system. 'An operational definition of change involves transcendence of a particular time and space, as follows:

1. the learner could not do x at time a (the "gap");
2. the learner co-adapted x at time b ("social construction");
3. the learner initiated x at time c in a similar context as in time b ("internalisation/self-regulation");
4. the learner employed x at time d in a new context ("transfer of learning"),

where x refers to some micro or macro feature of language or language use (for example, a specific lexical item, a particular genre, a pattern of participation in interaction). This definition assumes that change (and therefore learning) can occur at three different levels. Level 1 is where change originates in social activity – it is a scaffolded construct. To demonstrate this it is necessary to provide evidence that the learner could not perform x prior to the occasion when its jointly constructed use becomes evident. Level 2 is where the learner demonstrates the ability to use the newly acquired feature in a similar context to that in which it first appeared but independently of any interlocutor's scaffolding. Level 3 occurs when the learner can extend the use of the feature to an entirely different context. These levels reflect "depth" of learning. In other words, learning should not be viewed as an all-or-nothing phenomenon (that is, the learner "knows" or "does not know" something) but as incremental and continuous' (Ellis, this volume).

Learning issues and agendas

Research in L2 learning also needs to be conceptualised in terms of issues and agendas. In this section, I pick out the issues which have emerged in the collection in relation to language learning, and consider how these might create an agenda for future research. This builds on Myles's chapter, which poses six research questions intended to capture the three main research agendas which have prevailed in the field over the last 40 years or so, namely the cognitive, the social and the formal.

A common theme in a number of chapters in this collection is the issue of whether participation in classroom interaction can be equated with learning. Appel's chapter suggests that learning and participation are closely connected. He presents evidence to show that participation can support learning, but points out that there is also evidence that participation may actually constrain learning. It therefore seems reasonable to assume that participation cannot simply be equated with learning. The position taken in this chapter is that participation affects learning, for example by providing space and opportunities for cognitive processes. In order to understand instructed language learning, both participatory and cognitive aspects of learning have to be considered. Leung's chapter suggests that while participation in classroom activities can provide opportunities for meaning-making and meaning-taking, and understanding and learning can be achieved along the way, successful outcomes are not automatically assured. His empirical analysis shows that, despite active engagement with the teacher and with the task, Sairah and her teacher did not accomplish a shared understanding of mode in any explicit way. It is possible that one can talk and behave like a projected 'good' pupil in a seemingly supportive environment without achieving understanding and learning. Ohta interviews learners and reveals some of the limitations of social interaction as a context for language learning.

Leung's chapter also reminds us that instructed language learning does not take place in a political vacuum, and that macro-level policy decisions can have an enormous impact on micro-practices. Leung starts by considering policy developments which led to immigrant children being placed in mainstream classes in English secondary schools without specialist ELT support. He then looks at interaction in a specific classroom to exemplify the reality at classroom level. Leung's chapter exemplifies the relationship between macro-level educational policy and micro-level classroom practice, and clearly demonstrates the impact of government policy on learning in school settings. The overall picture in relation to L2 teaching gained in this study is that language learning is such a multifaceted and variable phenomenon that we should be wary of any teaching approach which concentrates exclusively on one aspect of a language, or one aspect of the learning process.

This collection has also developed the notion of classroom interactional competence (CIC) in relation to instructed L2 learning. This notion links learning to classroom pedagogy by considering how the teacher can maximise learning opportunities through interaction. CIC is defined in Seedhouse and Walsh's chapter as 'teachers' and learners' ability to use interaction as a tool for mediating and assisting learning'. The assumption is that by first understanding and then extending CIC, there will be greater opportunities for learning. A teacher who demonstrates CIC uses language which is both convergent to the pedagogic goal of the moment, and also appropriate to the learners. Second, CIC facilitates interactional space. Third, CIC entails teachers being able to *shape* learner contributions by scaffolding, paraphrasing, reiterating, modelling, or repairing learner input. In Appel's chapter we saw that the teacher has shown a remarkable sensitivity towards the potential of different participation formats for student learning. Pekarek Doehler argues that language competence cannot be seen as independent of the social-interactional dimensions of language practice.

Pekarek Doehler's chapter also illustrates a development which is receiving increasing attention and is certain to become increasingly important. This is the study of how classroom learning processes are intimately connected with non-verbal communication, and how multimodal technology and presentation can help uncover these connections. Pekarek Doehler shows how the evidence for learning of a linguistic item is embedded in gaze as well as sequential, prosodic and linguistic resources. Jenks's chapter demonstrates how technological development and applications continue to expand our notions of how learning may be organised. In this case, learners of English set up their own online voice-based chat rooms. Norms and standards vary from chat room to chat room, and there are often no pre-determined, fixed standards of language use and learning. Users develop their own methods of participation and organise their own methods of learning with people often from a different culture and thousands of miles away.

Perhaps the most promising area for fruitful collaboration between cognitive and social SLA is in the combination of perspectives on individual cognition and socially-shared cognition. Much work has been done over a lengthy period of time on individual cognition within cognitive SLA. More recently work on socially-shared cognition has been developed in Sociocultural Theory, in relation to the concept of mediation (see Ohta's chapter), as well as in CA (see Pekarek Doehler's and Seedhouse and Walsh's chapters). A perspective on individual cognition focuses on changes within an individual's mind. A CA perspective on socially-shared cognition aims to 'identify ways in which participants themselves orient to, display, and make sense of one another's cognitive states (among other things)' (Drew 1995: 79). There appear to be no a priori reasons why these two perspectives cannot be employed in the same study, and indeed the relationship between the two perspectives should be of great interest. Ellis's chapter argues for a sociocognitive research methodology in which the social and the cognitive are seen as inseparable, and which examines how convergence of the speaker's internal and external worlds might be achieved.

Much has been written in relation to the differences between social and cognitive research into L2 learning, and these are concisely summarised in Ellis's chapter. Traditionally, cognitive approaches have been represented as having a 'product' approach to learning. As Ellis (this collection) put it, 'in cognitive SLA, acquisition is seen as something that occurs inside the learner's head as a result of exposure to input and the activation of universal cognitive processes. Evidence that acquisition has taken place is found when it can be shown that a change has taken place in the learner's interlanguage as when the learner manifests the use of a new linguistic form or employs a previously acquired form with a new function. However, learning does not occur in language use; it only manifests itself in it.' In contrast, social approaches have been said to have a 'process' orientation. As Ellis puts it, 'L2 acquisition is "learning-in-action". It is a process rather than a product. That is, it manifests itself in the actual use of the L2 and thus no clear distinction can be drawn between use and acquisition. Thus learning is not a mental phenomenon but a social and collaborative one.'

Some researchers in this collection adopt a clearly cognitive standpoint (Pienemann; Myles; Elgort and Nation), whereas others adopt a social standpoint (Pekarek Doehler; Seedhouse and Walsh; Jenks; Ohta). However, one thing which has become clear in this collection is that learning is in practice treated as both a process and a product on both sides of the social/cognitive divide. In Pekarek Doehler's and Seedhouse and Walsh's chapters, the main emphasis is on portraying learning processes. However, both chapters also track the learning of a specific item (lexical and phonological respectively) by a specific individual over time, and evaluate the evidence of learning, that is, they show a product orientation as well. Similarly, Pienemann's chapter adopts a product orientation to learning, seeing it as a change in cognitive state. PT does not focus on the process of learning in the sense of observable activity in the L2 classroom. However, his study clearly does focus on the cognitive psycholinguistic processes or mechanisms which drive learning. His work also portrays grammar learning as a process in the sense of incremental movement along developmental trajectories, and in the sense that learner productions are generated by the language processor. Certainly, there are differences in the understanding of the term 'process': in cognitive SLA 'processes' are viewed as mental (internal), while in social SLA they are viewed as interactional (external).[1] A key finding of this collection is that learning is both a product and a process, and that one can take product and process orientations to learning. The two orientations are complementary, and there are many advantages to employing both orientations in the same research study.

Ways forward

If one were to take a global perspective from outside applied linguistics, it might well appear that we are creating a great quantity of knowledge in relation to both the products and processes of language learning. The question at present is therefore how to synthesise all of this knowledge. Several writers in this collection acknowledge the problems of opposition between different schools of SLA, and suggest ways of overcoming this. The discussion so far in this volume has provided a number of suggestions for ways forward which might enable cognitive and social approaches to learning to work together productively. I examine here how three of these proposals might work together in complementary fashion. These are: Epistemic Relativism, Sociocognitive Theory, and Complexity Theory.

Epistemic relativism

Myles's and Ellis's chapters propose epistemic relativism as a way forward. Ellis writes that 'such a stance acknowledges that theories are contextual and purposeful and thus need to be evaluated in terms of what they seek to explain. Such an approach would admit that cognitive and social theories both have a place in a broadly-defined SLA as they have been framed to account for different populations of learners and to emphasise different (but equally important) dimensions of learning.' Myles suggests that 'because second language acquisition is a multifaceted phenomenon and, like language itself, it is at the same time linguistic, cognitive and social, different theoretical and methodological paradigms are required to investigate different aspects of the SLA process. Each of the different facets of the SLA process is asking different research questions which require different theoretical and methodological tools.' Epistemic relativism, then, is a way forward on a philosophical or epistemological level. It suggests that it is perfectly acceptable for multiple research methodologies to be employed in language-learning research, and provides a springboard for considering how social and cognitive approaches might work together.

Sociocognitive Theory

Ellis also proposes a solution in terms of a research methodology, namely 'the development of a composite theory of L2 acquisition that includes both social and cognitive elements, drawing on recent work by Batstone (2010) and Atkinson (2002; Atkinson et al. 2007)'. Such work should ideally include the following: (1) longitudinal data collected from naturally-occurring social events that will enable the researcher to demonstrate to what extent 'change' takes place over time; (2) rich analyses of specific interactions involving learners based not just on the texts they produce but also on detailed information about the participants, their physical location and their artefacts. These analyses will need to examine a wide range of behaviours – para-linguistic as well as linguistic; and (3) data that directly address the cognitive aspects of sociocognitive events, (for example, stimulated recall protocols).

According to Batstone (2010), sociocognition is based on the view that all forms of language use always have both a social and a cognitive dimension, that understanding language acquisition involves understanding how these two dimensions interrelate, and that acquisition cannot be adequately explained in any other way. Such research might involve teams of researchers with members across the social and cognitive divide. The research would need to cover micro and macro practices, contain both longitudinal and cross-sectional studies, portray learning as both product and process, and provide perspectives on both individual and socially shared cognition.

Complexity Theory

Larsen-Freeman places the different schools of SLA on a having-doing continuum, and proposes Complexity Theory as a way of overcoming this polarisation. Complexity Theory (as presented in Larsen-Freeman's chapter) places the study of second language learning in a much broader perspective. It suggests that second language learning as a system shares many fundamental characteristics with other complex adaptive systems in the world. This suggests the possibility of major progress in our understanding of second language learning as a system, and also the integration of the study of second language learning into a much larger scientific project. Advances in the study of complex adaptive systems in any field could potentially have implications for our understanding of second language learning.

From a Complexity Theory perspective, when we study language learning as a system we are in effect studying the interactions of a number of complex systems which are 'nested' 'at different levels of granularity' (Larsen-Freeman and Cameron 2008b). So, for example, language is considered 'an open dynamic system of language-using patterns' (Larsen-Freeman and Cameron 2008a). Learning is a complex adaptive system: 'Learners are not engaged in simply learning fixed forms or sentences, but rather in learning to adapt their behavior to an increasingly complex environment. Learning is not a linear, additive process, but an iterative one' (Larsen-Freeman, this volume). Learner discourse is viewed as 'a complex, dynamic, adaptive system' (Larsen-Freeman and Cameron 2008a).

I now return to the theme of the multiplexity of language learning with which I started this chapter, and consider this from a Complexity Theory perspective. Language learning exhibits multiplexity at all levels. When researching language learning, we are studying the interaction of a number of 'nested' complex adaptive systems which together create a system. The study of the individual systems requires a different approach or perspective, which explains why there are so many different approaches. Complexity Theory offers the possibility of understanding how the complex systems work together, and how the various research approaches can work together to understand them.

Moving the perspective further out onto the meta level, the study of language learning is itself a complex adaptive system. The interactions of researchers in conferences, journals, emails and meeting themselves form a complex adaptive system. This edited collection has functioned as a complex adaptive system, starting with a seminar which brought researchers together from the cognitive and social schools of SLA. Complexity Theory, then, provides us not only with a perspective to understand how the components and issues of L2 learning relate to one another, but also with one which shows how researchers are able to work together to investigate the phenomenon.

Summary

I now recap on the discussion in this chapter. The framework for conceptualising language learning which has emerged from this collection is of necessity a loose one, and consists of the three following components:

a) a definition of learning;
b) a protocol;
c) three complementary ways forward.

Definition of learning

Second language learning involves both a sociocognitive process and a change in cognitive state. It involves adapting linguistic and other semiotic resources to communicative needs. It represents an adjustment in a complex adaptive system. An operational definition of change involves transcendence of a particular time and space, as follows:

1. the learner could not do x at time a (the 'gap');
2. the learner co-adapted x at time b ('social construction');
3. the learner initiated x at time c in a similar context as in time b ('internalisation/self-regulation');
4. the learner employed x at time d in a new context ('transfer of learning');

where x refers to some micro or macro feature of language or language use (for example, a specific lexical item, a particular genre, or a pattern of participation in interaction).[2]

Protocol

Because there is such heterogeneity in conceptualising learning in applied linguistics, it would be helpful if future studies into 'learning' could include a brief statement of the conceptualisation of learning which is involved. This would include:

a) the meaning of 'language' involved (preferably using Cook's scheme);
b) the component(s) of language or language use learnt (vocabulary, syntax, patterns of participation, and so on);
c) the definition or conceptualisation of learning employed;
d) the criteria employed for the evaluation of learning;
e) the research methodology and epistemology employed;
f) the aims of the research, or research questions;
g) the circumstances of learning;
h) whether learning is being understood as a process, a product, or both.

Three complementary ways forward

The three ways forward discussed in the previous section operate on different levels, but appear to be broadly complementary. Epistimic Relativism is an epistemological position, Sociocognitive Theory is a research methodology to be developed specifically to investigate L2 learning, and Complexity Theory is a much broader enterprise, relevant to virtually every academic discipline. Larsen-Freeman and Cameron (2008b) specify the methodological principles for researching language and language development from a Complexity Theory perspective, and a Sociocognitive methodology seems to conform to these principles. Each of the three ways forward provides ways of bridging the cognitive/ social divide.

Notes

1. Thanks to Rod Ellis for making this point.
2. This definition derives primarily from Ellis's chapter.

Bibliography

Abdesslem, H. 1993. Analysing foreign language lesson discourse. *International Review of Applied Linguistics*, 31: 221–35.

Adolphs, S. and N. Schmitt. 2004. Vocabulary coverage according to spoken discourse context. In P. Bogaards and B. Laufer (eds), *Vocabulary in a Second Language*. Amsterdam: John Benjamins, pp. 39–52.

Agar, M. 2005. Local discourses and global research: The role of local knowledge. *Language in Society*, 34(1): 1–22.

Alanen, R., A.K. Jäppinen and T. Nikula. 2008. 'But big is funny word': A multiple perspective on concept formation in a foreign-language-mediated classroom. *Journal of Applied Linguistics*, 3: 69–90.

Aljaafreh, A. and J. Lantolf. 1994. Negative feedback as regulation and second language learning in the Zone of Proximal Development. *The Modern Language Journal*, 78: 465–83.

Allwright, D. 1988. *Observation in the Language Classroom*. London: Longman.

Anderson, B. 1983. *Imagined Communities*. New York: Verso.

Andersen, R. 1983. Transfer to somewhere. In S. Gass and L. Selinker (eds), *Language Transfer in Language Learning*. Rowley, MA: Newbury House.

Anton, M. and F.J. DiCamilla. 1998. Socio-cognitive functions of L1 collaborative interaction in the L2 classroom. *The Canadian Modern Language Review*, 54(3): 314–42.

Appel, J. 2007. Language teaching in performance. *International Journal of Applied Linguistics*, 17: 277–93.

Archibald, J. 2004. Interfaces in the prosodic hierarchy: New structure and the phonolgical parser. *The International Journal of Bilingualism*, 8: 29–50.

Archibald, J. 2005. Second language phonology as redeployment of L1 phonological knowledge. *Canadian Journal of Linguistics*, 50: 285–314.

Archibald, J. 2009. Phonological feature re-assembly and the importance of phonetic cues. *Second Langauge Research*, 25: 231–3.

Aronoff, M. 1992. Segmentalism in linguistics: The alphabetic basis of phonological theory. In P. Downing, S.D. Lima and M. Noonan (eds), *The Linguistics of Literacy*. Amsterdam: Benjamins, pp. 71–82.

Atkins, P.W.B. and A.D. Baddeley. 1998. Working memory and distributed vocabulary learning. *Applied Psycholinguistics*, 19: 537–52.

Atkinson, D. 2002. Toward a sociocognitive approach to second language acquisition. *The Modern Language Journal*, 86: 525–45.

Atkinson, D., E. Churchill, T. Nishino and H. Okada. 2007. Alignment and interaction in a sociocognitive approach to second language acquisition. *The Modern Language Journal*, 91(2): 169–88.

Au, K.H. 1980. Participation structures in a reading lesson with Hawaiian children: Analysis of a culturally appropriate instruction event. *Anthropology and Education Quarterly*, 11: 91–115.

Auer, P. 1992. Introduction: John Gumperz' approach to contextualization. In P. Auer and A. di Luzio (eds), *The Contextualization of Language*, Amsterdam: John Benjamins, pp. 1–37.

Auer, P. 1995. The pragmatics of code-switching: A sequential approach. In L. Milroy and P. Muysken (eds), *One Speaker, Two Languages: Cross-Disciplinary Perspectives on Code-Switching*. Cambridge: Cambridge University Press, pp. 115–35.

Auer, P. 2009. On-line syntax: Thoughts on the temporality of spoken language. *Language Sciences*, 31: 1–13.

Bakhtin, M. 1981. *The Dialogic Imagination: Four Essays by M.M. Bakhtin*. Austin, TX: University of Texas Press.

Batstone, R. 2010. Issues and options in sociocognition. In R. Batstone (ed.) *Sociocognitive Perspectives on Language Use and Language Learning*. Oxford: Oxford University Press.

Beretta, A. 1991. Theory construction in SLA: Complementarity and opposition. *Studies in Second Language Acquisition*, 13: 493–511.

Beretta, A. 1993. "As God said, and I think, rightly...". Perspectives on theory construction in SLA: An introduction. *Applied Linguistics*, 14: 221–4.

Berk, L.E. and M.E. Diaz (eds) 1992. *Private Speech: From Social Interaction to Self-Regulation*. Hillsdale, NJ: Lawrence Erlbaum and Associates.

Berns, M. 1990. 'Second' and 'foreign' in second language acquisition/foreign language learning: A sociolinguistic perspective. In VanPatten and J.F. Lee (eds), *Second Language Acquisition-Foreign Language Learning*. Clevedon: Multilingual Matters, pp. 3–12.

Bhattacharya, R., S. Gupta, C. Jewitt, D. Newfold, Y. Reed and P. Stein. 2007. The policy-practice nexus in English classrooms in Delhi, Johannesburg, and London: Teachers and the textual cycle. *TESOL Quarterly*, 41: 465–87.

Bialystok, E. 1978. A theoretical model of second language learning. *Language Learning*, 28: 69–84.

Bialystok, E. and K. Hakuta. 1999. Confounded age: Linguistic and cognitive factors in age differences for second language acquisition. In D. Birdsong (ed.), *Second Language Acquisition and the Critical Period Hypothesis*. Mahwah, NJ: Lawrence Erlbaum, pp. 161–81.

Biko, S. 1978. *I Write What I Like*. The Bowerdan Press. Reprinted by Penguin, London. 1998.

Birdsong, D. 1999. Introduction: Whys and why nots of the critical period hypothesis for second language acquisition. In D. Birdsong (ed), *Second Language Acquisition and the Critical Period Hypothesis*. Mahwah, NJ: Lawrence Erlbaum, pp. 1–22.

Block, D. 1996. Not so fast! Some thoughts on theory culling, relativism, accepted findings and the heart and soul of SLA. *Applied Linguistics*, 17: 65–83.

Block, D. 2003. *The Social Turn in Second Language Acquisition*. Edinburgh: Edinburgh University Press.

Bloomfield, L. 1926. A set of postulates for the science of language. *Language*, 2: 153–64.

Bobb, S.C., N. Hoshino and J.F. Kroll. 2008. The role of language cues in constraining cross-language activity. *EUROSLA Yearbook*, 8: 6–31.

Boss. 1996. German grammar for beginners – the teachability hypothesis and its relevance to the classroom. In C. Arbones Sola, J. Rolin-Ianziti and R. Sussex (eds), *Working Papers in Applied Linguistics, 1*. Brisbane: University of Queensland, Centre for Language Teaching and Research, pp. 93–103.

Bourdieu, P. 1991. *Language and Symbolic Power*. London: Polity Press.

Bourne, J. and J. McPake. 1991. *Partnership Teaching: Co-Operative Teaching Strategies for English Language Support in Multilingual Classrooms.* London: HMSO.

Brecht, R. and W. Rivers. 2005. Language needs analysis at the societal level. In M. Long (Ed.), *Second language needs analysis.* Cambridge: Cambridge University Press, pp. 79–104.

Breen, M.P. 1999. Navigating the discourse: On what is learned in the language classroom. In W.A. Renandya and G.M. Jacobs (eds), *Learners and Language Learning. Anthology Series 39.* Singapore: SEAMO Regional Language Centre, pp. 115–44.

Bremer, K., C. Roberst, M. Vasseur, M. Simonot, and P. Broeder. 1996. *Achieving Understanding: Discourse in Intercultural Encounters.* Harlow: Longman.

Bresnan, J. 2001. *Lexical-Functional Syntax.* Malden, MA: Blackwell.

Brooks, F. 1992. Spanish III learners talking to one another through a jigsaw task. *Canadian Modern Language Review,* 48: 696–717.

Brouwer, C.E. 2003. Word searches in NNS-NS interaction: Opportunities for language learning? *The Modern Language Journal,* 87(4): 534–45.

Brouwer, C.E. 2008. Ways to apply CA to second language acquisition: Six – maybe seven. Paper presented at the Methodologies and practices for approaching learning as a social phenomenon inside and outside of school conference. Luxembourg University, December.

Brouwer, C.E. and J. Wagner. 2004. Developmental issues in second language conversation. *Journal of Applied Linguistics* 1(1): 29–47.

Brown, A. 2003. Interviewer variation and the co-construction of speaking proficiency. *Language Testing,* 20(1): 1–25.

Bruner, J. 1983. *Child's Talk. Learning to Use Language.* New York and London: Norton.

Brutt-Griffler, J. 2002. *World English: A Study of Its Development.* Clevedon: Multilingual Matters.

Bryson, B. 1991. *Mother Tongue: The English Language.* London: Penguin.

Budd Rowe, M. 1986. Wait time: Slowing down may be a way of speeding up! *Journal of Teacher Education,* 37: 43–50.

Bullock, A. 1975. *A Language for Life: Report of the Committee of Inquiry Appointed by the Secretary of State for Education and Science under the Chairmanship of Sir Alan Bullock* / [Committee of Inquiry into Reading and the Use of English]. London: HMSO.

Bybee, J. 2006. From usage to grammar: The mind's response to repetition. *Language,* 82(4): 711–33.

Cameron, D. 2001. *Working with Spoken Discourse.* London: Sage.

Cameron, L. 2003. Challenges for ELT from the expansion in teaching children. *ELT Journal,* 57(2): 105–12.

Canagarajah, A.S. 2005. Reconstructing local knowledge, reconfiguring language studies. In A.S. Canagarajah (ed.), *Reclaiming the Local in Language Policy and Practice.* New Jersey: Lawrence Erlbaum Associates, pp. 3–24.

Canagarajah, S. 2007. Lingua franca English, multilingual communities, and language acquisition. *The Modern Language Journal,* 91: 923–39.

Canale, M. 1983. On some dimensions of language proficiency. In J. Oller (ed.), *Issues in Language Testing Research.* Rowley, MA: Newbury House, pp. 333–42.

Carr, D. (ed.) 2006. *Teacher Training DVD Series* (Set of 15 DVDs). London: International House.

Cekaite, A. 2007. A child's development of interactional competence in a Swedish L2 classroom. *The Modern Language Journal*, 91(1): 45–62.

Chaiklin, S. 2003. The zone of proximal development in Vygotsky's analysis of learning and instruction. In A. Kozulin (ed.), *Vygotsky's Educational Theory in Cultural Context*. Cambridge: Cambridge University Press, pp. 39–64.

Chee, M.W.L., C.S. Soon, H.L. Lee and C. Pallier. 2004. Left insula activation: A marker for language attainment in bilinguals. *PNAS*, 101/42: 15265–70.

Chomsky, N. 1957. *Syntactic Structures*. The Hague: Mouton.

Chomsky, N. 1965. *Aspects of the Theory of Syntax*. Boston, MA: MIT Press.

Chomsky, N. 2005. Three factors in language design. *Linguistic Inquiry*, 36(1): 1–22.

Christiansen, M. and N. Chater. 2008. Language as shaped by the brain. *Behavioural and Brain Sciences*, 31: 480–509.

Churchill, S. 2004. *Official Languages in Canada: Changing the Language Landscape*. Canadian Heritage: Official Languages Support Program Branch.

Cicero. 55BC. *De Inventione*, I, IV. http://scrineum.unipv.it/wight/invs1.htm. Translation by C.D. Yonge in *The Orations of Marcus Tullius Cicero*. London: George Bell & Sons.

Clahsen, H. 1992. Learnability theory and the problem of development in language acquisition. In J. Weissenborn, H. Goodluck, and T. Roeper (eds), *Theoretical Issues in Language Acquisition: Continuity and Change*. Hillsdale, NJ: Lawrence Erlbaum. pp. 53–76.

Clahsen, H. and P. Muysken. 1989. The UG paradox in L2 acquisition. *Second Language Research*, 5: 1–29.

Cobb, T. and M. Horst. 2004. Is there an academic word list in French? In P. Bogaards and B. Laufer (eds), *Vocabulary in a Second Language*. Amsterdam: John Benjamins, pp. 15–38.

Commission For Racial Equality. 1986. *Teaching English as a Second Language*. London: CRE.

Cook, V. 1979. The English are only human. *English Language Teaching Journal*, 33(3): 163–7.

Cook, V. 2001a. *Second Language Learning and Language Teaching*. London: Arnold.

Cook, V. 2001b. Using the first language in the classroom. *Canadian Modern Language Review*, 57(3): 402–23.

Cook, V. (ed.) 2003. *Effects of the Second Language on the First*. Clevedon: Multilingual Matters.

Cook, V. 2007. The nature of the L2 user. In L. Roberts, A. Gurel, S. Tatar and L. Marti (eds), *EUROSLA Yearbook*, 7: 205–20.

Cook, V. 2008. Review of *Handbook of Bilingualism: Psycholinguistic Approaches*. *Language*, 84(1): 196–8

Cook, V. 2009. Language user groups and language teaching. In V. Cook and L.Wei (eds), *Contemporary Applied Linguistics, Vol 1*. London: Continuum, pp. 54–74.

Cook, G. and B. Seidlhofer (eds) 1995. *Principle and Practice in Applied Linguistics*. Oxford: Oxford University Press.

Cook, V., B. Bassetti, C. Kasai, M. Sasaki and J. Takahashi. 2006. Do bilinguals have different concepts? The case of shape and material in Japanese L2 users of English. *International Journal of Bilingualism*, 10: 137–52.

Cooper, D. 1999. *Linguistic Attractors: The Cognitive Dynamics of Language Acquisition and Change*. Amsterdam: John Benjamins.

Council of Europe. 1997. *Language Policies for a Multilingual and Multicultural Europe*. Strasburg: Council for Cultural Cooperation Committee CC-LANG, (98)1.

Coupland, N. 2001. Introduction: Sociolinguistic theory and social theory. In N. Coupland, S. Sarangi, and C. Candlin (eds), *Sociolinguistic and Social Theory*. Harlow: Pearson Education, pp. 1–26.

Coxhead, A. 2000. A new academic word list. *TESOL Quarterly*, 34: 213–238.

Creese, A. 2002. EAL and ethnicity issues in teacher professional and institutional discourses. In Leung, C. (ed.), *Language and Additional/Second Language Issues for School Education: A Reader for Teachers*. Watford, National Association for Language Development in the Curriculum, pp. 14–24.

Creese, A. 2005. *Teacher Collaboration and Talk in Multilingual Classrooms*. Clevedon: Multilingual Matters.

Cummins, J. 1984. *Bilingualism and Special Education: Issues in Assessment and Pedagogy*. Clevedon: Multilingual Matters.

Cummins, J. 1992. Language proficiency, bilingualism, and academic achievement. In P.A. Richard-Amato and M.A. Snow (eds), *The Multicultural Classroom: Readings for Content-Area Teachers*. New York: Longman, pp. 16–26.

Cummins, J. 1993. Bilingualism and second language learning. *Annual Review of Applied Linguistics*, 13: 51–70.

Cummins, J. 2000. *Language, Power and Pedagogy: Bilingual Children in the Crossfire*. Clevedon: Multilingual Matters.

Cummins, J. 2008. BICS and CALP: Empirical and theoretical status of the distinction. In B.V. Street and N.H. Hornberger (eds), *Encyclopedia of Language and Education*. New York: Springer, pp. 71–83.

Cummins, J. and Swain, M. 1986. *Bilingualism in Education*. New York: Longman.

Cullen, R. 1998. Teacher talk and the classroom context. *English Language Teaching Journal*, 52(3): 179–87.

Dale, R. and M. Spivey. 2006. Unraveling the dyad: Using recurrence analysis to explore patterns of syntactic coordination between children and caregivers in conversation. *Language Learning*, 56(3): 391–430.

Daller, H., J. Milton and J. Treffers-Daller (eds) 2007. *Modelling and Assessing Vocabulary Knowledge*. Cambridge: Cambridge University Press.

David, A. 2008a. A developmental perspective on productive lexical knowledge in L2 oral interlanguage. *Journal of French Language Studies*, 18(3): 315–31.

David, A. 2008b. Vocabulary breadth in French L2 learners. *Language Learning Journal*, 36: 167–80.

David, A., F. Myles, V. Rogers and S. Rule. 2009. Lexical development in instructed L2 learners of French: Is there a relationship with morphosyntactic development? In Daller, H., D. Malvern, P. Meara, J. Milton, B. Richards and J. Treffers-Daller (eds), *Vocabulary Studies in First and Second Language Acquisition: The Interface Between Theory and Application*. Basingstoke: Palgrave, pp. 147–63.

De Groot, A.M.B. and J.G. van Hell. 2005. The learning of foreign language vocabulary. In Kroll and De Groot (eds), *Handbook of Bilingualism: Psycholinguistic Approaches*. Oxford: Oxford University Press, pp. 9–29.

de Guerrero, M.C.M. 2005. *Inner Speech—L2: Thinking Words in a Second Language*. New York: Springer.

De Houwer, A. 2005. Early bilingual acquisition: Focus on morphosyntax and the Separate Development Hypothesis. In Kroll and De Groot (eds), pp. 30–48.

de Saussure, F. 1915/1976. *Cours de Linguistique Générale*. In Bally, C. and A. Sechehaye (eds). Paris: Payothèque, Payot.

De Swaan, A. 2001. *Words of the World: The Global Language System*. Cambridge: Polity Press.

DeKeyser, R. 2000. The robustness of critical period effects in second language acquisition. *Studies in Second Language Acquisition*, 22: 499–533.

DeKeyser, R.M. 1998. Beyond focus on form: Cognitive perspective on learning and practical second language grammar. In C. Doughty and J. Williams (eds), *Focus on form in classroom second language acquisition*. Cambridge: Cambridge University Press, pp. 42–63.

Dekydtspotter, L. 2001. The Universal Parser and interlanguage: Domain-specific mental organization in the comprehension of combien interrogatives in English-French interlanguage. *Second Language Research*, 17: 91–143.

Dekydtspotter, L., R. Sprouse and D. Anderson. 1998. Interlanguage A-bar dependencies: Binding construals, null prepostitions and Universal Grammar. *Second Language Research*, 14: 341–58.

Dekydtspotter, L. and R.A. Sprouse. 2001. Mental design and (second) language epistemology: Adjectival restrictions of *wh*-quantifiers and tense in English-French interlanguage. *Second Language Research*, 17: 1–35.

Dekydtspotter, L., R.A. Sprouse, K. Swanson and R. Thyre. 1999. Semantics, pragmatics and second language acquisition: The case of *combien* extractions. In A. Greenhill, H. Littlefield and C. Tano (eds), *Proceedings of the 23rd Annual Boston University Conference on Language Development*. Somerville, MA: Cascadilla Press, pp. 162–71.

Department for Children, Schools and Families. 2008. Pupil characteristics and class sizes in maintained schools in England, January. From http://www.dcsf. gov.uk/rsgateway/DB/SFR/s000786/index.shtml. Retrieved on 7 July 2009.

Department for Education and Employment. 1998. *The National Literacy Strategy*, London: DfEE.

Department for Education and Employment. 2001. *Key Stage 3 National Strategy – Literacy Across the Curriculum*. London: DfEE.

Department for Education and Skills. 2003. *Aiming High: Raising the Achievement of Minority Ethnic Pupils*. Nottingham: DfES.

Department for Education and Skills. 2005. *Aiming High: Guidance on Assessment of Pupils Learning English as an Additional Language*. Nottingham: DfES.

Department for Education and Skills. 2006. *Secondary National Strategy: Pupils Learning English as an Additional Language*. London: DfES.

Department for Education and Skills. 2007. *Making the Grade*. Nottingham: DfES.

DiCamilla, F.J. and J.P. Lantolf. 1995. The linguistic analysis of private writing. *Language Sciences*, 16(3–4): 347–69.

Dijkstra, A. and W.J.B. van Heuven. 2002. The architecture of the bilingual word recognition system: From identification to decision. *Bilingualism: Language and Cognition*, 23: 175–97.

Dittmar, N., B. Spolsky and J. Walters. 1998. Language and identity in immigrant language acquisition and use. In *Contemporary Approaches to Second Language Acquisition in Social Context*. University College Dublin Press, 124–36.

Donato, R. 1994. Collective scaffolding in second language learning. In Lantolf, J.P. and Appel, G. (eds), *Vygotskian approaches to second language research*. Norwood, NJ: Ablex. pp. 33–56.

Dörnyei, Z. 2003. Attitudes, orientations and motivation in language learning: Advances in theory, research and applications. *Language Learning*, 53: 3–32.

Dörnyei, Z. 2009. *The Psychology of Second Language Acquisition*. Oxford: Oxford University Press.

Dörnyei, Z. and P. Skehan (eds) 2002. *Individual Differences in Second Language Acquisition*. Amsterdam: John Benjamins.

Dörnyei, Z. and P. Skehan. 2003. Individual differences in second language learning. In C. Doughty, and M. Long (eds), *The Handbook of Second Language Acquisition*. Malden, MA: Blackwell, pp. 589–630.

Dorr-Bremme, D. 1990. Contextualization cues in the classroom: Discourse regulation and social control functions. *Language in Society*, 19: 379–402.

Doughty, C. and M. Long (eds) 2003. *Handbook of Second Language Acquisition*. Oxford: Blackwell.

Drew, P. 1995. Conversation analysis. In J.R. Smith, L. Harré, van Langenhove and P. Stearns (eds), *Rethinking Methods in Psychology*. London: Sage, pp. 64–79.

Drew, P. and J. Heritage (eds) 1992a. *Talk at Work: Interaction in Institutional Settings*. Cambridge: Cambridge University Press.

Drew, P. and J. Heritage. 1992b. Analyzing talk at work: An introduction. In P. Drew and J. Heritage (eds) *Talk at Work: Interaction in Institutional Settings*. Cambridge: Cambridge University Press, pp. 3–65.

Dulay, H.C., M. Burt and S. Krashen. 1982. *Language Two*. Rowley, MA: Newbury House.

Dunn, W. and J.P. Lantolf. 1998. I + 1 and the ZPD: Incommensurable constructs; incommensurable discourses. *Language Learning*, 48: 411–42.

Duranti, A. 1997. *Linguistic Anthropology*. Cambridge: Cambridge University Press.

Dyson, B. 1996. The debate on form-focused instruction: A teacher's perspective. *Australian Review of Applied Linguistics*, 19(2): 59–78.

Edwards, D. and N. Mercer. 1987. *Common Knowledge: The Development of Understanding in the Classroom*. London and New York: Methuen.

Edwards, V. and A. Redfern. 1992. *The World in a Classroom: Language in Education in Britain and Canada*. Clevedon: Multilingual Matters.

Elgort, I. 2007. *The Role of Intentional Decontextualised Learning in Second Language Vocabulary Acquisition: Evidence from Primed Lexical Decision Tasks with Advanced Bilinguals*. PhD thesis. Wellington: Victoria University of Wellington.

Elgort, I. 2011 (in press). Deliberate learning and vocabulary acquisition in a second language. *Language Learning*, 61(2).

Elio, R. and Anderson, J.R. 1981. The effects of category generalizations and instance similarity on schema abstraction. *Journal of Experimental Psychology: Human Learning and Memory*, 7: 397–417.

Elio, R. and Anderson, J.R. 1984. The effects of information order and learning mode on schema abstraction. *Memory & Cognition*, 12: 20–30.

Ellis, N. 1994. Vocabulary acquisition: The implicit ins and outs of explicit cognitive mediation. In N. Ellis (ed.) *Implicit and Explicit Learning of Languages*. London: Academic Press, pp. 211–82.

Ellis, N. 2002a. Frequency effects in language processing: A review with implications for theories of implicit and explicit language acquisition. *Studies in
Second Language Acquisition*, 24: 143–88.

Ellis, N. 2002b. Reflections on frequency effects in language processing. *Studies
in Second Language Acquisition*, 24: 297–339.

Ellis, N. 2003. Constructionism, chunking, and connectionism: The emergence
of second language structure. In C.J. Doughty and M.H. Long (eds), *Handbook
of Second Language Acquisition*. Malden, MA: Blackwell, pp. 63–103.

Ellis, N. 2006. Selective attention and transfer phenomena in SLA: Contingency,
cue competition, salience, interference, overshadowing, blocking, and perceptual learning. *Applied Linguistics*, 27(2): 1–31.

Ellis, N. 2008. Usage-based and form-focused language acquisition. In
P. Robinson and N.C. Ellis (eds), *Handbook of Cognitive Linguistics and Second
Language Acquisition*. New York: Routledge, pp. 372–405.

Ellis, N. and F. Ferreira-Junior. 2009. Construction learning as a function of frequency, frequency distribution, and function. *Modern Language Journal*, 93(3):
370–85.

Ellis, N. and D. Larsen-Freeman (eds) 2006. Language emergence: Implications
for applied linguistics. Introduction to the special issue. *Applied Linguistics*,
27(4): 558–89.

Ellis, N. with D. Larsen-Freeman. 2009a. Constructing a second language:
Analyses and computational simulations of the emergence of linguistic constructions from usage. Special issue. *Language Learning*, 59: 90–125.

Ellis, N. and D. Larsen-Freeman (eds) 2009b. Language as a complex adaptive
system. Special issue. *Language Learning*, 59: v–vii.

Ellis, N. and R. Schmidt. 1998. Rules or associations in the acquisition of morphology? The frequency by regularity interaction in human and PDP learning of
morphosyntax. *Language and Cognitive Processes*, 13: 307–36.

Ellis, R. 1985. *Understanding Second Language Acquisition*. Oxford: Oxford University Press.

Ellis, R. 1989. Are classroom and naturalistic acquisition the same? A study of the
classroom acquisition of German word order rules. *Studies in Second Language
Acuisition*, 11: 303–28.

Ellis, R. 1994. *The Study of Second Language Acquisition*. Oxford: Oxford University
Press.

Ellis, R. 1995. Appraising second language acquisition theory in relation to
language pedagogy. In G. Cook and B. Seidlhofer (eds), *Principle and Practice
in Applied Linguistics: Studies in Honour of H. G. Widdowson*. Oxford: Oxford
University Press.

Ellis, R. (ed.) 2001. *Form-Focused Instruction and Second Language Learning*.
Malden, MA: Blackwell.

Ellis, R. 2008. *The Study of Second Language Acquisition. 2nd Edition*. Oxford:
Oxford University Press.

Epstein, S., S. Flynn and G. Martohardjono. 1996. Second language acquisition:
Theoretical and experimental issues in contemporary research. *Brain and
Behavioral Sciences*, 19: 677–758.

Erickson, F. 1982. Classroom discourse as improvisation: Relationships between
academic task structure and social participation structure in lessons. In
Wilkinson, L. (ed.), *Communicating in the Classroom*. New York: Academic
Press, pp. 153–81.

Bibliography 265

Eun, B., S.E. Knotek and A.L. Heining-Boynton. 2008. Reconceptualizing the zone of proximal development: The importance of the third voice. *Educational Psychology Review*, 20: 133–47.

Feldman, M. 2006. *From Molecule to Metaphor: A Neural Theory of Language*. Cambridge, MA: The MIT Press.

Felix, S.W. 1984. Maturational aspects of universal grammar. In A. Davies, C. Criper and A. Howatt (eds), *Interlanguage*. Edinburgh: Edinburgh University Press, pp. 133–61.

Feyerabend, P. 1975. *Against Method*. London: Verso.

Firth, A. 2009. Doing *not* being a foreign language learner: English as a *lingua franca* in the workplace and (some) implications for SLA. *International Review of Applied Linguistics in Language Teaching*, 47(1): 127–56.

Firth, A. and J. Wagner. 1997. On discourse, communication, and (some) fundamental concepts in SLA research. *Modern Language Journal*, 81: 285–300.

Firth, A. and J. Wagner. 2007. Second/foreign language learning as a social accomplishment: Elaborations on a 'reconceptualised' SLA. *Modern Language Journal*, 91: 800–19.

Flege, J.E., I.R.A. Mackay and T. Piske. 2002. Assessing bilingual dominance. *Applied Psycholinguistics*, 23: 567–98.

Fodor, J. 1998. *In Critical Condition: Polemical Essays on Cognitive Science and the Philosophy of the Mind*. Cambridge, MA: MIT Press.

Franceschina, F. 2001. Morphological or syntactic deficits in near-native speakers? An assessment of some current proposals. *Second Language Research*, 17: 213–47.

Francis, D. and S. Hester. 2004. *An Invitation to Ethnomethodology: Language, Society and Interaction*. London: Sage.

Franson, C. 1999. Mainstreaming learners of English as an additional language: The class teacher's perspective. *Language, Culture and Curriculum*, 12: 59–71.

Gánem Gutiérrez, G.A. 2008. Microgenesis, method and object: A study of collaborative activity in a Spanish as a foreign language classroom. *Applied Linguistics*, 29: 120–48.

Gardner, R. 1985. *Social Psychology and Second Language Learning: The Role of Attitude and Motivation*. London: Edward Arnold.

Gardner, R. 2006. The socio-educational model of second language acquisition. A research paradigm. *EUROSLA Yearbook*, 6: 237–60.

Gardner, R. and J. Wagner (eds) 2004. *Second Language Conversations*. London: Continuum.

Garfinkel, H. 1967. *Studies in Ethnomethodology*. Englewood Cliffs, NJ: Prentice-Hall.

Gass, S. 1997. *Input, Interaction, and the Development of Second Languages*. Mahwah, NJ: Lawrence Erlbaum and Associates.

Gass, S.M. 1998. Apples and oranges: Or, why apples are not oranges and don't need to be. A response to Firth and Wagner. *The Modern Language Journal*, 88(4): 597–616.

Gass, S. 2003. Input and interaction. In C. Doughty and M. Long (eds), *The Handbook of Second Language Acquisition*. Malden, MA: Blackwell, pp. 224–55.

Gass, S. and A. Mackey. 2000. *Stimulated Recall Methodology in Second Language Research*. Mahwah, NJ: Lawrence Erlbaum.

Gass, S.M. and L. Selinker. 2001. *Second Language Acquisition: An Introductory Course*. Mahwah, NJ: Lawrence Erlbaum Associates.

Gass, S. and E. Varonis. 1994. Input, interaction and second language production. *Studies in Second Language Acquisition*, 16: 283–302.

Gathercole, S.E. and S.J. Pickering. 1999. Estimating the capacity of phonological short-term memory. *International Journal of Psychology*, 34: 378–82.

Geekie, P. and B. Raban. 1994. Language learning at home and at school. In C. Gallawayand and B.J. Richards (eds), *Input and Interaction in Language Acquisition*. Cambridge: Cambridge University Press, pp. 153–80.

Gentner, T.Q., K.M. Fenn, D. Margoliash and H.C. Nusbaum. 2006. Recursive syntactic pattern learning by songbirds. *Nature*, 440: 1204–7.

Giles, H. and J. Byrne. 1982. An intergroup approach to second language acquisition. *Journal of Multicultural and Multilingual Development*, 3: 17–40.

Givón, T. 1999. Generativity and variation: The notion 'rule of grammar' revisited. In MacWhinney, B. (ed.), *The Emergence of Language*. Mahwah, NJ: Lawrence Erlbaum Associates, pp. 81–114.

Gleick, J. 1987. *Chaos: Making a New Science*. New York: Penguin Books.

Gleitman, L., E. Newport and H. Gleitman. 1984. The current state of the motherese hypothesis. *Journal of Child Language*, 11: 43–79.

Goffman, E. 1981. *Forms of Talk*. Philadelphia, PA: University of Pennsylvania.

Goldberg, A. 2006. *Constructions at Work: The Nature of Generalization in Language*. Oxford: Oxford University Press

Goodwin, C. 1979. The interactive construction of a sentence in natural conversation. In G. Psathas (ed.), *Everyday Language: Studies in Ethnomethodology*. New York: Irvington Publishers, pp. 97–121.

Goodwin, C. and M. Harness Goodwin. 2004. Participation. In A. Duranti (ed.), *A Companion to Linguistic Anthropology*, Oxford: Blackwell, pp. 222–44.

Gordon, R.G. Jr. (ed.) 2005. *Ethnologue: Languages of the World. Fifteenth Edition*. Dallas, TX: SIL International. Online version: http://www.ethnologue.com/.

Gregg, K. 2000. A theory for every occasion: Postmodernism and SLA. *Second Language Research*, 16: 383–99.

Gregg, K. 2002. A garden ripe for weeding: A reply to Lantolf. *Second Language Research*, 18: 79–81.

Gregg, K. 2003. The state of emergentism in second language acquisition. *Second Language Research*, 19: 95–128.

Gregg, K., M. Long, G. Jordan and A. Beretta. 1997. Rationality and its discontents in SLA. *Applied Linguistics*, 18(4): 538–58.

Grosjean, F. 1982. *Life with Two Languages: An Introduction to Bilingualism*. Cambridge, MA: Harvard University Press.

Grosjean, F. 1997. The bilingual individual. *Interpreting*, 2: 163–87.

Guilford, J.P. 1942. *Fundamental Statistics in Psychology and Education*. New York: McGraw Hill.

Guk, I. and D. Kellogg. 2007. The ZPD and whole class teaching: Teacher-led and student-led interactional mediation of tasks. *Language Teaching Research*, 11(3), 281–99.

Gumperz, J. 1982. *Discourse Strategies*. Cambridge: Cambridge University Press.

Gumperz, J. 1992a. Contextualization and understanding. In A. Duranti and C. Goodwin (eds), *Rethinking Context. Language as an Interactive Phenomenon*, Cambridge: Cambridge University Press, pp. 229–52.

Gumperz, J. 1992b. Contextualization Revisited. In P. Auer and A. di Luzio (eds), *The Contextualization of Language*. Amsterdam: John Benjamins, pp. 39–53.

Hakuta, K. 1974. A preliminary report on the development of grammatical morphemes in a Japanese girl learning English as a second language. *Working Papers on Bilingualism*, 3: 18–43.

Hall, J.K. 1995. « Aw man, where you goin' ?». Classroom interaction and the development of L2 interactional competence. *Issues in Applied Linguistics*, 6(2): 37–62.

Hall, J.K. 1998. Differential teacher attention to student utterances: The construction of different opportunities for learning in the IRF. In *Linguistics and Education*, 9: 287–311.

Hall, J.K. 2004. Language learning as an interactional event. *The Modern Language Journal*, 88(4): 607–11.

Halliday, M.A.K. and C.M.IM. Matthiessen. 2000. *Construing Experience Through Meaning: A Language-Based Approach to Cognition*. London: Continuum.

Hamers, J. and M. Blanc. 2000. *Bilinguality and Bilingualism*. Cambridge: Cambridge University Press.

Harrington, M. 2002. Sentence processing. In P. Robinson (ed.), Harris, R. 1997. Romantic bilingualism: Time for a change? In C. Leung and C. Cable (eds), *English as an Additional Language: Changing Perspectives*. Watford, National Association for Language Development in the Curriculum (NALDIC), pp. 14–27.

Hatch, E.M. 1978a. Discourse analysis and second language acquisition. In E. Hatch (ed.) *Second Language Acquisition: A Book of Readings*. Rowley, MA: Newbury House, pp. 402–35.

Hatch, E.M. (ed.) 1978b. *Second Language Acquisition: A Book of Readings*. Mahwah, NJ: Newbury House.

Hauser, M.D., N. Chomsky and T.M. Fitch. 2002. The faculty of language: What is it, who has it and how did it evolve. *Science*, 298: 1569–79.

Hawkins, R. 2001. *Second Language Syntax: A Generative Introduction*. Oxford: Blackwell.

Hawkins, R. 2004. The contribution of the theory of Universal Grammar to our understanding of the acquisition of French as a second language. *Journal of French language studies*, 14: 233–55.

Hawkins, R. and F. Franceschina. 2004. Explaining the acquisition and non-acquisition of determiner-noun gender concord in French and Spanish. In P. Prévost and J. Paradis (eds), *The Acquisition of French in Different Contexts: Focus on Functional Categories*. Amsterdam: John Benjamins, pp. 175–205.

He, A.W. 2003. Novices and their speech roles in Chinese heritage language classes. In R. Bayley and R. Schecter (eds), *Language Socialization in Bilingual and Multilingual Societies*. Clevedon: Multilingual Matters, pp. 128–46.

He, A.W. 2004. CA for SLA: Arguments from the Chinese language classroom. *The Modern Language Journal*, 88(4): 568–82.

Hebb, D.O. 1949. *The Organization of Behaviour*. New York: John Wiley and Sons.

Hellermann, J. 2007. The development of practices for action in classroom dyadic interaction: Focus on task openings. *The Modern Language Journal*, 91(1): 83–96.

Hellermann, J. 2008. *Social Actions for Classroom Language Learning*. Clevedon: Multilingual Matters.

Henriksen, B. 1999. Three dimensions of vocabulary development. *Studies in Second Language Acquisition*, 21(2): 303–17.

268   *Bibliography*

Herschensohn, J. 2004. Functional categories and the acquisition of object clit-
ics in L2 French. In P. Prevost and J. Paradis (eds), *The Acquisition of French in
Different Contexts: Focus on Functional Categories*. Amsterdam: John Benjamins,
pp. 269–70.
Hinkel, E. (ed.) 2005. *Handbook of Research in Second Language Teaching and
Learning*. Mahwah, NJ: Lawrence Erlbaum Associates.
Hjelmslev, L. 1943/1961. *Prolegomena to a Theory of Language*. Madison, WI:
University of Madison Press.
Hopper, P.J. 1988. Emergent grammar and the a priori grammar postulate. In D.
Tannen (ed.), *Linguistics in Context: Connecting Observation and Understanding*.
Norwood, NJ: Ablex, pp. 117–34.
Hopper, P.J. 1998. Emergent grammar. In M. Tomasello (ed.), *The New Psychology
of Language: Cognitive and Functional Approaches to Language Structure*. Mahwah,
NJ: Erlbaum, pp. 155–76.
Housen, A. 2002. A corpus-based study of the L2 acquisition of the English
verb system. In S. Granger, J. Hung and S. Petch-Tyson (eds), *Computer Learner
Corpora, Second Language Acquisition and Foreign Language Learning*. Amsterdam:
John Benjamins, pp. 77–116.
Howatt, A. 1984. *A History of English Language Teaching*. Oxford: Oxford University
Press.
Hu, M. and I.S.P. Nation. 2000. Unknown vocabulary density and reading com-
prehension. *Reading in a Foreign Language*, 13: 403–30.
Hulstijn, J.H. 2002. Towards a unified account of the representation, processing
and acquisition of second language knowledge. *Second Language Research*, 18:
193–223.
Humboldt, W. von. 1836/1999. *On Language*. Translated by P. Heath. Cambridge:
Cambridge University Press.
Hunt, A. and D. Beglar. 2005. A framework for developing EFL reading vocabu-
lary. *Reading in a foreign language*, 17: 23–59.
Huong, L.P.H. 2007. The more knowledgeable peer, target language use, and
group participation. *The Canadian Modern Language Review*, 64(2): 329–50.
Hymes, D. 1972. On communicative competence. In J.B. Pride and J. Holmes
(eds), *Sociolinguistics*. London: Penguin, pp. 269–93.
Irvine, J. 1996. Shadow Conversations: The Indeterminacy of Participant Roles.
In M. Silverstein and G. Urban (eds), *Natural Histories of Discourse*. London:
The University of Chicago Press, pp. 131–59.
Ishida, M. 2009. Development of interactional competence: Changes in the use
of *ne* in L2 Japanese during study abroad. In H. Nguyen and G. Kasper (eds),
Talk-in-Interaction: Multilingual Perspectives. University of Hawaii, pp. 351–87.
Ivanič, R. 2006. Language, learning and identification. In R. Kiely, P. Rea-
Dickens, H. Woodfield and G. Clibbon (eds), *Language, Culture and Identity in
Applied Linguistics*. London: Equinox.
Jackendoff, R. 2002. *Foundations of Language: Brain, Meaning, Grammar, Evolution*.
New York: Oxford University Press
Jarvis, J. and Robinson, M. 1997. Analysing educational discourse: An exploratory
study of teacher response and support to pupils' learning. *Applied Linguistics*,
18(2): 212–28.
Jefferson, G., H. Sacks and E.A. Schegloff. 1987. Notes on laughter in the pursuit
of intimacy. In G. Button and J.R.E. Lee (eds), *Talk and Social Organization*.
Clevedon: Multilingual Matters, pp. 153–205.

Jenkins, J. 2007. *English as a Lingua Franca: Attitude and Identity*. Oxford: Oxford University Press.

Jenks, C.J. 2009a. Getting acquainted in Skypecasts: Aspects of social organization in online chat rooms. *International Journal of Applied Linguistics*, 18(2): 26–46.

Jenks, C.J. 2009b. When is it appropriate to talk? Managing overlapping talk in multi-participant voice-based chat rooms. *Computer Assisted Language Learning*, 22(1): 19–30.

Jessner, U. 2008. Teaching third languages: Findings, trends and challenges. *Language Teaching*, 41(1): 15–56.

Jiang, N. 2000. Lexical representation and development in a second language. *Applied Linguistics*, 21: 47–77.

Jiang, N. 2002. Form–meaning mapping in vocabulary acquisition in a second language. *Studies in Second Language Acquisition*, 24: 617–37.

Jiang, N. 2004. Semantic transfer and development in adult L2 vocabulary acquisition. In P. Bogaards and B. Laufer (eds), *Vocabulary in a Second Language: Description, Acquisition, and Testing*. Amsterdam: Benjamins, pp. 416–32.

Johnson, K.E. 1995. *Understanding Communication in Second Language Classrooms*, Cambridge: Cambridge University Press.

Johnson, K. 2001. *An Introduction to Foreign Language Learning and Teaching*. Harlow: Longman.

Johnson, M. 2004. *A Philosophy of Second Language Acquisition*. New Haven, CT: Yale University Press.

Jordan, G. 2003. *Theory Construction in Second Language Acquisition*. Amsterdam: John Benjamins.

Juffs, A. 2000. An overview of the second language acquisition of links between verb semantics and morpho-syntax. In J. Archibald (ed.) *Second Language Acquisition and Linguistic Theory*. Oxford: Blackwell, pp. 187–227.

Juffs, A. 2004. Representation, processing and working memory in a second language. *Transactions of the Philological Society*, 102: 199–225.

Kanagy, R. 1999. Interactional routines as a mechanism for L2 acquisition and socialization in an immersion context. *Journal of Pragmatics*, 31: 1467–92.

Kasper, G. 1997. 'A' stands for acquisition. *The Modern Language Journal*, 81: 307–12.

Kasper, G. 2004. Participant orientations in German conversation-for-learning. *The Modern Language Journal*, 88(4): 551–67.

Kasper, G. 2009. Locating cognition in second language interaction and learning: Inside the skull or in public view? *International Review of Applied Linguistics in Language Teaching*, 47(1): 11–36.

Kawaguchi, S. 2005. Argument structure and syntactic development in Japanese as a second language. In Pienemann, M. (ed.), *Cross-Linguistic Aspects of Processability Theory*. Amsterdam: John Benjamins, pp. 253–98.

Kempen, G. and E. Hoenkamp. 1987. An incremental procedural grammar for sentence formulation. *Cognitive Science*, 11: 201–58.

Klein, W. 1986. *Second Language Acquisition*. Cambridge: Cambridge University Press.

Kojic-Sabo, I. and P.M. Lightbown. 1999. Students' approaches to vocabulary learning and their relationship to success. *The Modern Language Journal*, 83: 176–92.

Koshik, I. 2002. Designedly incomplete utterances: A pedagogical practice for eliciting knowledge displays in error correction sequences. *Research on Language and Social Interaction*, 35: 277–309.

Kramsch, C. 1986. From language proficiency to interactional competence. *The Modern Language Journal*, 70(4): 366–72.

Kramsch, C. (ed.) 2002. *Language Acquisition and Language Socialization*. London: Continuum.

Kramsch, C. 2009. Third culture and language education. In V. Cook and L. Wei (eds), *Contemporary Applied Linguistics. Volume 1*. London: Continuum, pp. 233–54.

Krashen, S.D. 1981. *Second Language Acquisition and Second Language Learning*. Oxford: Pergamon.

Krashen, S.D. 1982. *Principles and Practice in Second Language Acquistion*. Oxford: Pergamon.

Krashen, S.D. 1985. *The Input Hypothesis*. New York: Longman.

Krashen, S.D. 1989. We acquire vocabulary and spelling by reading: Additional evidence for the input hypothesis. *The Modern Language Journal*, 73: 440–63.

Kroll, J.F. and A.M.B. De Groot (eds) 2005. *Handbook of Bilingualism: Psycholinguistic Approaches*. Oxford: Oxford University Press.

Kroll, J.F. and J.A. Linck. 2007. Representation and skill in second language learners and proficient bilinguals. In I. Kecskes and L. Albertazzi (eds), *Cognitive Aspects of Bilingualism*. Springer, pp. 237–269.

Kroll, J.F., E. Michael, N. Tokowicz and R. Dufour. 2002. The development of lexical fluency in a second language. *Second Language Research*, 18: 137–171.

Kroll, J.F. and E. Stewart. 1994. Category interference in translation and picture naming: Evidence for asymmetric connections between bilingual memory representations. *Journal of Memory and Language*, 33: 149–74.

Kroll, J.F., B.M. Sumutka and A.I. Schwartz. 2005. A cognitive view of the bilingual lexicon: Reading and speaking words in two languages. *International Journal of Bilingualism*, 9: 27–48.

Kuhn, T.S. 1962. *The Structure of Scientific Revolutions*. Chicago, IL: University of Chicago Press.

Kurhila, S. 2004. Clients or language learners: Being a second language speaker in institutional interaction. In R. Gardner and J. Wagner (eds), *Second Language Conversations*. London: Continuum, pp. 58–74.

Lakshmanan, U. and L. Selinker. 2001. Analysing interlanguage: How do we know what learners know? *Second Language Research*, 17: 393–420.

Lambert, W.E. 1955. Measurement of the linguistic dominance of bilinguals. *Journal of Abnormal and Social Psychology*, 50: 197–200.

Lantolf, J.P. 1994. Sociocultural theory and second language learning. *The Modern Language Journal*, 78: 418–20.

Lantolf, J.P. 1996. Second language theory building: Letting all the flowers bloom! *Language Learning*, 46: 713–49.

Lantolf, J.P. (ed.) 2000. *Sociocultural Theory and Second Language Learning*. Oxford: Oxford University Press.

Lantolf, J.P. 2002. Commentary from the flower garden: Responding to Gregg 2000. *Second Language Research*, 18: 72–8.

Lantolf, J.P. 2005. Sociocultural and second language learning research: An exegesis. In E. Hinkel (ed.), *Handbook of Research on Second Language Teaching and Learning*. Mahway, NJ: Lawrence Erlbaum.

Lantolf, J.P. and A. Aljaafreh. 1996. Second language learning in the zone of proximal development: A revolutionary experience. *International Journal of Educational Research*, 23: 619–32.

Lantolf, J.P. and G. Appel (eds) 1994. *Vygotskian Approaches to Second Language Research.* Norwood, NJ: Ablex.

Lantolf, J.P. and M. Poehner. 2008. *Sociocultural Theory and the Teaching of Second Languages.* London: Equinox.

Lantolf, J. and S. Thorne. 2006. *Sociocultural Theory and the Genesis of Second Language Development.* Oxford: Oxford University Press.

Lardiere, D. 2009. Some thoughts on the contrastive analysis of features in second language acquisition. *Second Langauge Research,* 25: 173–227.

Larsen-Freeman, D. 1997. Chaos/complexity science and second language acquisition. *Applied Linguistics,* 18: 141–65.

Larsen-Freeman, D. 2003. *Teaching Language: From Grammar to Grammaring.* Boston, MA: Thomson/Heinle.

Larsen-Freeman, D. 2005. Second language acquisition and the issue of fossilization: There is no end, and there is no state. In Z-H. Han and T. Odlin (eds), *Studies of Fossilization in Second Language Acquisition.* Clevedon: Multilingual Matters, pp. 189–200.

Larsen-Freeman, D. 2007. Reflecting on the cognitive-social debate in second language acquisition. *The Modern language Journal,* 91: 773–87.

Larsen-Freeman, D. and L. Cameron. 2008a. *Complex Systems and Applied Linguistics.* Oxford: Oxford University Press.

Larsen-Freeman, D. and L. Cameron. 2008b. Research methodology on language development from a Complex Systems Perspective. *The Modern Language Journal,* 92(2): 200–13.

Larsen-Freeman, D. and M. Long. 1991. *An Introduction to Second Language Acquisition Research.* London: Longman.

Laufer, B. 2005. Focus on form in second language vocabulary acquisition. In S.H. Foster-Cohen, M.P. Garcia-Mayo and J. Cenoz (eds), *EUROSLA Yearbook 5.* Amsterdam: John Benjamins, pp. 223–250.

Laufer, B. 2006. Comparing focus on form and focus on forms in second-language vocabulary learning. *The Canadian Modern Language Review,* 63(1): 149–166.

Laufer, B. and N. Girsai. 2008. Form-focused instruction in second language vocabulary learning: A case for contrastive analysis and translation. *Applied Linguistics,* 29(4): 694–716.

Laufer, B. and J. Hulstijn. 2001. Incidental vocabulary acquisition in a second language: The construct of task-induced involvement. *Applied Linguistics,* 22: 1–26.

Lave, J. and E. Wenger. 1991. *Situated Learning: Legitimate Peripheral Participation.* Cambridge: Cambridge University Press.

Lee, Y. 2006. Towards respecification of communicative competence: Condition of L2 instruction of its objective? *Applied Linguistics,* 27(3): 349–76.

Lee, N. and J. Schumann. 2005. Neurobiological and evolutionary bases for child language acquisition abilities. Paper presented at the 14th World Congress of Applied Linguistics. Madison, Wisconsin, July.

Lemke, J.L. 1990. *Talking Science. Language, Learning, and Values.* Norwood, NJ: Ablex.

Lenneberg, E. 1967. *Biological Foundations of Language.* New York: Wiley.

Lerner, G. 1991. On the syntax of sentences-in-progress. *Language in Society,* 20: 441–58.

Lerner, G. 1993. Collectivities in action: Establishing the relevance of conjoined participation in conversation. *Text,* 13: 213–45.

Leung, C. 1996. Context, content and language. In T. Cline and N. Frederickson (eds), *Curriculum Related Assessment, Cummins and Bilingual Children*. Clevedon: Multilingual Matters, pp. 26–40.

Leung, C. 1997. Language content and learning process in curriculum tasks. In C. Leung and C. Cable (eds), *English as an Additional Language: Changing Perspectives*. Watford: National Association for Language Development in the Curriculum (NALDIC), pp. 1–13.

Leung, C. 2001. English as an additional language: Distinctive language focus or diffused curriculum concerns? *Language and Education*, 15: 33–55.

Leung, C. (ed.) 2002. *Language and Additional/Second Language Issues for School Education: A Reader for Teachers*. Watford: National Association for Language Development in the Curriculum (NALDIC).

Leung, C. 2005a. Convivial communication: Recontextualizing communicative communication. *International Journal of Applied Linguistics*, 15(2): 119–44.

Leung, C. 2005b. Language and content in bilingual education. *Linguistics and Education*, 16: 238–52.

Leung, C. 2009. Mainstreaming: Language policies and pedagogies. In I. Goglin and U. Neumann (eds), *Streitfall Zweisprachigkeit – The Bilingualism Controversy*. Wiesbaden: VS Verlag für Sozialwissenschaften, pp. 215–31.

Leung, C. and C. Cable (eds) 1997. *English as an Additional Language: Changing Perspectives*. Watford: National Association for Language Development in the Curriculum (NALDIC).

Leung, C. and A. Creese. 2008. Professional issues in working with ethno-linguistic difference: Inclusive policy in practice. In D.E. Murray (ed.), *Planning Change, Changing Plans*. Ann Arbor, MI: University of Michigan Press, pp. 155–73.

Leung, C. and C. Franson. 2001. Curriculum identity and professional development: System-wide questions. In B. Mohan, C. Leung and C. Davison (eds), *English as a Second Language in the Mainstream: Teaching, Learning and Identity*. London, Longman, pp. 55–71.

Levelt, W.J.M. 1989. *Speaking: From Intention to Articulation*. Cambridge, MA: MIT Press.

Levinson, S. 1988. Putting linguistics on a proper footing: Explorations in Goffman's concepts of participation. In P. Drew and A. Wooton (eds), *Erving Goffman. Exploring the Interaction Order*. Cambridge: Polity Press, pp. 161–227.

Lightbown, P. 2000. Anniversary article. Classroom SLA research and second language teaching. *Applied Linguistics*, 21: 431–62.

Lightbown, P. and N. Spada. 2006. *How Languages are Learned*. Oxford: Oxford University Press.

Loewen, S. 2002. The occurrence and effectiveness of incidental focus on form in meaning-focussed esl lessons. Unpublished doctoral thesis. New Zealand: University of Auckland.

Long, M. 1990. The least a second language acquisition theory needs to explain. *TESOL Quarterly*, 24: 649–66.

Long, M. 1993. Assessment strategies for SLA theories. *Applied Linguistics*, 14: 225–49.

Long, M. 1996. The role of the linguistic environment in second language acquisition. In W. Ritchie and T. Bhatia (eds), *Handbook of Second Language Acquisition*. San Diego: Academic Press, pp. 413–68.

Long, M. 1997. Construct validity in SLA research: A response to Firth and Wagner. *The Modern Language Journal*, 81(3): 318–23.

Long, M. 1998. SLA breaking the siege. *University of Hawaii Working Papers in ESL*, 17: 79–129.

Long, M. (ed.) 2006. *Problems in SLA*. Mahwah, NJ: Lawrence Erlbaum.

Lörscher, W. 1986. Conversational structures in the foreign language classroom. In G. Kasper (ed), *Learning, Teaching and Communication in the Foreign Language Classroom*. Aarhus: Aarhus University Press, pp. 11–22.

Mackey, A. 1999. Input, interaction and second language development: An empirical study of question formation in ESL. *Studies in Second Language Acquisition*, 21: 557–87.

Mackey, A. (ed.) 2007. *Conversational Interaction in Second Language Acquisition*. New York: Oxford University Press.

Mackey, A. and S.M. Gass. 2005. *Second Language Research: Methodology and Design*. Mahwah, NJ: Lawrence Erlbaum Associates.

Mackey, A., M. Al-Khalil, G. Atanassowa, M. Hama and A. Logan-Terry. 2007. Teachers' intentions and learners' perceptions about corrective feedback in the L2 classroom. *Innovation in Language Learning and Teaching*, 1: 129–52.

Mackey, A., R. Oliver, J. Leeman. 2003. Interactional input and the incorporation of feedback: An exploration of NS-NNS adult and child dyads. *Language Learning*, 53: 35–56.

Mackey, W.F. 1972. The description of bilingualism. In J.A. Fishman (ed.), *Readings in the Sociology of Language*. The Hague: Mouton, pp. 554–84.

MacWhinney, B. 2001. The competition model: The input, the context, and the brain. In P. Robinson (ed.), *Cognition and Second Language Instruction*. Cambridge: Cambridge University Press, pp. 69–90.

MacWhinney, B. 2006. Emergentism – Use often and with care. *Applied Linguistics* 27(4): 729–40.

MacWhinney, B. 2008. A unified model. In P. Robinson and N. C. Ellis (eds). *Handbook of Cognitive Linguistics and Second Language Acquisition*. New York: Routledge, pp. 341–70.

Malinowski, B. 1923. The problem of meaning in primitive languages. In C.K. Ogden and I.A. Richards (eds), *The Meaning of Meaning*. New York: Harcourt, Brace and World, pp. 296–336.

Mansouri, F. and L. Duffy. 2005. The pedagogic effectiveness of developmental readiness in ESL grammer instruction. *Australian Review of Applied Linguistics*, 28(1): 81–99.

Markee, N. 2000. *Conversation Analysis*. Mahwah, NJ: Lawrence Erlbaum Associates.

Markee, N. 2004. Zones of interactional transition in ESL classes. *The Modern Language Journal*, 88(4): 583–96.

Markee, N. 2008. Toward a learning behavior tracking methodology for CA-for SLA. *Applied Linguistics*, 29: 404–27.

Markee, N. and G. Kasper. 2004. Classroom talks: An Introduction. *The Modern Language Journal*, 88(4): 491–500.

Markee, N. and Seo, M.-S. 2009. Learning talk analysis. *International Review of Applied Linguistics in Language Teaching*, 47(1): 37–63.

McCafferty, S. 2002. Gesture and creating zones of proximal development for second language learning. *The Modern Language Journal*, 86(2): 192–203.

McLaughlin, B. 1987. *Theories of Second Language Learning.* London: Edward Arnold.

McLaughlin, B. and R. Heredia. 1996. Information-processing approaches to research on second language acquisition and use. In W. Ritchie and T. Bhatia (eds), *Handbook of Second Language Acquisition.* San Diego: Academic Press, pp. 213–28.

Meek, M. (ed.) 1996. *Developing Pedagogies in the Multilingual Classroom: The Writings of Josie Levine.* Stoke-on-Trent: Trentham Books.

Michael, E. and T.H. Gollan. 2005. Being and becoming bilingual: Individual Differences and consequences for language production. In J.F. Kroll and A.M.B. de Groot (eds), *The Handbook of Bilingualism: Psycholinguistic Approaches.* New York: Oxford University Press, pp. 389–407.

Mitchell, R. 2003a. Rationales for foreign language education in the 21st century. In S. Sarangi and T. van Leeuwen (eds), *Applied Linguistics and Communities of Practice: British Studies in Applied Linguistics.* Continuum, pp. 114–31.

Mitchell, R. 2003b. Rethinking the concept of progression in the National Curriculum for Modern Foreign Languages: A research perspective. *Language Learning Journal,* 27: 15–23.

Mitchell, R. 2004. Scaffolding and microgenesis in early learner French. Paper presented at the *Annual Conference of the American Association for Applied Linguistics.* Portland: Oregon.

Mitchell, R. 2006. Using second language corpora to validate assessment models for second language learning. Paper presented at the conference for the *British Association for Applied Linguistics.* Cork: Ireland.

Mitchell, R. and F. Myles. 1998. *Second Language Learning Theories.* London: Arnold.

Mitchell, R. and Myles F. 2004. *Second Language Learning Theories.* Second Edition. London: Arnold.

Mitchell, S. 2003. *Biological Complexity and Integrative Pluralism.* Cambridge: Cambridge University Press.

Mohan, B. 1986. *Language and Content.* Reading, MA: Addison-Wesley.

Mohan, B. 1990. LEP students and the integration of language and content: Knowledge structures and tasks. In C. Simich-Dudgeon (ed.), *Proceedings of the First Research Symposium on Limited English Proficient Students' Issues.* Washington, DC: Office of Bilingual Education and Minority Languages Affairs.

Mohan, B. and T. Slater. 2004. The evaluation of causal discourse and language as a resource for meaning. In J.A. Foley (ed.), *Language, Education, and Discourse: Functional Approaches.* New York: Continuum, pp. 65–79.

Mohanan, K.P. 1992. Emergence of complexity in phonological development. In C. Ferguson, L. Menn, and C. Stoel-Gammon (eds), *Phonological Development.* Timonium, MD: York Press.

Molder, H. and J. Potter. 2005. *Conversation and Cognition.* Cambridge: Cambridge University Press.

Mondada, L. and S. Pekarek Doehler. 2000. Interaction sociale et cognition située: quels modèles pour la recherche sur l'acquisition des langues? *Acquisition et Interaction en Langue Etrangère,* 12: 147–74. From http://aile.revues.org/document947.html.

Mondada, L. and S. Pekarek Doehler. 2004. Second language acquisition as situated practice: Task accomplishment in the French second language classroom. *The Modern Language Journal,* 88(4): 501–18.

Mori, J. 2004. Negotiating sequential boundaries and learning opportunities: A case from a Japanese language classroom. *The Modern Language Journal*, 88(4): 536–50.

Mori, J. and A. Hasegawa. 2009. Doing being a foreign language learner in a classroom: Embodiment of cognitive states as social events. *International Review of Applied Linguistics in Language Teaching*, 47(1): 65–94.

Muñoz, C. 2008a. Age-related differences in foreign language learning: Revisiting the empirical evidence. *International Review of Applied Linguistics*, 46: 197–220.

Muñoz, C. 2008b. Symmetries and asymmetries of age effects in naturalistic and instructed L2 learning. *Applied Linguistics*, 29: 578–96.

Myhill, J. 2003. The native speaker, identity and the authenticity hierarchy. *Language Sciences*, 25(1): 77–97.

Myles, F. 1995. Interaction between linguistic theory and language processing in SLA. *Second Language Research*, 11: 235–66.

Myles, F. 2003. The early development of L2 narratives: A longitudinal study. *Marges Linguistiques*, 5: 40–55.

Myles, F. 2004. From data to theory: The over-representation of linguistic knowledge in SLA. In R. Towell and R. Hawkins (eds), *Empirical Evidence and Theories of Representation in Current Research in Second Language Acquisition*. Transactions of the Philological Society, pp. 139–68.

Myles, F. 2005. The emergence of morpho-syntactic structure in French L2. In J-M Dewaele (ed.), *Focus on French as a Foreign Language: Multidisciplinary Approaches*. Clevedon: Multilingual Matters, pp. 88–113.

Myles, F., J. Hooper and R. Mitchell. 1998. Rote or rule? Exploring the role of formulaic language in classroom foreign language learning. *Language Learning*, 48: 323–63.

Myles, F., R. Mitchell and J. Hooper. 1999. Interrogative chunks in French L2: A basis for creative construction? *Studies in Second Language Acquisition*, 21: 49–80.

Nagy, W.E. and P.A. Herman. 1987. Breadth and depth of vocabulary knowledge: Implications for acquisition and instruction. In M. McKeown and M. Curtis (eds), *The Nature of Vocabulary Acquisition*. Hillsdale, NJ: Erlbaum Associates, pp. 19–35.

Nassaji, H. and A. Cumming. 2000. What's in a ZPD? A case study of a young ESL student and teacher interacting through dialogue journals. *Language Teaching Research*, 4(2): 95–121.

Nassaji, H. and G. Wells. 2000. What's the use of 'Triadic Dialogue'? An investigation of teacher-student interaction. *Applied Linguistics*, 21: 376–406.

Nation, I.S.P. 2001. *Learning Vocabulary in Another Language*. Cambridge: Cambridge University Press.

Nation, I.S.P. 2006. How large a vocabulary is needed for reading and listening? *The Canadian Modern Language Review*, 63: 59–82.

Nation, I.S.P. 2007. The four strands. *Innovation in Language Learning and Teaching*, 1: 1–12.

National Curriculum Council. 1991. Circular number 11: Linguistic diversity and the National Curriculum. York: NCC.

Negueruela, E. 2008. Revolutionary pedagogies: Learning that leads (to) second language development. In J.P. Lantolf and M. Poehner (eds), *Sociocultural Theory and the Teaching of Second Languages*. London: Equinox, pp. 189–227.

Nelson, R. 2007. The stability-plasticity dilemma and SLA. Paper presented at American Association for Applied Linguistics Conference. Costa Mesa, California, April.

Newman, F. and Holzman, L. 1993. *Lev Vygotsky: Revolutionary Scientist.* New York: Routledge.

Nofsinger, R.E. 1975. The demand ticket: A conversational device for getting the floor. *Speech Monographs,* 42: 1–9.

Norris, J. and L. Ortega. 2003. Defining and measuring SLA. In C. Doughty and M. Long (eds). *Handbook of Second Language Acquisition.* Oxford: Blackwell, pp. 717–61.

Norton, B. 2000. *Identity and Language Learning: Gender, Ethnicity and Educational Change.* Harlow: Longman.

Norton, B. and K. Toohey. 2002. Identity and language learning. In R. Kaplan (ed.), *The Oxford Handbook of Applied Linguistics.* New York: Oxford University Press, pp. 113–23.

Nystrand, M., L.L. Wu, A. Gamoran, S. Zeiser and D.A. Long. 2003. Questions in time: Investigating the structure and dynamics of unfolding classroom discourse. *Discourse Processes,* 35: 135–98.

Ochs, E., E.A. Schegloff and S. Thompson (eds) 1996. *Interaction and Grammar.* Cambridge: Cambridge University Press.

Ochs, E., B.B. Schieffelin and M. Platt. 1979. Propositions across utterances and speakers. In E. Ochs and B.B.Schieffelin (eds), *Developmental Pragmatics,* New York: Academic Press, pp. 251–68.

Odlin, T. 1989. *Language Transfer: Cross-Linguistic Influence in Language Learning.* Cambridge: Cambridge University Press.

Odlin, T. 2003. Cross-linguistic influence. In C. Doughty and M. Long (eds), *The Handbook of Second Language Acquisition.* Malden, MA: Blackwell, pp. 436–86.

Office for Standards in Education. 2001. *Inspecting English as an Additional Language.* London: OFSTED.

Office for Standards in Education. 2008. Schools & Inspection: Information and Guidance for Inspectors of Maintained Schools, Independent Schools and Teacher Education Providers. London: OFSTED.

Official Languages Act. 2006. Canada: Department of Justice.

Ohta, A.S. 1995. Applying sociocultural theory to an analysis of learner discourse: Learner-learner collaborative interaction in the zone of proximal development. *Issues in Applied Linguistics,* 6: 93–121.

Ohta, A.S. 2000a. Re-thinking interaction in SLA: Developmentally appropriate assistance in the zone of proximal development and the acquisition of L2 grammar. In J.P. Lantolf (ed.), *Sociocultural Theory and Second Language Learning.* Oxford University Press, pp. 51–78.

Ohta, A.S. 2000b. Re-thinking recasts: A learner-centered examination of corrective feedback in the Japanese language classroom. In J.K. Hall and L. Verplaeste (eds), *The Construction of Second and Foreign Language Learning through Classroom Interaction.* Mahwah, NJ: Lawrence Erlbaum, pp. 47–71.

Ohta, A.S. 2001a. *Second Language Acquisition Processes in the Classroom: Learning Japanese.* Mahwah, NJ: Lawrence Erlbaum Associates.

Ohta, A.S. 2001b. From acknowledgement to alignment: A longitudinal study of the development of expressions of alignment by two classroom learners of Japanese. In K. Rose and G. Kasper (eds), *Pragmatics in Language Teaching.* New York: Cambridge University Press, pp. 103–20.

Ohta, A.S. 2006. The zone of proximal development and second language acquisition: beyond social interaction. In Asako Yoshitomi, Tae Umino and Masashi Negishi, (eds), *Readings in Second Language Acquisition and Second Language Pedagogy in a Japanese Context*. Amsterdam: John Benjamins, pp. 155–78.

Olsher, D. 2004. Talk and gesture: The embodied completion of sequential actions in spoken interaction. In R. Gardner and J. Wagner (eds), *Second Language Conversations*. London: Continuum, pp. 221–45.

Ortega, L. 2009. *Understanding Second Language Acquisition*. London: Hodder Education.

Oxford English Dictionary (OED). 2009. On-line version. Oxford: Oxford University Press. From www.oed.com/.

Paradis, M. 2007. The neurofunctional components of the bilingual cognitive system. In I. Kecskes and L. Albertazzi (eds), *Cognitive Aspects of Bilingualism*. Springer, pp. 3–28.

Paradis, M. 2009. *Declarative and Procedural Determinants of Second Languages*. Amsterdam: John Benjamins.

Parrini, P. 1998. *Knowledge and Reality: An Essay in Positive Philosophy*. Dordrecht: Kluwer.

Pavlenko, A. 2005. Bilingualism and thought. In J.F. Kroll and A.M.B. de Groot (eds), *Handbook of Bilingualism: Psycholinguistic Perspectives*. Oxford: Oxford University Press, pp. 433–53.

Pavlenko, A. and A. Blackledge (eds) 2004. *Negotiation of Identities in Multilingual Contexts*. Clevedon: Multilingual Matters.

Pekarek Doehler, S. 2002. Mediation revisited: The interactive organization of mediation in learning environments. *Mind, Culture and Activity*, 9(1): 22–42.

Pekarek Doehler, S. 2006a. «CA for SLA»: Analyse conversationnelle et recherche sur l'acquisition des langues. *Revue Française de Linguistique appliquée*, 2: 123–37.

Pekarek Doehler, S. 2006b. Compétence et langage en action. *Bulletin Suisse de Linguistique Appliqué*, 84: 9–45.

Pekarek Doehler, S. (in press). Emergent grammar for all practical purposes: The on-line formating of dislocated constructions in French conversation. In P. Auer and St. Pfänder (eds.), *Emergent Constructions*. Mouton de Gruyter.

Pekarek Doehler, S. and F. Steinbach Kohler. (Under review). Emergent L2 grammar: Socially situated learning and the on-line elaboration of grammatical constructions.

Pekarek Doehler, S. and G. Ziegler. 2007. Doing language, doing science and the sequential organization of the immersion classroom. In Z. Hua, P. Seedhouse and V. Cook (eds), *Language Learning and Teaching as Social Interaction*. Basingstoke: Palgrave Macmillan, pp. 72–87.

Peters, A.M. and S.T. Boggs. 1986. Interactional routines as cultural influences upon language acquisition. In I. Schieffelin and B.H. Ochs (eds), *Language Socialization Across Cultures*. Cambridge: Cambridge University Press, pp. 80–96.

Phillips, N.A., N. Segalowitz, I. O'Brien and N. Yamasakia. 2004. Semantic priming in a first and second language: Evidence from reaction time variability and event-related brain potentials. *Journal of Neurolinguistics*, 17: 237–62.

Philips, S. 1972. Participant structures and communicative competence: Warm Springs Children in community and classroom. In C. Cazden, V. John and D. Hymes (eds), *Functions of Language in the Classroom*. New York: Teachers College Press, pp. 370–94.

278 Bibliography

Philips, S. 1983. *The Invisible Culture: Communication in Classroom and Community on the Warm Springs Indian Reservation*. New York: Longman.

Pickering, M.J., H.P. Branigan and J.F. McLean. 2002. Constituent structure is formulated in one stage. *Journal of Memory and Language*, 46: 586–605.

Pienemann, M. 1984. Psychological constraints on the teachability of languages. *Studies in Second Language Acquisition*, 6: 186–214.

Pienemann, M. 1998. *Language Processing and Second Language Acquisition: Processability Theory*. Amsterdam: John Benjamins.

Pienemann, M. 2003. Language processing capacity. In C. Doughty and M. Long (eds), *The Handbook of Second Language Acquisition*. Malden, MA: Blackwell, pp. 679–714.

Pienemann, M. (ed.) 2005. *Cross-Linguistic Aspects of Processability Theory*. Amsterdam: John Benjamins.

Pienemann, M. 2008. Processability Theory. In B. VanPatten and J. Williams (eds), *Theories in Second Language Acquisition*. New York: Routledge, pp. 137–54.

Pienemann, M., B. Di Biase and S. Kawaguchi. 2005. Extending processability theory. In M. Pienemann (ed.), *Cross-Linguistic Aspects of Processability Theory*. Amsterdam: John Benjamins, pp. 199–251.

Pienemann, M. and J.-U. Keßler. 2007. Measuring bilingualism. In P. Auer and L. Wei (eds), *Handbook of Applied Linguistics, Vol. 5: Multilingualism and Multilingual Communication*. Berlin: Mouton/de Gruyter, pp. 247–75.

Pinker, S. 1979. Formal models of language learning. *Cognition*, 7: 217–83.

Pinker, S. 1984. *Language Learnability and Language Development*. Cambridge, MA: Harvard University Press.

Poehner, M.E. and J.P. Lantolf. 2005. Dynamic assessment in the language classroom. *Language Teaching Research*, 9: 233–65.

Poole, D. 1992. Language socialization in the second language classroom. *Language Learning*, 42: 593–616.

Popper, K.R. 1972. *Objective Knowledge*. Oxford: Clarendon Press.

Port, R. and T. van Gelder. 1995. *Mind as Motion: Explorations in the Dynamics of Cognition*. Cambridge, MA: The MIT Press.

Psathas, G. 1995. *Conversation Analysis: The Study of Talk-in-Interaction*. London: Sage.

Qualifications and Curriculum Authority. 2000. *A Language in Common: Assessing English as an Additional Language*. London: QCA.

Quirk, R., S. Greenbaum, G. Leech and J. Svartvik. 1972. *A Grammar of Contemporary English*. London: Longman.

Rampton, B., R. Harris and C. Leung. 1997. Multilingualism in England. *Annual Review of Applied Linguistics*, 17: 224–41.

Read, J. 2000. *Assessing Vocabulary*. London: Cambridge University Press.

Read, J. 2004. Plumbing the depths: How should the construct of vocabulary knowledge be defined. In P. Bogaards and B. Laufer (eds), *Vocabulary in a Second Language*. Amsterdam: John Benjamins, pp. 209–28.

Robinson, P. (ed.) 2002. *Individual Differences and Instructed Language Learning*. Amsterdam: John Benjamins.

Rogoff, B. 2003. *The Cultural Nature of Human Development*. Oxford: Oxford University Press.

Rule, S. 2004. French interlanguage orla corpora: Recent developments. *Journal of French Language Studies*, 14: 343–56.

Rule, S. and E. Marsden. 2006. The acquisition of functional categories in early French second languages grammars: The use finite and non-finite verbs in negative contexts. *Second Language Research*, 22: 1–31.

Ryberg, T. and E. Christiansen. 2008. Community and social network sites as technology enhanced learning environments. *Technology, Pedagogy, and Education*, 17(3): 207–19.

Sacks, H. 1992. *Lectures on Conversation*. Oxford: Basil Blackwell.

Sacks, H., E.A. Schegloff and G. Jefferson. 1974. A simplest systematics for the organization of turn-taking for conversation. *Language*, 50: 696–735.

Sampson, E.E. 1989. The challenge of social change for psychology: Globalization and psychology's theory of the person. *American Psychologist*, 44: 914–21.

Sapir, E. 1921. *Language: An Introduction to the Study of Speech*. New York: Harcourt, Brace and Company.

Saville-Troike, M. and J.A. Kleifgen. 1986. Scripts for school: Cross-cultural communication in elementary classrooms. *Text*, 6: 207–21.

Sawyer, M. and L. Ranta. 2001. Aptitude, individual differences, and instructional design. In P. Robinson (ed.), *Cognition and Second Language Instruction*. Cambridge: Cambridge University Press, pp. 319–53.

Scarcella, R. 2003. *Academic English: A Conceptual Framework*. Irvine: Linguistic Minority Research Institute, University of California.

Schatzki, T.R. 1996. *Social Practices: A Wittgensteinian Approach to Human Activity and the Social*. Cambridge: Cambridge University Press.

Schegloff, E.A. 1986. The routine as achievement. *Human Studies*, 9: 111–51.

Schegloff, E.A. 1991. Conversation analysis and socially shared cognition. In L.B. Resnick, J.M. Levine and St. D. Teasley (eds), *Perspectives on Socially Shared Cognition*. American Psychological Association, pp. 150–71.

Schegloff, E. 1996. Turn organization: One intersection of grammar and interaction. In E. Ochs, E.A. Schegloff and S.A. Thompson (eds), *Interaction and Grammar*. Cambridge: Cambridge University Press, pp. 52–133.

Schegloff, E.A. 2000. Overlapping talk and the organization of turn-taking for conversation. *Language in Society*, 29: 1–63.

Schegloff, E.A. 2006. Interaction: The infrastructure for social institutions, the natural ecological niche for language, and the arena in which culture is enacted. In N.J. Enfield and St. C. Levinson (eds), *Roots of Human Society*. Oxford: Berg, pp. 70–96.

Schegloff, E.A., I. Koshik, S. Jacoby and A. Olsher. 2002. Conversation Analysis and applied linguistics. *Annual Review of Applied Linguistics*, 22: 3–31.

Schegloff, E.A., H. Sacks and G. Jefferson. 1977. The preference for self correction in the organisation of repair in conversation. *Language*, 53(2): 361–82.

Schleppegrell, M.J. and M.C. Colombi (eds) 2002. *Developing Advanced Literacy in First and Second Languages: Meaning with Power*. Mahwah, NJ: Lawrence Erlbaum Associates.

Schmidt, R. 1994. Deconstructing consciousness in search of useful definitions for applied linguistics. *AILA Review*, 11: 11–26.

Schmitt, N. 2000. *Vocabulary in Language Teaching*. Cambridge: Cambridge University Press.

Schumann, J. 1978. *The Pidginization Process: A Model for Second Language Acquisition*. Rowley, MA: Newbury House.

Schumann, J. 1993. Some problems with falsification: An illustration from SLA research. *Applied Linguistics*, 14: 295–306.

Schwab, G. 2007. Schülerbeteiligung im Englischunterricht der Hauptschule: Eine empirische Studie zu Partizipationsstrukturen eines kommunikativ geführten Fremdsprachenunterrichts in einer Hauptschulklasse. Unpublished PhD thesis. Ludwigsburg.

Schwartz, B. and R. Sprouse. 1996. L2 cognitive states and the full transfer/full access model. *Second Language Research*, 12: 40–72.

Schwartz, B. and R. Sprouse. 2000. When syntactic theories evolve: Consequences for L2 acquisition research. In J. Archibald (ed.), *Second Language Acquisition and Linguistic Theory*. Malden, MA: Blackwell, pp. 56–86.

Schwarze, C. 2002. Representation and variation: On the development of Romance auxiliary syntax. In M. Butt and T. Holloway King (eds), *Time ver Matter: Diachronic Perspectives in Morphosyntax*. Stanford, CA: CSLI.

Scollon, R. 1996. Discourse identity, social identity, and confusion in intercultural communication. *Intercultural Communication Studies*, 6: 1–16.

Seedhouse, P. 2004. *The Interactional Architecture of the Language Classroom: A Conversation Analysis Perspective*. Malden, MA: Blackwell.

Seedhouse, P. 2005. Conversation analysis and language learning. *Language Teaching*, 38: 165–87.

Seedhouse, P. 2007. On ethnomethodological CA and 'linguistic CA': A reply to Hall. *The Modern Language Journal*, 91(4): 527–33.

Seedhouse, P. and M. Egbert. 2006. The Interactional Organisation of the IELTS Speaking Test. *IELTS Research Reports*, 6: 161–206.

Segalowitz, N. 2000. Automaticity and attentional skill in fluent performance. In H. Riggenbach (ed.), *Perspectives on Fluency*. Ann Arbor, MI: University of Michigan Press, pp. 200–19.

Segalowitz, N.S. and S.J. Segalowitz. 1993. Skilled performance, practice, and the differentiation of speed-up from automatisation effects: Evidence from second language word recognition. *Applied Psycholinguistics*, 14: 369–85.

Seidlhofer, B. 2002. Pedagogy and local learner corpora: Working with learning-driven data. In S. Granger, J. Hung and S. Petch-Tyson (eds), *Computer Learner Corpora, Second Language Acquisition and Foreign Language Teaching*, pp. 213–34.

Selinker, L. 1972. Interlanguage. *International Review of Applied Linguistics*, 10(3): 209–31.

Selinker, L. and U. Lakshmanan. 1992. Language transfer and fossilization: The 'multiple effects' principle. In S. Gass and L. Selinker (eds), *Language Transfer in Language Learning*. Rowley, MA: Newbury House, pp. 393–420.

Sfard, A. 1998. On two metaphors for learning and the dangers of choosing just one. *Educational Researcher*, 27(4): 4–13.

Sfard, A. and C. Kieran. 2001. Cognition as communication: Rethinking learning-by-talking through multi-faceted analysis of students mathematical interactions. *Mind, Culture, and Activity*, 8: 42–76.

Skehan, P. 1989. *Individual Differences in Foreign Language Learning*. London: Arnold.

Snape, N., Y.I. Leung and M. Sharwood Smith (eds) 2009. *Representational Deficits in SLA: Studies in Honor of Roger Hawkins*. Amsterdam: John Benjamins.

Spolsky, B. 1990. Introduction to a colloquium: The scope and form of a theory of second language learning. *TESOL Quarterly*, 24: 609–16.

Steinbach Kohler, F. 2008. Co-construction dans l'interaction en classe de FLE: De la dialogitité du langage vers a dialogicité de l'apprentissage. *Travaux Neuchâtelois de Linguistique*, pp. 25–42.

Stern, H.H. 1983. *Fundamental Concepts of Language Teaching*. Oxford: Oxford University Press.

Stern, H.H. 1992. *Issues and Options in Language Teaching*. Oxford: Oxford University Press.

Stow, C. and B. Dodd. 2003. Providing an equitable service to bilingual children in the UK: Areview. *International Journal of Language Communication Disorders*, 38(4): 351–77.

Swain, M. 1972. Bilingualism as a First Language. PhD Dissertation. Irvine: University of California.

Swain, M. 2005. The output hypothesis: Theory and research. In E. Hinkel (ed.), *Handbook of Research in Second Language Teaching and Learning*. Mahwah, NJ: Lawrence Erlbaum Associates, pp. 471–83.

Swain, M. and S. Lapkin. 1998. Interaction and second language learning: Two adolescent French immersion students working together. *The Modern Language Journal*, 82: 320–37.

Swann Report. 1985. *Education for All*. London: HMSO.

Takac, V.P. 2008. *Vocabulary Learning Strategies and Foreign Language Acquisition*. Clevedon: Multilingual Matters.

Talamas, A., J.F. Kroll and R. Dufour. 1999. Form related errors in second language learning: A preliminary stage in the acquisition of L2 vocabulary. *Bilingualism: Language and Cognition*, 2: 45–58.

Tarone, E. 2000. Still wrestling with context in interlanguage theory. *Annual Review of Applied Linguistics*, 20: 182–98.

Tarone, E. and G. Liu. 1995. Situational context, variation, and second language acquisition theory. In G. Cook and B. Seidlhofer (eds), *Principle and Practice in Applied Linguistics: Studies in Honour of H. G. Widdowson*. Oxford: Oxford University Press, pp. 107–24.

Thelen, E. and E. Bates. 2003. Connectionism and dynamic systems: Are they really different? *Developmental Science*, 6: 378–91.

Thelen, E. and L. Smith. 1994. *A Dynamic Systems Approach to the Development of Cognition and Action*. Cambridge, MA: The MIT Press.

Tokowicz, N., E. Michael and J.F. Kroll. 2004. The roles of study abroad experience and working memory capacity in the types of errors made during translation. *Bilingualism: Language and Cognition*, 7: 255–272.

Tomasello, M. 2003. *Constructing a Language*. Cambridge, MA: Harvard University Press.

Toohey, K. 2000. *Learning English at School: Identity, Social Relations and Classroom Practice*. Clevedon: Multilingual Matters.

Toohey, K. 2001. Disputes in Child L2 Learning. *TESOL Quarterly*, 35: 257–78.

Towell, R. 2003. Introduction: Second language acquisition research in search of an interface. In R. van Hout, A. Hulk, F. Kuiken, R. Towell (eds), *The Lexicon-Syntax Interface in Second Language Acquisition*. Amsterdam: John Benjamins, pp. 1–20.

Towell, R. 2007. Complexity, accuracy and fluency in second language acquisition research. In S. van Daele, A. Housen, F. Kuiken, M. Pierrard and I. Vedder (eds), *Complexity, Accuracy and Fluency in Second Language Use, Learning and Teaching*. Brussels: KVAB, pp. 285–93.

Towell, R. and J.M. Dewaele. 2005. The role of psycholinguistic factors in the development of fluency amongst advanced learners of French. In J-M. Dewaele (ed.), *Focus on French as a Foreign Language: Multidisciplinary Approaches*. Clevedon: Multilingual Matters, pp. 210–39.

Towell, R. and R. Hawkins. 1994. *Approaches to Second Language Acquisition*. Clevedon: Multilingual Matters.

Travers, P. and L. Higgs. 2004. Beyond the naming of parts: Working with pupils at Key Stages 3 and 4 in the English curriculum. In P. Travers and G. Klein (eds), *Equal Measures: Ethnic Minority and Bilingual Pupils in Secondary Schools*. Stoke on Trent: Trentham Books.

Tucker, M. and K. Hirsh-Pasek. 1993. Systems and language: Implications for acquisition. In L. Smith and E. Thelen (eds), *A Dynamic Systems Approach to Development: Applications*. Cambridge, MA: The MIT Press, pp. 359–84.

Tseng, W. and N. Schmitt. 2008. Toward a model of motivated vocabulary learning: A structural equation modeling approach. *Language Learning*, 58(2): 357–400.

Ushioda, E. 2001. Language learning at university: Exploring the role of motivational thinking. In Z. Dörnyei and R. Schmidt (eds), *Motivation und Second Language Acquisition*. Honolulu, HI: University of Hawaii Press, pp. 93–125.

Ushioda, E. 2007. Motivation, autonomy and sociocultural theory. In P. Benson (ed.), *Learner Autonomy 8: Teacher and Learner Perspectives*. Dublin: Authentik, pp. 5–24.

van Berkel, A. 2005. The role of the phonological strategy in learning to spell in English as a second language. In V. Cook and B. Bassetti (eds), *Second Language Writing Systems*. Clevedon: Multilingual Matters, pp. 97–121.

van Dam, J. 2002. Ritual, face, and play in a first English lesson: Bootstrapping a classroom culture. In C. Kramsch (ed.), *Language Acquisition and Language Socialization: Ecological Perspectives*. London: Continuum, pp. 237–65.

van Dam, J. 2003. Language acquisition behind the scenes: Collusion and play in educational settings. In J. Leather and J. van Dam (eds), *Ecology of Language Acquisition*. Dordrecht: Kluwer Academic Publishers, pp. 203–21.

van Geert, P. 2003. Dynamic systems approaches and modeling of developmental processes. In J. Valsiner and K. Connolly (eds), *Handbook of Developmental Psychology*. London: Sage, pp. 640–72.

van Hell, J.G. and T. Dijkstra. 2002. Foreign language knowledge can influence native language performance on exclusively native contexts. *Psychonomic Bulletin and Review*, 9(4): 780–9.

van Lier, L. 2000. From input to affordance: Social-interactive learning from an ecological perspective. In J. Lantolf (ed.), *Sociocultural Theory and Second Language Learning*. Oxford: Oxford University Press, pp. 245–59.

van Lier, L. 2004. *The Ecology and Semiotics of Language Learning: A Sociocultural Perspective*. New York: Springer.

VanPatten, B. 1996. *Input Processing and Grammar Instruction: Theory and Research*. Norwood, NJ: Ablex.

VanPatten, B. 2002. Processing instruction: An update. *Language Learning*, 52: 755–803.

VanPatten, B. and J.F. Lee (eds) 1990. *Second Language Acquisition-Foreign Language Learning.* Clevedon: Multilingual Matters.

VanPatten, B. and J. Williams (eds) 2006. *Theories in Second Language Acquisition.* Mahwah, NJ: Lawrence Erlbaum.

VanPatten, B. and J. Williams. 2007. *Theories in Second Language Acquisition.* Mahwah, NJ: Lawrence Erlbaum.

Vo, G. 2004. Speaking from experience. In P. Travers and Klein, G. (eds), *Equal Measures: Ethnic Minority and Bilingual Pupils in Secondary Schools.* Stoke on trent: Trentham Books, pp. 24–6.

Volosinov, V.N. 1973. *Marxism and the Philosophy of Language.* Cambridge, MA: Harvard University Press.

Vygotsky, L.S. 1934/1962. *Thought and Language.* Cambridge, MA: MIT Press.

Vygotsky, L.S. 1978. *Mind in Society: The Development of Higher Psychological Processes.* Cambridge, MA: Harvard University Press.

Vygotsky, L.S. 1987. Thinking and Speech. In R.W. Rieber and A.S. Carton (eds), *The Collected Works of L. S. Vygotsky.* Volume 1. New York: Plenum Press, pp. 39–285.

Wagner, J. and R. Gardner. 2004. Introduction. In R. Gardner and J. Wagner (eds), *Second Language Conversations.* London: Continuum, pp. 1–17.

Walsh, S. 2003. Developing interactional awareness in the second language classroom. *Language Awareness,* 12: 124–42.

Walsh, S. 2006. *Investigating Classroom Discourse.* London: Routledge.

Watanabe, Y. and M. Swain. 2007. Effects of proficiency differences and patterns of pair interaction on second language learning: Collaborative dialogue between adult ESL learners. *Language Teaching Research,* 11(2): 121–42.

Watson-Gegeo, K. 2004. Mind, language and epistemology: Toward a language socialization paradigm for SLA. *The Modern Language Journal,* 88(3): 331–50.

Weinreich, U. 1953. *Languages in Contact.* The Hague: Mouton.

Wells, G. 1993. Re-evaluating the IRF Sequence: A proposal for the articulation of theories of activity and discourse for the analysis of teaching and learning in the classroom. *Linguistics and Education,* 5: 1–37.

Wells, G. 1995. Language and the inquiry-oriented curriculum. *Curriculum Enquiry,* 25: 233–69.

Wells, G. 2002. The role of dialogue in activity theory. *Mind, Culture and Activity,* 9: 43–66.

Wertsch, J.V. 1985. *Vygotsky and the Social Formation of Mind.* Cambridge, MA: Harvard University Press.

Wesche, M. and T.S. Paribakht. 1996. Assessing second language vocabulary knowledge: Depth versus breadth. *Canadian Modern Language Review,* 53: 13–40.

Wexler, K. 1982. A principle theory for language acquisition. In E. Wanner and L.R. Gleitman (eds), 1982. *Language Acquisition: The State of the Art.* Cambridge: Cambridge University Press, pp. 288–315.

Wexler, K. and P. Culicover. 1980. *Formal Principles of Language Acquisition.* Cambridge, MA: MIT Press.

White, L. 1996. Clitics in L2 French. In H. Clashen (ed.), *Generative Perspectives on Language Acquisition. Empirical Findings, Theoretical Considerations and Crosslinguistic Comparisons.* Amsterdam: John Benjamins, pp. 335–68.

White, L. 2003. *Second Language Acquisition and Universal Grammar*. Cambridge: Cambridge University Press.

White, L. 2007. Linguistic theory, Universal Grammar, and second language acquisition. In B. VanPatten and J. Williams (eds), *Theories in Second Language Acquisition*. pp. 37–55.

Wittgenstein, L. 1953/2001. *Philosophical Investigations (tr. G.E.M.Anscombe)*. 3rd edition. Oxford: Blackwell.

Young, R. 1999. Sociolinguistic approaches to SLA. *Annual Review of Applied Linguistics*, 19: 105–132.

Young, R. 2003. Learning to talk the talk and walk the walk: Interactional competence in academic spoken English. *North Eastern Illinois University Working Papers in Linguistics*, 2: 26–44.

Young, R. and E. Miller. 2004. Learning as changing participation: Discourse roles in ESL writing conferences. *The Modern Language Journal*, 88(4): 519–35.

Zipf, G.K. 1935. *The Psycho-Biology of Language*. Boston, MA: Houghton Mifflin.

Index

286 *Index*